T0314957

Seafaring in the Contemporary Pacific Islands

SEAFARING

in the Contemporary Pacific Islands

Studies in Continuity and Change

Edited by

Richard Feinberg

📖

Northern Illinois

University

Press

DeKalb

1995

Design by Julia Fauci

Library of Congress Cataloging-in-Publication Data
Seafaring in the contemporary Pacific islands: studies in
continuity and change / edited by Richard Feinberg.
      p.   cm.
    Includes bibliographical references and index.
    ISBN 0-87580-201-X (clothbound : acid-free paper)
    1. Maritime anthropology—Oceania. 2. Naviga-
tion—Oceania. 3. Seafaring life—Oceania. 4. Fishing
villages—Oceania. 5. Division of labor—Oceania. 6.
Oceania—Social life and customs. I. Feinberg, Richard.
GN662.S43   1995
303.48'32'099—dc20   95-11622
                              CIP

Contents

Acknowledgments

Seafaring in the Contemporary Pacific Islands grows out of sessions at the 1987, 1990, and 1991 meetings of the Association for Social Anthropology in Oceania. Not all contributions to those sessions appear in this volume; the pages that follow, however, bear the imprint of all session participants. In particular, we wish to thank Tim Bayliss-Smith, Philip deVita, Ben Finney, Charles Frake, Robert Franco, Tommy Holmes, and Craig Severance for their input and support at various stages in the book's development.

This volume has benefited from thoughtful criticism and encouragement by Daniel R. Coran, acquisitions editor at Northern Illinois University Press, and three anonymous reviewers. In addition, we are grateful to Kent State University graduate students Carrie Kelley and Jill McEldery-Maxwell, who assisted in preparation of the manuscript.

Above all we extend our warm appreciation to the mariners who generously shared their time and expertise with us. This collection is a tribute to the skill and determination with which they have adapted old traditions to the ever-changing circumstances of Pacific Island life. We hope it is a fitting tribute.

Seafaring in the Contemporary Pacific Islands

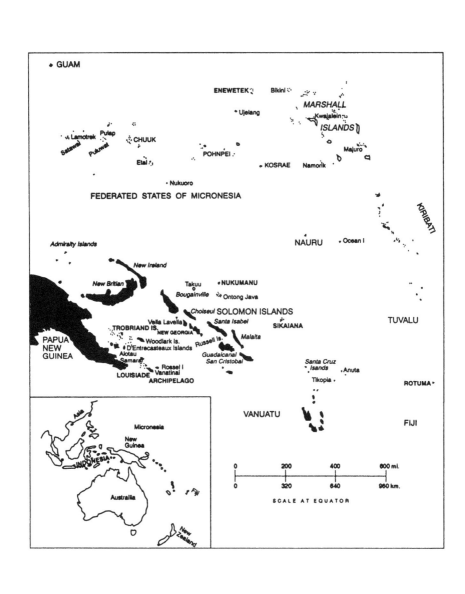

GUAM

ENEWETEK Bikini
MARSHALL
Ujelang
Kwajalein
ISLANDS

Pulap CHUUK
Lamotrek
Satawal Puluwat
Etal POHNPEI
Majuro

KOSRAE Namorik

Nukuoro
FEDERATED STATES OF MICRONESIA

KIRIBATI

NAURU Ocean I

Admiralty Islands

New Ireland

New Britian
Takuu NUKUMANU
Bougainville Ontong Java

Choiseul SOLOMON ISLANDS

TUVALU

Vella Lavella Santa Isabel
TROBRIAND IS. SIKAIANA
NEW GEORGIA
Woodlark Is. Malaita
D'Entrecasteaux Islands Russell Is.
PAPUA Alotau
NEW Samarai Guadalcanal
GUINEA Rossel I San Cristobal
Vanatinai Santa Cruz
LOUISIADE Isands Anuta
ARCHIPELAGO Tikopia
ROTUMA

VANUATU FIJI

Asia
Micronesia
New
Guinea
INDONESIA
Fiji
Australia
New
Zealand

0   200   400   600 mi.
0   320   640   960 km.
SCALE AT EQUATOR

INTRODUCTION
Theme and Variation in Pacific Island Seafaring

Richard Feinberg

• Pacific Island peoples are renowned among scholars and in popular imagination for their seafaring abilities. Meticulously honed skills enabled early voyagers to reach the many islands their descendants presently inhabit, and contemporary islanders rely upon those skills for a wide range of purposes. The sea remains a source of sustenance, an avenue for social contacts and exchange, a focus of symbolic interest, and a major site for recreational activities.

The Pacific is our planet's largest ocean, covering a third of the earth's surface—more than all land area combined. Scattered through this vast expanse are thousands of islands, many little more than sandbars barely visible above the surface at high tide and separated by hundreds of kilometers of open sea. Yet, by the time of European contact, almost every habitable speck of land strewn across the tropical Pacific evidenced some human habitation.

Until recently, Pacific Islanders traversed their watery milieu in craft fashioned from hollowed logs, built up of planks, or both in combination. Single-outrigger canoes were used throughout the Pacific, reaching their highest level of sophistication in the Micronesian archipelagoes of northwestern Oceania. Simultaneously, great double-hulled canoes plied the waters of the Polynesian Triangle on lengthy interisland voyages. Melanesian vessels ranged from the imposing double-hulled sailing craft of the Mailu to graceful, outriggerless war canoes paddled on head-hunting raids among the islands of the western Solomons. By contrast, many islanders are now content with tiny dugouts, used solely for fishing and for inshore transportation.

Before the time of European contact, vessels were propelled exclusively by paddle, pole, or sail. On the more elaborate craft, steering was performed by manipulation of the sail or with the aid of a large steering oar, braced against or fastened to the hull. On smaller craft, ordinary paddles often were employed.

The most important navigational "instruments" during the precontact period were the stars and sun. During inclement weather, wind and groundswell were employed to hold a steady course, while reflected waves, flight patterns of birds, and an assortment of auxiliary techniques were used to locate land. A navigator's position at sea was calculated by dead reckoning. Yet, despite the absence of magnetic compass, printed charts, sextant, and other aids familiar to the Western mariner, the islanders' equipment and techniques have proved remarkably proficient.

Most writing on Pacific Island seafaring and navigation has focused on the spectacular exploits of those peoples who have managed to retain a large proportion of the old technology and skills. Prominent in this literature are mariners from Puluwat (Gladwin 1970) and Satawal (Thomas 1987) in Micronesia's Caroline Islands. Through a series of books, articles, and films, these people are now famous for their wayfinding abilities.[1] The *Hōkūle'a,* a reconstructed double-hulled Hawaiian voyaging canoe, has earned comparable fame for sailing through the isles of Polynesia under the guidance of Mau Piailug, a master navigator from Satawal, and later, Nainoa Thompson, a Native Hawaiian who learned his trade from Piailug (see Finney 1979, 1985, 1991; Finney et al. 1989; Kyselka 1987). Yet, impressive as these feats may be, the sea is equally important to islanders who have abandoned—or who never had—great voyaging traditions.

In contrast with most literature on Oceanic seafaring, the present volume focuses on what one might describe as ordinary people doing ordinary things. Yet these "ordinary things" can make the difference between life and death, provide a sense of cultural identity, and determine people's psychological well-being. This book is about people who depend upon the sea for food and transportation, who paddle their canoes or fire up their outboard motors to deliver copra to the local trader, whose children swim and surf until their leisure is cut short by work or school, whose songs and dances depict maritime themes, who travel on the ocean in fiberglass canoes and European ships, and for whom the sea provides a metaphor for all the vagaries of life. To borrow an expression from a different realm of discourse (Montague and Morais 1976), Hipour, Mau Piailug, and Nainoa Thompson are the "superstars" of Oceanic wayfinding. Such heroic figures draw attention to spheres of endeavor worthy of investigation. However, anthropology's ultimate objective is to learn about the *human* condition, something we cannot accomplish if we limit our observations to the accomplishments of superstars. Few people have the combination of natural ability, rigorous training, and the opportunity for practice necessary to become standard-bearers. Exceptional people are—by definition after all—exceptional.

Our shift of focus to the ordinary, we believe, reflects a maturation in the study of Pacific Island maritime activities. As in other areas of anthropological concern, interest was initially sparked by startling "discoveries." Only later did we learn that such activities as house building, yam harvesting, and food preparation often tell us more about a people than do arcane rituals or seemingly strange forms of marriage. This was Malinowski's point in his injunction that we focus more attention on the "imponderabilia of actual life" (Malinowski 1961 [1922]:18–21). The issue is not, as Jarvie (1964) has suggested, that we sacrifice the interesting for the mundane. Rather, the ordinary can be as fascinating and informative as the unusual, if we take time to look at it and ask the right questions.

COMMON ELEMENTS IN PACIFIC SEAFARING

This volume covers a broad spectrum of Pacific maritime communities, ranging from Nukumanu Atoll and the Massim region of Papua New Guinea, where much of the old knowledge and technique remains intact, to Sikaiana and Rotuma, where "seafaring" has for years been largely limited to working as deckhands on European ships and where local boats are used almost exclusively for inshore fishing. Despite these differences, however, all of the communities depicted here have much in common. They all consist of Austronesian speakers who presumably developed from a common source (see Goodenough and Feinberg, epilogue), and they share many geographical and ecological constraints.

The communities presented here are found on small tropical islands, making it virtually inevitable that people orient their lives toward the ocean. In times past, canoes were necessary if one was to use the sea effectively, and they could only be constructed from locally available, natural materials. These included wood for hulls, masts, outriggers, and paddles; sennit cord for lashing and rigging; sap, bark cloth, and similar materials for caulking; and pandanus leaves for sails.

Design was also largely dictated by environmental factors. Sailing vessels need some mechanism to provide resistance against leeway drift, both for navigation and effective tacking. Typically, this is provided either by a keel or an outrigger. A deep keel makes for better tracking and enables one to beat into a head wind. In waters studded with shallow reefs, however, particularly where vessels usually are stored on shore between expeditions, a keel is inconvenient and sometimes dangerous. The most practical solution, therefore, is some variety of outrigger or double-hulled canoe, generally combined with a deep-V hull design. This is especially true for long-distance voyaging canoes and may be seen from Polynesian Nukumanu and Takuu (Feinberg, essay 8; for Polynesia see also Feinberg 1988) and the Massim area of Melanesia (Lepowsky, essay 2; Montague, essay 3; Powell, essay 4) to many Micronesian atolls (see Carucci, essay 1; Gladwin 1970).

Few Pacific Islanders today make lengthy canoe voyages. Those who do, however, all rely on similar techniques (e.g., see Lewis 1972). Certain stars and constellations are particularly significant for these purposes, appearing in the navigational repertoires of many communities.[2] Even when islanders pilot modern ships, they are likely to rely on stars and wave patterns as much as instruments (see Ammarell, essay 9). Moreover, waves are often used to hold a steady course for inshore piloting and sailing on atoll lagoons as well as deep-sea navigation.

The communities presented in this volume depend on the sea for a variety of economic purposes. All rely on fish and shellfish as a major source of protein. Canoes are often used to transport crops from gardens to home villages. Interisland trade may have important consequences for comfort and survival, and maritime activities have been incorporated into the cash economy.

This point is most clearly illustrated by the Bugis, who procure their livelihood as commercial traders. Market exchange is less pervasive in the lives of other peoples discussed in this volume; still it is an essential fact of life. In Kaduwaga (Montague, essay 3) visitors pay handsomely to use the harbor for canoe repair. On Nukumanu

(Feinberg, essay 8) bêche-de-mer and trochus are, along with copra, the leading source of income. Rotumans (Howard, essay 6) have experimented with commercial fisheries. They have dispersed through Fiji, traveling primarily on European ships, in pursuit of education and employment opportunities, and many work as deckhands. Donner (essay 7) makes comparable points for Sikaiana.

Another common element through most of Oceania is the association of men with the sea and women with the land. In most island communities, the division of labor between men and women reflects the conceptual division between land and sea. Men usually sail, navigate, engage in deep-sea fishing, and participate in interisland trade. Women's responsibilities involve such pursuits as cooking, gardening, and mat making. The reef flat is a meeting ground where men and women search for shellfish and perform communal fish drives. This division of labor, however, is not universal. Girls as well as boys paddle canoes in Manus of Papua New Guinea's Admiralty Islands (Mead 1930). In Fanalei of Small Malaita in the Solomons, both men and women are adept at handling canoes.[3] On Nukumanu, women sometimes paddle on the lagoon as they hunt for shellfish, and they occasionally spearfish or bottom-fish with hook and line from a canoe. Such practices, however, are exceptional; and even in these cases, women rarely operate a sail or handle an outboard motor. Every essay in this volume comments upon the association of men with the sea and women with land-based activities. In this light, Lepowsky's observations (essay 2) in the Louisiade Archipelago of Papua New Guinea take on special significance. There, women not only sail and navigate their own canoes but also organize major trading expeditions. Such initiative might be somewhat expectable, as women typically enjoy greater autonomy in matrilineal societies than in their patrilineal counterparts. The extent of economic and political initiative and freedom of movement described by Lepowsky, however, is exceptional even for the matrilineal regions of Oceania. I am unaware of comparable seafaring exploits by women in either the matrilineal societies of Micronesia or in other Massim communities such as the Trobriand Islands (see Montague this volume; Powell this volume).

In a maritime environment, the sea becomes a potent symbol. Associated with the common gender-based division of labor is a widespread system of sociospatial symbolism in which male is identified with sea, front, up, right, and chiefly, while female is identified with inland, rear, down, left, and commoner. This is clearly seen in Fiji (Sahlins 1976) and Anuta (Feinberg 1980); it is best illustrated in this volume by Enewetak and Nukumanu. However, even in the matrilineal Trobriands, where women play important social roles and control important forms of wealth (e.g., see Weiner 1976), the ocean is a predominantly male domain (Montague this volume; Powell this volume).

The ocean often provides symbols through which a community constructs and reinforces its sense of cultural identity. Many peoples view themselves as uniquely in tune with the sea and contrast themselves with others whom they see as less adept at dealing with the ocean. In this regard, the Enewetak emphasize the sleek designs of their own craft and disparage what they view as clumsy vessels of their Marshallese neighbors. Similarly, people of Marovo (Hviding, essay 5) take pride in their graceful war canoes of yesteryear, whose high prows warned prospective victims of impending doom. Today each Marovo community is identified by the unique design of its canoes.[4] Pride in aggressive command of the seaways is expressed by men who drive motor-powered boats at top speed over the lagoon at night and paint their vessels with bright colors to warn occupants of small paddle canoes to move aside. Plans to build a replica of an old war canoe for a goodwill voyage through the central Solomons and the prominence of canoe races at the tenth anniversary of Solomon Islands independence in 1988 further verify the value attached to seamanship as a symbol of island identity and pride. Nukumanu comments on Anutan canoe design (Feinberg, essay 8) make the same point.[5]

For many communities, the sea is a guide to social history. Certain reefs, channels, passages, and seamarks are associated with particular spirit beings—sometimes dangerous, sometimes benevolent (Lepowsky, essay 2; Hviding, essay 5). Places on the ocean are often identified as sites of great historical events, both encoding and lending credibility to oral traditions (Hviding, essay 5). In other instances, the sea becomes a metaphor for crucial aspects of social life. Maritime themes are embossed on islanders' bodies in the form of tattoos, and people speak of "sailing through life" (Carucci, essay 1). Canoes and ocean voyaging serve as metaphors for romance and sexual experience (Feinberg 1988; Donner, essay 7; Carucci, essay 1), and marital relations are compared to the relationship between canoe and outrigger (Carucci, essay 1). The possibilities seem endless.

POINTS OF DIFFERENTIATION AMONG SEAFARING TRADITIONS

The underlying commonality notwithstanding, differences among island communities in manner of relating to the sea are striking. Such differences may be attributed to several factors, largely geographic and historic.

Prominent among the forces leading to abandonment of old technology and practice are the intensity and length of Western contact. It is hardly accidental that those communities that have retained the most in terms of their old knowledge and technique are located on small, isolated islands, largely devoid of commercially exploitable resources. Puluwat and Satawal fit into this category. Similarly, Anuta experienced little systematic contact until the past two decades. By contrast, islanders in contact with the Western world have had the opportunity to observe and copy European maritime techniques. They have seen European technology in operation and have come to appreciate its virtues. Through wage labor, cash cropping, and commercial exploitation of marine resources, they have obtained the financial resources to purchase fiberglass boats, outboard motors, and other accoutrements of Western civilization. Still, for many generations, no Pacific island has been wholly free of European contact. Therefore, contact by itself cannot explain the differences.

In addition to length and intensity, the *kind* of Western contact is a major factor. In this regard, geography is crucial. The Austronesian-speaking Bugis, like other Indonesians, are centrally located among several major population centers; thus they have been in contact with outsiders, have had intimate associations with people from a wide variety of cultural backgrounds, and have borrowed a great deal from peoples whom they have encountered. As a result, much of their technology appears quite alien to what is seen in the Pacific proper. Yet even this divergence is largely superficial. In boat design and navigational technique, the similarity between Bugis and other Austronesian seafarers is clear.

Among Pacific Islanders themselves, a wide variety of geographical forces impinge on the way in which people utilize their maritime environments. Some of these forces, including isolation and availability of commercially exploitable resources, directly influence the frequency and kinds of contact, as discussed above.

Geography can influence the use of marine resources in other ways as well. For example, sea conditions affect the size of vessels. On an atoll with a protected lagoon, or on the leeward side of a large island, one may safely use a small canoe or dinghy with marginal stability and little freeboard. Sikaiana and Nukumanu fit into this category. By contrast, on islands with only a fringing reef, where vessels must be used upon the open sea and passage to the ocean usually is rough, small boats are not a viable alternative. This is why Anutan canoes are relatively large and stable, with high gunwales, wide hulls, and large outriggers (see Feinberg 1988).[6] Rotuma, an isolated volcanic island like Anuta, is likely to have had to deal with similar constraints. Because of greater access to Western technology, however, the Rotumans' solution has been to resort to European craft.

Contours of the sea bottom affect methods of propulsion. If there are large areas of shallow water, as is often true of atoll lagoons, poling is the preferred means for moving one's canoe. In deeper water, a paddle, sail, or outboard motor is essential. By contrast, in very shallow water, particularly if surf is breaking on a reef, a motor may become a liability. The prop can easily be damaged on the bottom, while the engine, when it is not running, makes the vessel heavier and somewhat awkward to maneuver.

As important as propulsion techniques is the care of boats while they are not in use. Since most islanders still use canoes constructed from local materials and wood deteriorates upon exposure to the elements, care must be taken to preserve the vessels. If there is a good natural harbor, as in Kaduwaga of the Trobriands, boats may be moored for lengthy periods. This prevents the wood from drying out, with the attendant contraction, swelling, cracking, and damage to caulking and (perhaps) paint. On the other hand, it is difficult to repair boats while they are in the water, and in rough weather they are likely to be damaged by wave action. For this reason, Kaduwaga is exceptional, and most communities pull their vessels up onto the beach between uses. In such instances, hulls must be protected from the sun and rain. Canoe sheds are often made for this purpose. In other cases, boats are covered with leaves—sometimes more or less perfunctorily, as on Nukumanu; sometimes with great care and effort, as on Anuta.

Islanders depend upon the sea for much of their sustenance. Even island communities that have given up long-distance voyaging continue to fish and collect other forms of marine life. Different varieties of fish and shellfish require different methods of collection. Such methods include casting a hook and line from shore, wading on a reef, or swimming and diving. In addition, most communities rely on fishing from canoes. Precisely how this is accomplished depends on the species sought, reef and bottom contours, and other environmental details.

The degree to which traditional voyaging techniques have been retained largely depends on the presence of other islands close enough to invite interisland visitation, yet far enough apart to present a challenge. True isolates like Rotuma appear to have lost their seafaring traditions relatively early. A similar point could be made about such social isolates as Sikaiana. For a voyager from Sikaiana, the large island of Malaita is a fairly easy navigational target. Sikaiana, however, considered the culturally alien Malaitans to be hostile and aggressive; therefore, they avoided making landfall there, preferring to risk longer voyages to more elusive destinations. Like the Rotumans, Sikaiana gave up canoe voyaging relatively early and no longer even make outrigger vessels.

Those islands that have most effectively retained their old knowledge and technique, in contrast with Rotuma and Sikaiana, have potential destinations within a day or two at sea. Puluwat men regularly sail to Pikelot, an uninhabited island 160 kilometers distant, to hunt for turtles (Gladwin 1970:38, 41–43). Anutans sail to Patutaka, a distance of fifty kilometers, to hunt birds, and until the last few decades, they voyaged to Tikopia, 120 kilometers away (Feinberg 1988). Trobrianders sail to other islands of the *kula* area; Vanatinai voyage through the Louisiade Archipelago for purposes of trade, utilitarian as well as ceremonial; and Marovo look toward the many islands of the western and central Solomons as potential destinations.

In general, seafaring has typified atolls and small islands rather than the large volcanic ones (see Goodenough and Feinberg, epilogue). In Micronesia, the great navigational centers are such remote outposts as Puluwat (Gladwin 1970), Lamotrek (Alkire 1965), and Satawal (Thomas 1987) rather than high islands of the Marianas, Yap, or Chuuk. Anutans evidently voyaged to the larger (albeit still small) Tikopia more frequently than the reverse,[7] and they continue interisland voyaging while their more worldly neighbors abandoned the practice decades ago (Feinberg 1988, 1991). Likewise, Melanesia's voyaging centers are not found on Guadalcanal, Bougainville, New Britain, or New Guinea; rather, they are on the smaller islands of the Massim region and New Georgia in the western Solomons.

Reasons for this pattern are easy to imagine. The larger islands have more resources and larger populations; therefore, residents have less incentive to risk lengthy ocean voyages. People on the smaller islands are more vulnerable to natural disasters and sometimes find it necessary to travel to their neighbors for "relief supplies"—a point emphasized by Alkire both in his book and a critique of my discussion of Anutan seafaring (Alkire 1965, 1990). This may be accomplished through trade, as among Elato, Lamotrek, and Satawal (Alkire 1965); the Trobriands and other islands in the *kula* area (Malinowski 1961 [1922]; Powell this volume; Lepowsky this volume); and between Tikopia and Anuta (Firth 1954). Alternately, it may be accomplished through the exploitation of uninhabited reefs or islands, as in Puluwat turtle hunting on Pikelot (Gladwin 1970) or Anutan bird hunting on Patutaka (Feinberg 1988:chapter 7).[8]

On islands with small populations, interisland travel also increases the pool of

acceptable marriage partners. The resulting marriages, in turn, create kinship networks that sometimes extend to several islands, providing further incentive for
travel. This may well be the case for Puluwat, Pulap, and Pulusuk of western
Chuuk State, and for Elato, Lamotrek, and Satawal of eastern Yap State in the Micronesian Carolines. It is certainly the case for Tikopia and Anuta (e.g., see Firth
1954; Feinberg 1981) and for Nukumanu and Ontong Java.

Another incentive for interisland travel may be to trade for objects of ritual
value. This, of course, is the essential point of Malinowski's classic, *Argonauts of the
Western Pacific*, as well as many subsequent works (e.g., see Leach and Leach 1983).
Control of such exchange may, in part, determine political leadership and ritual
rank, as discussed by Powell (this volume, also 1960, 1969).

A further impetus for interisland voyaging is warfare. Incentives to engage in
warfare include the following: to obtain commodities of either ritual or practical
significance; to take prisoners of war, perhaps with the thought of ultimately marry-
ing some of them; or to expand or re-assert political dominion. Warfare, however,
is distinctive in that it favors big communities and motivates people on larger islands to engage, at least occasionally, in overseas expeditions. Thus, peoples of New
Georgia, a group of midsized islands in the western Solomons, until recently, were
widely known for raiding weaker neighbors.

Vessels and their use have changed over time. Most Pacific Islanders once possessed large, elaborate voyaging canoes. There is evidence that at some time—often
in the not too distant past—all of the communities appearing in this volume had
large canoes routinely used for interisland travel. This, of course, is not surprising in
that vessels capable of lengthy voyages were required for initial settlement.

In some parts of the Pacific, such impressive vessels are still regularly made and
sailed. This is true in the Central Carolines (Alkire 1965; Gladwin 1970; Lewis
1972; Thomas 1987), Anuta (Feinberg 1988) and the Massim area (Lepowsky;
Montague; Powell, all this volume; see also Malinowski 1961 [1922]; Lauer 1976).
On other islands, old-style voyaging canoes have not been built or sailed for many
years, but details of construction and operation are well remembered, and small
models sometimes made. This is true of Enewetak, Nukumanu, Takuu, and
Marovo as well as Taumako (Davenport 1968; Lewis 1972). Elsewhere, although
details may have faded from even the keenest memories, archival records document
existence of large voyaging canoes at some time in the islands' histories. Such communities are represented in the present volume by Sikaiana and Rotuma.

Even among the more elaborate canoes, there are important points of variation.
For example, the Kiriwinans of Omarakana in the northeastern Trobriands emphasize cargo space at the expense of tacking ability and speed. Anutans favor speed
over maneuverability. Micronesians maximize both speed and maneuverability but
compromise somewhat on cargo capacity. The Marovo had a rather different set of
problems to confront. Much of their voyaging was for purposes of raiding. In order
to maneuver quickly in close quarters and efficiently transport a maximum number
of warriors, they developed slender, graceful paddling canoes with high prows and
sterns, equipped with neither outrigger nor sail.

With the few exceptions described above, the old voyaging canoes have been abandoned throughout the Pacific. However, that does not entail abandonment of interisland voyaging. As of 1984, the largest canoes on Nukumanu measured fifteen meters—as long as the old *vaka hai laa*. They were less well crafted than their predecessors—rough hewn with round-bottomed hulls, much like paddling canoes in overall design; and they were not sailed to distant archipelagoes. Still, these boats were fitted with small outboard engines and used on almost a weekly basis for the eighty-kilometer round-trip voyage to Ontong Java, where similar canoes were made and used.

Likewise, most communities at one time had more skillful navigators than they do at present. Still, islanders from Nukumanu, Ontong Java, Marovo, the Louisiade Archipelago, and the Trobriands, as well as the better-known Micronesian centers of marine activity, continue to make interisland voyages, sometimes out of sight of land, relying on the stars, sun, waves, and seamarks for their safe arrival. The extent to which the old skills and equipment are maintained depends on their potential use and the availability of viable alternatives. Where outboard motors, fiberglass canoes, and European ships are accessible and affordable, they have—to some degree—replaced the older vessels and materials. Yet, even in such instances, feelings for the sea have often been retained. Thus, islanders from Sikaiana and Rotuma have gained reputations as outstanding sailors and deckhands. Meanwhile, old techniques have been adapted to the new conditions. Interest in overseas contacts, emigration, and voyaging has been maintained—perhaps even increased—among Pacific Islanders in recent years. The sea remains an avenue of communication as well as a source for the necessities of life. Appreciation of the sea has been retained in such symbolic forms as stories, dances, songs, tattoo designs, and rites of passage. This volume explores these issues and concerns among communities distributed through Oceania today.

*T*his book grew out of sessions at the 1987, 1990, and 1991 annual meetings of the Association for Social Anthropology in Oceania. Specific foci of the essays vary somewhat. Those on Sikaiana, Nukumanu, Rotuma, Marovo, and the Louisiade Archipelago attempt a general overview of these communities and their relations, past and present, to the ocean. Powell's essay on Kiriwina adds to an ongoing discussion of the source of hierarchy in the Trobriands (see Powell 1960, 1969, 1978; Irwin 1983). In particular, it explores the implications of geography and seafaring abilities for systems of exchange and political hegemony. Montague examines the significance of a natural harbor at Kaduwaga village in the Trobriands for the establishment of regional social networks and as a source of wealth for local residents. Lepowsky also gives special attention to interisland trade networks within the Massim region. Carucci explores the modern use of symbolic imagery drawn from canoes and from the sea on Enewetak in the Marshall Islands. Howard's focus is largely historic, exploring Rotumans' establishment of a new seafaring tradition within the context of a cash economy, based on travel and employment aboard

European ships. Donner examines the same issue with respect to Sikaiana.

Ammarell's discussion of the Indonesian Bugis helps to broaden the volume's scope. Although it sometimes is convenient to treat Austronesian speakers as if they could be neatly divided into discrete culture areas—I have even done so at times in this introduction—assumptions underlying such divisions have been vigorously challenged over the past decade. Prominent among these challenges has been deconstruction of the supposedly rigid Polynesia-Melanesia division, especially in terms of political organization and styles of leadership (e.g., see Douglas 1979; Thomas 1989; Godelier 1986; Godelier and Strathern 1991; Feinberg 1993; Feinberg and Watson-Gegeo n.d.). For a long time similar questions have been raised about the soundness of a stark division between Micronesia and Polynesia (e.g., see Shapiro 1933; Irwin 1992). And scholars have been tracing the historical and cultural connections among Austronesian-speaking peoples well beyond the bounds of what is usually considered to be Oceania. For this reason, a 1981 volume on siblingship in the Pacific contained a chapter on Malaysia (McKinley 1981). The recent Austronesian Project at the Australian National University's Research School for Pacific Studies included scholars focusing on regions as far-flung as Island Southeast Asia and even Madagascar. And a 1991 National Endowment for the Humanities seminar, "Politics of Culture: Pacific Island Perspectives," included specialists on Indonesia and Malaysia (Feinberg and Zimmer-Tamakoshi 1995). Goodenough and Feinberg, in the epilogue, attempt to demonstrate how the case studies in this volume represent, each in its own way, a common Austronesian heritage. And Ammarell's discussion of the Bugis brings the issue sharply into focus.

The Bugis, like the other peoples discussed here, are Austronesian speakers. They have been influenced, however, by a history of contact with a number of "great civilizations," and they ply the seas in vessels that look superficially like European sailing ships. Indonesian law requires ships to be equipped with radio and compass, and unlike contemporary Pacific Islanders, many Bugis make their homes aboard their vessels for months at a time while they engage in interisland commerce. Yet they show remarkable resemblances to peoples of the insular Pacific, both in worldview and seafaring technique. The length of their journeys notwithstanding, Bugis interisland voyages are now as routine as Nukumanu canoe trips to Ontong Java and Vanatinai trading expeditions to other islands of the Louisiade Archipelago. The Bugis share with their Pacific Island cousins an economic and symbolic association of the land with women and the sea with men. Like Pacific Islanders, they depend upon the movements of celestial bodies for navigation; indeed, Ammarell's account of Bugis astronomic reckoning is reminiscent of Goodenough's (1953) and Gladwin's (1970) works on Carolinian astronomy. Furthermore, the Bugis share with their Pacific neighbors dependence on such secondary navigational aids as wave configurations, flight patterns of birds, and subtle shifts of color in the sky and sea.

Finally, this volume bears on several broader issues in contemporary anthropological discourse. Anthropologists, in recent years, have grown increasingly concerned with history and insist on seeing local communities as part of a larger "world system." The shift of emphasis reflects dissatisfaction with older views of the communities we study as insulated, self-sufficient, homogeneous, and integrated (e.g., see Carrier 1992; Keesing 1989; Said 1978). This volume highlights history and a variety of outside influences upon the development of maritime activities in Oceania. At the same time, the book recognizes the active participation of local communities in incorporating external elements into living systems of cultural and social interaction.

NOTES

1. Kyselka (1987) suggests "wayfinding" for Pacific voyagers' abilities to locate distant islands. It denotes what other writers call "noninstrument navigation" but focuses on what the islanders do, not what they lack.

2. Prominent among these are Sirius, Orion, Altair, the Southern Cross, Polaris, and Arcturus.

3. This observation is based on a short visit in 1973. Even in this area, however, it should be noted that the more spectacular maritime activities, such as communal dolphin hunting, are masculine endeavors (Meltzoff, personal communication).

4. Lepowsky (essay 2) makes a comparable observation about Massim vessels.

5. It should be noted that although sea and maritime activities are central to the sense of self and cultural identity of many islanders, they are also often viewed with some ambivalence. The ocean is a source of life but at the same time may be fraught with danger. It is an avenue of communication with the outside world, providing opportunities for trade and acquisition of new ideas and technology. But outsiders also pose a threat, both physically and culturally, and are, therefore, often treated with suspicion. This issue is implied in several essays and is discussed explicitly with respect to Sikaiana and Rotuma.

6. When Anutans move to the central Solomons, where they have easy access to calm water, they build small canoes without deck covers and splash rails. Such vessels would be almost useless on Anuta.

7. Anuta is more or less circular, with a diameter of about one kilometer and a resident population of approximately two hundred people; Tikopia is about six kilometers long and three kilometers wide, with a resident population of approximately 1,500. In addition to size and location, Anuta's isolation is increased by a rough passage through its fringing reef, which makes landing a canoe or dinghy difficult in any but the calmest weather.

8. For a discussion of the limitations of practical explanations for Anutan interisland voyaging, see Feinberg (1988:chapter 8).

REFERENCES

Alkire, William
1965   *Lamotrek Atoll and Inter-island Socioeconomic Ties.* Illinois Studies in Anthropology No. 5. Urbana: University of Illinois Press.
1990   Review of *Polynesian Seafaring and Navigation: Ocean Travel in Anutan Culture and Society,* by Richard Feinberg. *American Ethnologist* 17:588–89.
Carrier, James (editor)
1992   *History and Tradition in Melanesian Anthropology.* Berkeley: University of California Press.
Davenport, William H.
1968   Social organization in the Northern Santa Cruz Islands: The Duff Islands

(Taumako). *Baessler-Archiv* (Neuefolge) 16:207–75.

Douglas, Brownen

1979   Rank, power, and authority: a reassessment of traditional leadership in South Pacific societies. *Journal of Pacific History* 14:2–27.

Feinberg, Richard

1980   History and structure: a case of Polynesian dualism. *Journal of Anthropological Research* 36: 361–78.

1981   *Anuta: Social Structure of a Polynesian Island*. Copenhagen and Lā'ie: National Museum of Denmark, in cooperation with the Institute for Polynesian Studies.

1988   *Polynesian Seafaring and Navigation: Ocean Travel in Anutan Culture and Society*. Kent, Ohio: Kent State University Press.

1991   A long-distance voyage in contemporary Polynesia. *Journal of the Polynesian Society* 100:25–44.

1993   Elements of leadership in Oceania. Paper presented to symposium entitled "Chiefs Today" at the annual meeting of the Association for Social Anthropology in Oceania, Kona, Hawai'i.

Feinberg, Richard, and Karen Ann Watson-Gegeo (editors)

n.d.   *Leadership and Change in the Western Pacific: Essays Presented to Sir Raymond Firth on the Occasion of his Ninetieth Birthday*. London School of Economics Monographs on Social Anthropology. London: Athlone. In press.

Feinberg, Richard, and Laura Zimmer-Tamakoshi (editors)

1995   *Politics of Culture in the Pacific Islands*. *Ethnology* 34:89–209. Special Issue.

Finney, Ben R.

1979   *Hōkūle'a: The Way to Tahiti*. New York: Dodd, Mead and Company.

1985   Anomalous westerlies, El Niño, and the colonization of Polynesia. *American Anthropologist* 87:9–26.

1991   Myth, experiment, and the reinvention of Polynesian voyaging. *American Anthropologist* 93:383–404.

Finney, Ben, Paul Frost, Richard Rhodes, and Nainoa Thompson

1989   Wait for the west wind. *Journal of the Polynesian Society* 98:261–302.

Firth, Raymond

1954   Anuta and Tikopia: symbiotic elements in social organisation. *Journal of the Polynesian Society* 63:87–131.

Gladwin, Thomas

1970   *East is a Big Bird: Navigation and Logic on Puluwat Atoll*. Cambridge: Harvard University Press.

Godelier, Maurice

1986   *The Making of Great Men: Male Domination and Power among the New Guinea Baruya*. (1982) Translated by Rupert Swyer. Cambridge: Cambridge University Press.

Godelier, Maurice, and Marilyn Strathern (editors)

1991   *Big Men and Great Men*. Cambridge: Cambridge University Press.

Goodenough, Ward H.

1953   *Native Astronomy in the Central Caroline Islands*. Museum Monographs. Philadelphia: University Museum, University of Pennsylvania.

Irwin, Geoffrey

1983   Chieftainship, kula, and trade in Massim prehistory. In *The Kula*, edited by Jerry W. Leach and Edmund Leach, pp. 29–72. Cambridge: Cambridge University Press.

1992   *Prehistoric Exploration and Colonisation of the Pacific*. Cambridge: Cambridge University Press.

Jarvie, I. C.
1964   *The Revolution in Anthropology*. London: Routledge and Kegan Paul.

Keesing, Roger M.
1989   Creating the past: custom and identity in the contemporary Pacific. *The Contemporary Pacific* 1:19–42.

Kyselka, Will
1987   *An Ocean in Mind*. Honolulu: University of Hawai'i Press.

Lauer, Peter K.
1976   Sailing with the Amphlett Islanders. In *Pacific Navigation and Voyaging*, edited by Ben R. Finney, pp. 72–89. Polynesian Society Memoir No. 39. Wellington, N.Z.: Polynesian Society.

Leach, Jerry W., and Edmund Leach (editors)
1983   *The Kula*. Cambridge: Cambridge University Press.

Lewis, David
1972   *We, the Navigators*. Honolulu: University of Hawai'i Press.

McKinley, Robert
1981   Cain and Abel on the Malay Peninsula. In *Siblingship in Oceania: Studies in the Meaning of Kin Relations*, edited by Mac Marshall, pp. 335–87. ASAO Monograph No. 8. Ann Arbor: University of Michigan Press.

Malinowski, Bronislaw
1961   *Argonauts of the Western Pacific*. (1922) New York: E. P. Dutton.

Mead, Margaret
1930   *Growing Up in New Guinea*. New York: William Morrow.

Montague, Susan P., and Robert Morais
1976   Football games and rock concerts: the ritual enactment. In *The American Dimension: Cultural Myths and Social Realities*, edited by William Arens and Susan P. Montague, pp. 33–52. Port Washington, N.Y.: Alfred.

Powell, Harry
1960   Competitive leadership in Trobriand political organisation. *Journal of the Royal Anthropological Institute* 90:118–45.
1969   Territory, hierarchy and kinship in Kiriwina. *Man* 4:580–604.
1978   The kula in Trobriand politics? Paper read at first Kula Conference. Cambridge, U.K.

Sahlins, Marshall D.
1976   *Culture and Practical Reason*. Chicago: University of Chicago Press.

Said, Edward
1978   *Orientalism*. Harmondsworth, U.K.: Penguin.

Shapiro, Harry L.
1933   Are the Ontong Javanese Polynesian? *Oceania* 3:367–76.

Thomas, Nicholas
1989   The force of ethnology: origins and significance of the Melanesia/Polynesia division. *Current Anthropology* 30:27–41.

Thomas, Stephen D.
1987   *The Last Navigator*. New York: Henry Holt and Company.

Weiner, Annette
1976   *Women of Value, Men of Renown*. Austin: University of Texas Press.

SYMBOLIC IMAGERY OF ENEWETAK SAILING CANOES

Laurence Marshall Carucci

And behold! I was the one who had to look on in surprise, as, while we laboriously tacked about and gained very little on the wind, they, in their artfully constructed craft went straight ahead on the same route we went in a zig-zag fashion, hurried on ahead of us, and dropped their sails to await us.

—*Adelbert von Chamisso aboard the Brig Rurik, 1817*

TATTOOS, CANOES, COMMONERS, AND CHIEFS

• Persons in Kayapo society present themselves using intricate details sketched in body paint to convey critical components of social identity (Turner 1969). In a more perduring fashion, nineteenth-century Marshall Islanders, their earlobes distended from the use of large pandanus earrings, embossed abstract images into their skin using elaborate tattooing techniques (Krämer 1906; Choris 1822). These displays differentiated people by age, gender, and rank, but they included other layers of meaning as well. Chiefs and commoners, men and women, and even children had tattoos, but the most elaborate of these were, by far, among chiefs (Krämer and Nevermann 1938:iii–8). Given to humans by the primordial deities Lewoj and Lanij, the tattoo represents maturity and in the past was "essential to marriageability" (Krämer and Nevermann 1938:iii–17; Bwebwenato in Majel n.d.:4). The tattoo is also associated with immortality and with increased mana; in traditional times on Enebin, Ailinlablab (the high chiefly atoll of the Relik Chain), it was a central part of the yearly renewal festivities that accompanied the breadfruit harvest (Krämer and Nevermann 1938:iii–18). As Krämer and Nevermann note, Lewoj and Lanij gave the tattoo to humans "as an inalienable possession which is received from the ancestors and is taken even to the grave" (1938:iii–17). It is a critical part of the person and, like body parts and other objects that are core components of personal identity, it is marked by special linguistic forms.

Tattoos covered virtually the entire body of a chief, including the glans penis. Common men were not as heavily tattooed, and women were even less so. Krämer and Nevermann note that the female torso was not heavily tattooed and not at all below the waist, though the shoulders carried ornate designs (Choris 1822). Details of the tattoo varied, but the central motifs, according to Erdland (1910), focused on sailing. The upper pectoral triangle represented the body of the canoe, the lower pectoral triangle the ocean swells. The "belt-like band of wavy lines extending across the stomach are clouds, and the mast runs from neck to navel. The shoulder bands are barnacles, and the upper dorsal triangle is also known as *oa* 'sailing craft'" (Krämer and Nevermann 1938:9–12).

Though perplexing to Krämer and Nevermann, the detailed design of the canoe can easily be seen as a metaphor for life, uniting its ontogenetic and phylogenetic sources. The canoe's inverted form faces the gods, the phylogenetic renewable energy source, with its barnacles on the shoulders and clouds around the waist; the uppermost tip of the mast (not its base, as Krämer and Nevermann believed) emanates from the navel, amidst the clouds. Marshall Islanders consider the navel *(bwij-)* the ontogenetic source of every living human, and the lines *(ao)* of the tattoo replicate the line *(ao)* that links each child to its mother. (*Bwij* refers to the bilateral extended families as well—the lines or paths through which Enewetak and Ujelang people trace connections to living family members and deceased kin.) The mast also links the navel and the throat (*buru* 'the seat of Marshall Islanders' emotions' and, much like the Western heart, the source of life). The correlations, then, between mana, elimination of wrinkles (agelessness, immortality), marriage and birthing, and chiefly force can hardly be coincidental. The body, fully fashioned, is the vessel islanders used to face the voyage of life.

Elaborate tattoos no longer exist. They were denounced by the Congregationalist Mission (known at the time as ABCFM), outlawed by early administrators, and avoided on account of the severe fevers that accompanied the tattooing process (Krämer and Nevermann 1938:iii–18). They exist now as tiny marks—the embossed letters of a lost lover's name or the rough shape of a cross.

By the end of the twentieth century, sailing canoes will, in all likelihood, also disappear. Even now, they are but an ephemeral outline of their earlier form. The last traditional seaworthy canoes were constructed on Ujelang in 1976 and 1977. Of the four canoes built, only one was still sailing on Enewetak in 1983. Luta, its owner, was the most dedicated canoe maker of the recent era, his heavily tattooed chest reminiscent of a former age. This last canoe fell into disrepair in the mid-1980s due to the repatriation to Enewetak in 1980, the lack of canoe-manufacturing supplies on the recently replanted atoll, and Luta's advanced age. It is unlikely another one will ever be built.[1] Because of their small size, even the ten-meter craft depicted in the photographs from the 1970s that accompany this essay were unreliable on the open sea. They were only slightly over one-half the size of the canoes of the 1950s, and they are said to be less than one-third the length of the huge nineteenth-century vessels.

Today, most atoll residents own outboard motor boats, many of them costly

FIGURE 1.1.   The captain, Aluwo, and three sailors prepare to set sail in Ujelang's lagoon with their new craft. The captain and first mate adjust the rigging while sailors steady the canoe. Co-owner, Jitoken Chief Ioanej, sits amidst makeshift skids and watches preparations from the shore.

fiberglass boats purchased in the government center. Others build outboard boats from marine plywood skillfully placed on hand-hewn frames. Dependence upon these vessels, combined with a chronic fuel shortage, means that people spend less time at sea than they did in the past. Formerly, men sailed three or four days a week. They traveled to distant parts of the atoll to fish, catch birds, gather bird eggs, and *kemja* (capture turtles as they return to an islet to lay eggs). When men were not at sea, they made coir (coconut sennit), repaired boats, and fixed their nets. Today diligent men use their boats once or twice a week, and those less motivated or ill prepared may sail only a few days each year. Imported foods permit survival without a daily reliance upon the sea, and the rapidly fashioned outboard motor boats are relatively easy to repair. Consequently, far less time is spent on communal seafaring activities.

As canoes have disappeared, significant social organizational shifts have occurred. Women no longer work together weaving pandanus sails, and men do not give their attention to constructing and repairing sailing craft. Old men warmly reminisce about the days when they would gather to plait sennit, chant, and recount stories. Now they no longer need the support of others to dismantle and reassemble recaulked canoes, nor do men rush to the water's edge to assist in bringing

FIGURE 1.2. Bedecked with protective coconut fronds, Apinar's canoe is moved for final preparations and christening. The planking, lashed with coconut sennit, has joints filled with pandanus frond still to be caulked with breadfruit sap. The three-piece keel (*kaep* 'bottommost keel segment' and *baar* 'rising keel segment') and bow and stern segments *(jiim)* are hewn from local woods, while planks are hewn from driftwood *(ralap* 'large central planks' and *erip* 'planks adjacent to *jiim')*. The decking *(eddip)*, not yet trimmed to width, has in recent times been made from marine plywood. A canoe shed awning appears in the background, and coconut frond skids mark the path to the canoe's new resting place.

launches up on shore. This process, *aarik,* was always reciprocated with part of one's catch, and it involved men in solidarity-building exchanges that are remembered fondly by older residents. Today, the members of a crew beach their own lightweight craft.

Despite these changes in approach to seafaring and travel, Enewetak and Ujelang people, like the residents of Sikaiana, are unceasing sailors, whose love for the sea will long outlive the last canoe. The trope that equates life with canoe voyages dominates daily discussion now as in the past. Whether embossed in the flesh, embedded in discussions of the day, or used in practice to enhance human movement and transcend constraints of space and time, the value of canoe construction and seafaring remains a vital force in island life. For example, the full array of social relationships among deities and humans, chiefs and commoners, is mediated through performances and forms of talk that are vested in the lore of canoes. While deities are naturally empowered beings, humans are not. Nineteenth-century chiefs used the

FIGURE 1.3.   The Enewetak people's ever-changing world is seen in the juxtaposition of the government-owned supply ship (in background), outboard motor boat (anchored in middle foreground), and a pair of sailing canoes being loaded with supplies (left foreground). Rigging of canoe at rest is visible on the canoe nearest to the shore.

lines of canoes inscripted in tattoos to trace their power to its sacred, deified source, while high Marshall Islands chiefs now commandeer today's swiftest craft, Air Marshall Islands flights, on a moment's notice as public proclamations and expressions of their power. But dieties and high chiefs, whose rank is expressed by claims of access to pathways that lead to ancient chiefs and, ultimately, to gods, are inherently different from ordinary humans. As in Samoa, people claim that Marshall Islands chiefs should sit while others attend to their needs (Shore 1982). Their very movements in the world are dangerous to others who come in contact with them (cf. Sahlins 1985), and immobility limits these dangers. Ideally, Marshall Islands chiefs are the fixed points upon whom others depend for guidance (cf. Lutz 1988). Like stars, people expect their actions to be predictable, consistent, and moral. Indeed, most ancient deities are represented by stars that are also used for navigation. High chiefs make claims about their rank and access to extraordinary power through the use of personal names that link a chief to certain stars or to heaven (Carucci 1984) just as they attempt to lend legitimacy to their identities through claims along pathways that lead to ancient chiefs and, ultimately, to celestial deities. But only those chiefs who provide consistent guidance are honored as stars in the universe of daily life. They are the truly respected leaders who metaphorically replicate the characteristics of celestial bodies in the eyes of the navigator.

While the ritually inscribed lines of tattoos and navigational metaphors align chiefs with celestial deities in the Marshallese universe, other stories of sailing demonstrate ever-important practices for chiefs and commoners. As with Trobriand chiefs, moral Marshall Islands chiefs must balance danger, fear, and distance with reciprocal generosity to win the support of commoners (Weiner 1976). In spite of the affinities between chiefs and sacred force, ultimately it is the demonstration of proper behavior—sharing, watching over, and caring for others—that allows one to gain access to sacred force. This belief is illustrated in the story of Jebero, the youngest among a group of siblings born to the chiefly mother of the Marshall Islands (cf. Krämer and Nevermann 1938:chapter 6, p. 32). He is the least empowered of the sibling set and, in this respect, like the commoners. Yet, unlike his older brothers, he is portrayed as a kind figure who takes his mother on board during a canoe race to determine which sibling will rule. As a result, Loktanur, his mother, teaches Jebero how to sail (not just to paddle like his brothers), and with that ability he is able to secure rule over the earth from his inconsiderate older brothers (Carucci 1980; Carucci n.d.:introduction). Knowledge of sailing, which in accord with mythological precedent transforms the magical potency of the wind into directed activity, thus gives the low-ranked access to power beyond their inherent means. It gives ordinary humans the ability to attain renown and it provides the potential for one to hold a position of power.

Some specific dimensions of this ability are captured in the fragments of local knowledge that follow. In each subsequent section, I attempt to situate sailing as a historically grounded activity with cultural foci and elaborations. Since indigenous use sets the course for our analysis, it is important to note that Marshall Islanders measure human accomplishment with exemplary stories and parables known as *waanjonak*. (Literally, *waan-jonak* means 'a vehicle' or 'a sailing-class thing' with which 'to measure'.) It is this unique semiotic positioning of sailing that allows it to serve as an appropriate analogy for the course of human life.

SAILING THROUGH LIFE

The metaphor of sailing through life is used frequently in the morality plays that accompany the celebration of *Kurijmoj* 'Christmas'. In 1977 one songfest group used the sailing metaphor to describe its competitive travels to visit other groups. The opening phrases focused upon landing, and at the end of the performance, the speaker suggested that perhaps it was time for his group to "set sail." In 1982 one of the competing groups used the Morning Star (Ijuraan 'Venus'), the name early missionaries selected for their sailing craft, as the form of its tree (a piñata-like object that, when magically exploded, reveals the gifts the group presents to the minister, the earthly representative of God). The group's accompanying speeches focused on proper moral actions in life, relying upon commonly quoted biblical texts that emphasize love and sharing as well as an omnipotent God. The speaker couched his moral lessons in sailing terms by juxtaposing a sailing canoe that, incautiously captained, runs aground and sinks, to another canoe that, properly sailed, steers a peaceful and considerate course through life (Carucci n.d.).

The sailing canoe, which gains its legendary ability to "fly" from the wind, is the prototypical vehicle-class object *(wa)*. Its magical potency is extracted from the marginal region that separates the sky and the sea, and that potency reflects positively on those who build and sail these craft. Extended in the early contact period to European ships, *wa* is now used for bicycles, automobiles, airplanes, spacecraft, and satellites. Each of these instruments of locomotion shares a dimension of magical force with its prototype, the sailing canoe. Unlike walking and running, the sailing canoe captures the intangible force of the wind and multiplies manyfold the capabilities of those aboard. Walking is mundane and demeaning; riding in a vehicle *(wa)* represents personal accomplishment. On Enewetak, automobiles are abundant, although their utility is limited on an islet three miles long. Their representational value contributes to their owners' identity, and they epitomize the drivers' ability to manipulate the automobile's intangible force. On Majuro my Marshallese landlord refused to work when his company-owned vehicle was borrowed for a week. While he did not live far from his place of employment, walking to work was far too degrading.

As is true of most core belongings and pieces of a Marshallese self, the canoe takes on special semantic weight. The canoe is identified as *wa eo waam* 'sailing craft, the sailing craft class object of yours' or *wa eo warro* 'sailing craft, the sailing craft object of the two of us (inclusive)'. In innovating upon these usages, an automobile takes the same forms *(waam tiruk)*, and its steering wheel becomes an analogue of the *jebuei* (a paddlelike handheld rudder that is used to correct the course of the canoe).

More important than these semantic innovations are the life stories and the moral applications that use the metaphor of sailing, such as running aground *(loorek)*, floating around aimlessly *(ebebe bwajjik)*, and drifting helplessly downwind or ending up downwind from one's intended destination *(beilok)*. Also, while *bwabwe* indicates a direct course close to the wind, *jebwabwe* (*je-* is a prefix that, not unlike "im-" or "un-" in English, negates the condition that follows) means 'lost' or 'totally undirected' and refers to the lack of a consistent life's course. The opposites, sailing straight paths *(jimue)*, direct ones *(kajju)*, and fast, well-powered courses *(kakotkot)*, are associated with positive action.

The Enewetak voyagers of today, like those from Sikaiana and Rotuma (Donner, Howard this volume), gain great renown from their voyages. In recent decades, missionary voyages *(missen)* to other lands have become popular. After the mission in 1982 to Hawaii, people wondered, What is it that these (Enewetak) people could do for the people there? Well nothing. But it was a fine time for them to *travel around* and *see the way things are in that place and return and tell stories about it* (Benjamin Gideon, Enewetak Field Notes, 1982–1983). Similarly, people say the biggest reason men want to become council members is to travel, see distant places, and *come back and reveal the news about these places.* Voyagers hope to build renown by being like their predecessors who went to Saipan, Hawaii, New York, and Washington, D.C., to appeal for the community's compensation and repatriation to

Enewetak. These travelers also pattern their actions after ancient sailors—culture heroes remembered for their travels to other atolls where they "looked around," sometimes fought with foreign people, and came back to "tell the news" to those at home. Thus, voyagers achieve renown through their experience of the extraordinary and by sharing their uncommon knowledge with others who stayed behind. Again, this is a prototypical male quality, for Enewetak and Ujelang people contend that "while men travel around, women should stay put."

Different kinds of craft and voyage have become the templates to describe a wide range of life's affairs. The voyagers with intention, particularly ancient Enewetak sailors like Juraan and Niinjuraan, who set out to conquer other atolls and met with remarkable success against overwhelming odds, are held in highest esteem. The lowest-ranked pursuits include punting on the interior reef or using a paddling canoe to reach a nearby location. Intermediate are unintentional drift voyages, like that of two Enewetak men in 1982 who were within a "hundred miles or so of Guam" when they were rescued by a large ship. The story of the two men—an increasingly common tale in these days of undependable outboard motor boats—incorporates the intrigue and determination of the voyagers of old. They ventured far outside the reef, surviving on fish and the water they collected with their shirts and stored in their otherwise useless gasoline tank. But their story lacks the intent and subsequent fulfillment of purpose, the regularity of movement inherent in the story of Juraan and Niinjuraan. Still, it is recounted as a harrowing story that weaves images of ingenuity with the realities of life at sea.

At the same time, the story of the two Enewetak men exploits the relatively uncharted space between the sacred and profane. It is adduced as evidence of the good graces of God, the most highly ranked and foreign deity. But all activities beyond the reef share in this mediation of the unknown and the common. Indeed, the very sacredness of the most highly ranked paramount chiefs *(iroij lablab)* lies in their foreign character, the antithesis of local commoners in every respect. Foreigners of other sorts are treated with chiefly privilege, and their analogous position rests on characteristics they share with sacred chiefs and deities (Sahlins 1981; Carucci 1980, 1988).

Sailing gives ordinary humans extraordinary ability. It gives them a way to explore unknown, high-ranked, and supernaturally inhabited spaces beyond the outside reef. While these are dangerous pursuits, sailing and recounting details of one's voyage are sources of power. In local terms, they are "pathways" that allow people to develop significant sources of renown (see Feinberg 1991).

CANOES AND THE DIVISION OF LABOR

For Marshall Islanders, the canoe is a prototypically male object. From a young age, boys practice sailing skills by launching miniature canoes constructed from immature coconut fronds or by sailing more sophisticated proa made of sticks. Their landings are in play areas along the lagoon shore and their canoe houses are simple lean-tos beside undercut banks or arched coconut trees. Girls are not discouraged from such play but spend far less time engaged in it. On Ujelang, girls are more enamored by punting chains of laundry tubs, linked hand-to-hand by their occupants, along the shallows landward of the elevated interior reef.

In the process of becoming a man, a young male becomes part of a *wa*, a canoe group that shares a proa. The members of a canoe group build a sailing canoe, maintain it, rebuild it each year or two, and sail to distant islets to fish, gather birds, or wait for turtles. Fishing trips are also arranged on the open sea for tuna, jacks, mahimahi, and other large game fish. For such open ocean ventures, fewer fishermen board the craft (ideally three on the ten-meter craft of the late 1970s) since the outrigged vessel must be lightweight and ready to fly when a *wunaak* 'flock of plankton-feeding birds that marks a group of feeding fish' is located and pursued. In the 1970s most ocean-side trips of this sort were conducted in outboard motor boats. Even today these trips are considered very risky men's work, but the boats have much greater speed than canoes. This swiftness is critical in quickly reaching the fishing location, doubling back on the feeding-frenzied school of fish, and hooking the fish securely (see Tobin 1968; Carucci 1989).

Each *wa* must have a canoe-building specialist and a skilled sailor, or captain. In ancient times, chiefs are said never to have planned an open-sea voyage without the assistance of a seer who could predict the weather and the fortunes of the voyage. For a war canoe, this person also would foretell the outcome of the battle. A second specialist was the canoe bailer. Canoes chinked with pandanus fronds and caulked with breadfruit sap always leak, and a fast sailing canoe in choppy surf (especially when heavily laden) takes on a good bit of water through the open deck portals. The large oceangoing canoes of the nineteenth century, said to have been over thirty meters long, took on still more water. A skilled canoe bailer prevented this from occurring by using magical chants. Thus, while the canoes were very large, their holds were magically kept moisture-free.

The captain holds the highest rank among persons aboard a canoe. He sits on an elevated platform on the leeward side of the craft, controls the sail, and gives instructions to the sailor, or sailors, and canoe bailer. Traditionally, Marshallese captains sailed by observing wave patterns—the deflection of swells around atolls and the wave contours at their points of intersection. During the day, an astute sailor can read these cues in the differential light patterns reflected from major swells. At night, the most skilled sailors feel wave motions in the rocking of a boat. Even today a few captains of interisland Western ships rely upon this local method rather than on instruments (cf. Nukumanu [Feinberg this volume]; Bugis, Indonesia [Ammarell this volume]). Birds, stars, and fish also provide keys to navigation, but the location of atolls far beyond the horizon is coded in the different light patterns of waves that bounce back from, or lie in the lee of, their fringing reefs. Stories about ancient times tell of navigators who set sail for the most distant atolls using their knowledge of the stars. Long before the low-lying islets on the fringing reef came into view, it is said, the captain would correct his course by using the reflections from deflected swells.

The renowned Marshall Islands stick charts (Winkler 1901; Knight 1982) were of no use to skilled sailors who mapped details in their minds, and people claim they were never used on Enewetak, whose isolated location made them irrelevant.

Instead, islanders say the charts were employed in the Ratak and Relik Chains as training devices to remind young sailors of the major currents and wave patterns in the frequently traveled waters that connected nearby atolls. On Enewetak and Ujelang, the major sailing courses—a treacherous passage to Ujelang, a more frequently used path to Bikini, and a longer course to Aenenkio (Wake)—were traversed in stories that revealed prolific features of what, to outsiders, might be a totally undifferentiated sea. These stories paint a portrait of the sea in all its ambivalence: the choppy, indecisive waters on the course from Enewetak to Ujelang that could "damage a proa and throw it downwind to drift without recourse until it came ashore in the atolls of Truk, in bits and forever damaged" (Aluwo Atwar, Ujelang Field Notes, 1976–1978); or the lifesaving contours of the path between Enewetak and Bikini via a famous coral head marked by murky seas and sharks friendly to Enewetak people (an atoll formerly inhabited by many members of the shark clan). At this coral head, sailors are said to have dived for supplies of brackish water to satiate their thirst on the lengthy trip. From these stories the sailor gains the knowledge to captain a canoe. With the blessing of a chief, the assistance of a bailer, and one to watch the skies, a captain and his crew are ready to set sail.

Marshall Islands canoes keep their outriggers to windward. The captain accomplishes this task by reversing the bow and stern each time the boat must take a new tack. This maneuver, *riak*, replaces "coming about" on a Western sailing craft. Only the most skilled captains can do this single-handedly, and on the large proa of the past it required several sailors. The captain also directs a sailor to steer the craft, and he, single-handedly, raises the lower boom *(rojak korak* or *rojak kora)* when sailing into the wind to bring the craft into a tack square to the wind. In sailing close to the wind, it is his responsibility to lift the outrigger out of the sea to obtain maximum speed, a maneuver done smoothly only by the most skilled sailors.

The canoe is the captain's island. Whereas the land space of an atoll is metaphorically equated in local legends with women, safety, and protectiveness, the potentially violent sea is represented as the refuge of skilled sailors. It is said that in the worst typhoons ancient Enewetak people abandoned their atoll. They sailed out to sea, secured the sail and mast, filled the canoe with water, and sat out the storm. When the typhoon passed, the canoe was bailed and they set sail for home.

The canoe is also a metaphoric source of cooperative endeavor. The captain, bailer, and weather specialist provide metaphors through which storytellers describe hierarchical relationships, while the coordinated effort that allows members of the crew to perform as one represents people's interdependence in the voyage through life. Cooperative endeavor is equally expressed through stories that describe the righting of oceangoing outrigger canoes. The small canoes of Mokil can be righted by a single sailor who forces his feet down on the keel as he pulls the outrigger up and over his head, but the ten-meter Enewetak canoes require two men to accomplish this feat, and the canoes of old necessitated even more cooperative effort.[2]

As I have noted elsewhere (Carucci 1980), there is a separate sailing code to classify orientation according to wind direction and according to one's position vis-à-vis land. A different code is used to discuss directions of a fixed sort. This latter code resembles the European north-south-east-west schema. The sailing code, windward-leeward, is dynamic from any fixed point on earth. Windward ranks higher than leeward, and the canoe must always face the high-ranked windward. It is the captain's responsibility to maintain this trajectory, even in the summer months when the windward shifts rapidly.

In the sailing code, women generally occupy the leeward position. When male and female cross paths on a trail, for example, the woman should walk to the downwind side of the man. This is often complicated by the fact that the ocean side of the islets (and the open ocean itself) is the man's side and the lagoon side the woman's side. Likewise, on board a canoe, the outrigger is the woman's proper position. Ancient canoes had a small canoe hut constructed on the outrigger platform, slightly windward of the hull, where women were supposed to ride (see Haddon and Hornell 1975[1936]:366). This position places women on the windward side of men, a situation that allows for numerous negotiational possibilities. Thus, while women are upwind of the captain, they are also passengers—seated, immobile, and placed lower than the captain's platform. In the relatively egalitarian setting on Enewetak and Ujelang, ranked relationships between women and men are often negotiated through boasting and joking, drawing on spatial relationships that refer to interactions at sea as well as on land (cf. Feinberg 1988, this volume).

Canoes also provide material to depict the proper conjugal relations between adult men and women. By one such logic, a man is equated with the hull and a woman with the outrigger. Thus, when visiting neighbors, a common query directed to a man about his wife takes the form of *"Ewi kobaak eo?"* 'Where is the outrigger?' (the smaller, but equally critical, component that keeps the canoe afloat). Associated with this metaphor is another one that draws upon the way the outrigger platform is lashed to the hull. Lashings are made on both the windward and leeward sides of the craft, but the two knots on the leeward side are said to be the most critical. These must be properly tied in order to maintain the integrity of the craft as a whole. Not surprisingly, they are appropriated as the semantic fodder for the discussion of sound and shaky marital relationships as well, for it is at this critical point that the male and female segments of the canoe are linked. A second metaphor equates the lower boom and yard of the lateen sail, the 'tied' and 'front' spars *(korak* and *maan)*, with women *(kora)* and men *(emaan)*. Some informants even claimed the two had the same derivation. Most often this metaphoric material is used to describe sexual relations, where the man is on top and the woman on the bottom.

Similarly, one of my consultants taught his son that the *abit*, critical little pieces that provide rigidity between the outrigger and the outrigger platform and that are lashed in place as a canoe nears completion, were responsible for the verb *abidik(i)*, a term that refers to work that is no longer burdensome because its end is in sight. I am not convinced the two words share a common root, but the analogy is informative since it demonstrates the way in which directed activities of daily life are given logical order in terms of the prevailing relationships that typify the fashioning and sailing of canoes.

While the discourses of daily life simultaneously fashion and reflect the continued significance of sailing to these atoll dwellers, important changes have occurred in what British social anthropologists commonly have called the level of "actually existing social relations" (Radcliffe-Brown 1965:190). Indeed, when canoes were present, they were often the major focus of male endeavor, and females were excluded from most, but not all, of this activity. In older residents' memories, the manufacture and maintenance of a large craft occupied much of a sailing group's time, and when men were not sailing to fish or capture birds, they worked on their canoes. Spare time was used to repair canoes or was used in sennit-making circles where Enewetak sailors of old told stories and chanted special chants that built concentration and placed strength and excitement in their work *(itok limo in)*. Younger men remember playing as children around these circles of grizzled sailors, listening to their low, growling tones, and learning about sailing, canoe craft, and the separation of men's and women's labors. Indeed, the entire process of making sennit is a type of men's work that links sailing with the manufacture of coconut toddy, another prototypical male endeavor (Carucci 1987; Feinberg 1988:302, this volume).

The chants *(roro)* were not limited to sennit making. There were also sailing chants and chants to bring boats ashore. The chants ensured that the mediational work of sailing actually came into being. It is claimed to have made the most difficult of tasks bearable, and it brought strength to men's muscles in order to overcome the most dangerous and challenging obstacles. These fragmented chants, extremely difficult to translate, are discursive fragments that bring action into being. This sailing and fishing chant was taught to me by a renowned Ujelang sailor and canoe builder who is no longer alive:

> Kamuelik jitak ion buke
> Kamuelik jitak ion buke
> Io, io, kamelit io,
> kotkot io
> jone uaan
> Mona in jilu e wulep
> jalet bwebwe.

In rough translation, it shows how prototypically male activities are empowered:

> Making the canoe go out across the exterior reef,
> there, just to the windward of the fishing shoal.
> Making the canoe go out across the exterior reef,
> there, just to the windward of the fishing shoal.
> Me, me, make me intelligent
> Make me act swiftly
> Measure falsely (in the wild)
> The food of the largest of bluefin tuna
> Take the yellowfin tuna off the hook.

While canoe work and, particularly, chanting are men's activities, women still play a part in the manufacture of a canoe, for they stitch the sail. In recent times, they have sewn together lengths of heavy canvas, but the old women recall making sails from strips of pandanus, about a meter in width. These strips were made differently from sleeping mats, and today only a few women remember the technique. Women's place in canoe manufacture is not thought to be improper *(jekaar)*. It is a vital contribution, for just as Loktanur first revealed the sail to her youngest son and gave him the power to capture the force of the wind (and chiefly rule of the earth), so women give the same strength to sailors of today.

IDENTITY, ETHNICITY, AND ENEWETAK CANOES

While the Enewetak canoe-building tradition may be approaching its final days, most atoll residents continue to talk about canoes as if they were still a major part of daily life. Only the old canoe builders, saddened to see the passing of a central part of their lives, speak of canoes in the past tense. Others use the present tense, as if canoes were being constructed and sailed every day.[3] This discursive ploy allows Enewetak people to transcend the constraints of time and to draw on the symbolic potency of Enewetak canoes to make empowered statements about atoll identity.

Each Enewetak canoe is named, and each carries its own reputation for swiftness. Every time a new canoe is built, a race is organized. If supplies of driftwood allow, when one person begins a canoe, others with an interest in building a canoe also work. Those with older canoes repair their craft and, unless food is in short supply (requiring some canoes to be in service each day), they refit the planking and renew the pandanus and breadfruit sap caulking. Even before a canoe is completed, the tips of the bow and stern *(jiim)* are bedecked with coconut frond streamers. These ornaments are said to protect the craft, maintain its swiftness, and make it less vulnerable to magical attack.

Upon its completion, but before the canoe is moved to the shore to have the final pieces fitted, and before anyone other than the builders touches the craft, it is blessed *(aaje)*. A feast is given, the owners (heads of the canoe group) speak, and small gifts of soap, matches, and cloth that bedeck and enshroud the craft are given away. The minister says a prayer to wish the crew safe voyages, and then the hull is moved by all the men of the community to the area where canoes are beached.

The canoe's reputation for swiftness reflects upon the skill of the crew as much as upon the speed of the proa, but part of a canoe's reputation is captured in its markings. Each canoe is painted in bicolor. The draft below the waterline is painted 'black' (dark blues and other dark, highly saturated and reflective hues are included in this classification); the exposed part of the craft is painted in a light, contrasting color, usually white, but with slight variations in painting and design that, along with unique hatch covers, tie-down clamps, and other accoutrements, differentiate the owners. Each canoe also maintains its coconut frond streamers bow and stern to protect the craft and make it swift.

Other streamers may be placed on top of the mast, but in ancient times, multiple streamers atop the mast and on the lower boom *(rojak korak)* were found only on chiefly canoes. These are said to have been the same as the prohibitive markings a chief might place on trees that were not to be used or the markings around sacred shrines. The chief's canoe should be the swiftest of the fleet, and the prohibitive markings distinguish it from all other craft.

The story of Etao, the trickster, in his travels to Majuro Atoll (cf. Krämer and Nevermann 1938:chapter 5, p. 12), uses the swiftness of the chief's canoe as fodder for Etao's double-edged pursuits. Envious of Etao's swift new canoe, the chief of Majuro asks him to exchange the canoe for his own. Etao agrees but notes that he must first adjust and polish the canoe. Prior to the maiden voyage, each plank of the canoe to be given to the chief is replaced with a replica, identical in all respects except very smooth and shiny, which, the chief is convinced, will increase its speed. Its deceiving exterior, however, reflects only that it is made of *kone (Pemphis acidula)* the heaviest and hardest (as well as the shiniest) of indigenous woods. Etao plans to usurp the chiefly crown, and as the voyage approaches, he convinces the chief to lash himself soundly to the canoe since, in its swiftness of flight, he might be dislodged. Etao in the chief's old canoe and the chief in the shiny new craft set sail at the same time from the leeward end of Majuro. The chief, lashed to his canoe, sinks, to be fossilized in a famous coral head on the lagoon side of Ronron islet, while Etao easily escapes his pursuers and sails on to Arno to continue his sly primordial pursuits.

While the canoe captures distinctive elements of personal identity, of rank, and part of the craft's and crew's reputation in its very form, the most critical features of Enewetak canoes relate to their expression of atollwide identity. Enewetak people have always considered themselves the most skilled canoe builders in the region. They use their ability to represent themselves as superior to Marshall Islanders, who, in spite of superior numbers, were never able to conquer them and incorporate them into their chieftainships. While von Chamisso (1986:132) was impressed with the speed of Wotje canoes, Enewetak people consider Marshall Islands canoes 'fat' (*banban* in Enewetak dialect), small, and slow, the antithesis of what a good canoe should be. They respect the canoe-making abilities of the Mokil craftsmen (who say they learned their skill from the Marshallese) but consider their canoes so small as to be toylike, with little utility beyond the reef. In contrast, the Enewetak canoes, sleek and with the subtle differential curvature of an airplane wing, sail very rapidly and maintain a line close to the wind. Their extraordinary size makes them well suited to the large, crashing waves that predominate in the waters around Enewetak Atoll. (Von Chamisso measured a medium-sized Wotje canoe that was 17 feet 6 inches and notes that "Kotzebue measured two boats of 38 feet in length" [1986:133]. In contrast, the canoes Tobin pictured Enewetak people using on Ujelang were 65 feet [twenty meters] in length.) Canoes thus become a signifier that codes superior Enewetak abilities in the face of their negatively constructed backwoods image in the Marshall Islands (see Carucci 1989).

All of the congruences between identity and canoes, as well as the seemingly unjustified stereotyping of Enewetak people, were brought out in the Enewetak canoe project in 1992. The canoe project was a rite of revitalization that appropriated the historically grounded skills of Enewetak canoe builders to define and situate Enewetak identities in the context of the newly emergent Republic of the Marshall Islands. During the building phase on Majuro, the construction crew reported that

Marshall Islanders from other atolls believed the Enewetak canoe was too narrow and would collapse or sink when confronted with the swells of the open ocean. Enewetak people knew differently and waited for the chance to test the canoe against other Marshall Islands canoes. In these races in and around Majuro Atoll, the fifteen-meter Enewetak vessel came out far ahead, confirming for Enewetak people their superior skills and contradicting the backwoods image of them that is held by Marshall Islanders.

Once the canoe was built, Enewetak people planned to enter it in the Pan-Pacific race in the Cook Islands, while Marshall Islanders expected the crew to represent all of the Marshalls. Enewetak officials threatened to withdraw the canoe until, in the end, it was agreed that the captain and crew would be Enewetak people, but the navigator, whose skills deserved their own respect, would be Marshallese. While these events were given a variety of interpretations in different parts of the Marshalls, Enewetak saw them as a confirmation of their own superiority in sailing and of their own empowered atoll identity. When the Enewetak canoe won the outrigger class race in Rarotonga, further confirmation was provided for the canoe-building prowess of the Enewetak community and the concomitant realignment required by outsiders who had formerly treated the Enewetak and Ujelang people with disdain.

From the Enewetak and Ujelang perspective, their ethnic and canoe-building superiority is naturally and historically derived. By their accounts, Marshall Islands clans Ijjidik and Ejoa are derivative clans that came from Enewetak long ago, died out (in the case of Ejoa), and were reintroduced by women who married into Enewetak from the Marshalls. Related to this local cosmogony is a view that reinforces the primacy of Enewetak as the source of sailing knowledge. In this view, ancient deified beings came to Enewetak from Kabilin 'back side of heaven'. They traveled through Ujelang 'middle of heaven' and emerged on earth at Enewetak 'island opening to the windward'. From Enewetak these primordial beings began to create earthly locations—the northern fringes of Enewetak, the shallows between Enewetak and Bikini, and the tiny islets of Bikini. From there they proceeded to the central Relik Chain (*kabinmeto* 'the back side of the ocean').

In this view of primordial travel that I have pieced together from the stories of many people, Enewetak remains a critical point of juncture between heaven and earth, a point on the margin of the sacred and profane where the wind, the sea, and knowledge of sailing come together to provide a source of power to an isolated and overlooked group of people. The original travelers had an inherent source of power for they were *inea* 'superhuman'. They raced from Enewetak to Bikini on foot, as if across the sand. The humans that followed, however, had to seek their own sources of empowerment. These sources came in the form of tattoos, depictions of the lines of sacred force obtained through clan inheritance, and through capturing the wind with sailing canoes that could fly.

NOTES

Acknowledgments   Field research on which this essay is based was conducted in the Marshall Islands in 1976–1978, 1982–1983, and 1990–1991 under grants provided by the National Science Foundation and the National Endowment for the Humanities. All interpretations are those of the author, not those of the granting agencies.

1. Despite the Alele Museum's efforts to generate a sense of pride and renewed interest in canoe building throughout the Marshall Islands, there has been a radical reduction in canoe use since the beginning of the U.S. administration after World War II. This is particularly ironic since the canoe, to a greater degree, perhaps, than any other object, provided a core representation of island life for American visitors to the region after the war. As a result of the canoe-building project at the Alele, the presence of nuclear compensation monies on Enewetak, and even, perhaps, my own discussions about the canoe project with members of the community and about Enewetak canoes with the canoe project director, a seagoing canoe was built on Majuro Atoll by Enewetak people in 1992. It was raced in the Pacific Canoe Race in Rarotonga and subsequently shipped to New Zealand, where it awaits reassembly by visiting experts from Enewetak. While the canoe is an encouraging development, and the race might provide inspiration for a resurgence of interest in canoe building and navigation, the lack of integration of the new canoe into the life of the Enewetak community is notable. The canoe built on Majuro by visiting specialists from Enewetak was fashioned rapidly with the assistance of workers skilled in the use of power tools, and much of the sennit was purchased from various locations in the Caroline Islands. Unlike canoes on Ujelang and Enewetak, this one bears no name and resides in absentia. The canoe's very identity as an Enewetak canoe versus a Marshall Islands canoe was hotly disputed, and along with its current life as a museum piece, this contestation marks the new canoe's ambiguous position within the Enewetak community. While I argue below that the new canoe occupies a valuable symbolic place in the minds of Enewetak people, as a functional tool of daily subsistence, it might just as well not exist.

2. Ward Goodenough (personal communication) has noted that the people of Kiribati right their outriggers by forcing the outrigger boom under the hull, which helps to empty water from the hull as it is turned upright. Ujelang residents, like the people of Mokil (who claim to have learned their skills from the Marshallese) reverse the procedure. Ujelang people are evidently aware of the Gilbertese method, but they claim that it requires too much effort to force the outrigger under the water-filled hull of a very large canoe.

3. To capture the vitality of local discourse about canoes, I also use the present tense to talk about canoes in the paragraphs that follow.

REFERENCES

Bwebwenato in Majel
    n.d.   *Bwebwenato in Majel.* Compiled, edited, and typed by Billiet Edmond, Raynard Gideon, Saito Aine, and Peter Remail. Komman in MATCH Project eo. Jeje im Kopoje ilo Department eo an Education. Majuro: Aelon in Majol.
Carucci, Laurence Marshall
    1980   The Renewal of Life: A Ritual Encounter in the Marshall Islands. Ph.D. Dissertation, University of Chicago.
    1984   Significance of change or change of significance: a consideration of Marshallese personal names. *Ethnology* 23:143–55.

1987   *Jekero:* symbolizing the transition to manhood in the Marshall Islands. *Micronesica* 20:1–17.

1988   Small fish in a big sea: geographical dispersion and sociopolitical centralization in the Marshall Islands. In *State and Society: Emergence and Development of Social Hierarchy and Political Centralization,* edited by J. Gledhill, B. Bender, and M. Larsen. London: Unwin Hyman.

1989   The source of the force in Marshallese cosmology. In *The Pacific Theater: Island Representations of World War II,* edited by Geoffrey White and Lamont Lindstrom, pp. 73–96. Pacific Monograph Series No. 8. Honolulu: University of Hawai'i Press.

n.d.   The First Hour of Tomorrow: Ritual Renewal in an Island World. Forthcoming. DeKalb: Northern Illinois University Press.

Choris, L.
1822   *Voyage pittoresque autour du monde.* Paris: Firmin Didot.

Erdland, August
1910   Die Sternkunde bei den Seefahrern der Marschallinseln. *Anthropos* Bd. V.:16–26.

1914   *Die Marshall-Insulaner: Leben und Sitte, Sinn und Religion eines Sudsee-Volkes.* HRAF translation. Aschendorff.

Feinberg, Richard
1988   Socio-spatial symbolism and the logic of rank on two Polynesian outliers. *Ethnology* 27:291–310.

1991   A long-distance voyage in contemporary Polynesia. *Journal of the Polynesian Society* 100:25–44.

Finsch, O.
1893   *Ethnologische Efrahrungen und Belegstucke aus der Sudsee.* Translation available at University of Hawai'i Microfilms.

Haddon, A. C., and James Hornell
1975   *Canoes of Oceania,* Vol. 1. (1936) Special Publication No. 27. Honolulu: Bernice P. Bishop Museum Press.

Knight, Gerald
1982   *Man This Reef.* Majuro, Marshall Islands: The Micronitor.

Krämer, Augustin
1906   *Hawai'i Ostmikronesien und Samoa.* Stuttgart. Translation available at University of Hawai'i Microfilms.

Krämer, Augustin, and Hans Nevermann
1938   *Ralik Ratak.* Translation from the German text by Elizabeth A. Murphy, 1074 Sussex Turnpike, Randolph, N.J. 07869. Copy on deposit at the Pacific Islands Studies Program, University of Hawai'i.

Lutz, Catherine
1988   *Unnatural Emotions: Everyday Sentiments on a Micronesian Atoll and Their Challenge to a Western Theory.* Chicago: University of Chicago Press.

Radcliffe-Brown, A. R.
1965   On social structure. In *Structure and Function in Primitive Society,* pp. 188–204. (1940) New York: The Free Press.

Sahlins, Marshall
1981   *Historical Metaphors and Mythical Realities.* ASAO Special Publications No. 1. Ann Arbor: University of Michigan Press.

1985   *Islands of History.* Chicago: University of Chicago Press.

Shore, Bradd
1982   *Sala'ilua: A Samoan Mystery*. New York: Columbia University Press.
Tobin, Jack
1968   The Relocation of the Enewetak People. Ph.D. Dissertation, University of California, Berkeley.
Turner, Terence
1969   Tchikrin: a central Brazilian tribe and its language of bodily adornment. *Natural History* 78(8).
von Chamisso, Adelbert
1986   *A Voyage Around the World with the Romanzov Exploring Expedition in the Years 1815–1818 in the Brig Rurik, Captain Otto von Kotzebue*. Honolulu: University of Hawai'i Press.
Weiner, Annette B.
1976   *Women of Value, Men of Renown: New Perspectives in Trobriand Exchange*. Austin: University of Texas Press.
Winkler, Captain
1901   On sea charts formerly used in the Marshall Islands. *Annual Report of the Smithsonian Institution for 1899*, pp. 487–508. Washington, D.C.

VOYAGING AND CULTURAL IDENTITY IN THE LOUISIADE ARCHIPELAGO OF PAPUA NEW GUINEA

Maria Lepowsky

• Interisland canoe voyaging remains central to economy, ritual life, and cosmology on most islands in the Louisiade Archipelago of southeastern Papua New Guinea. Despite six generations of intermittent contact with white traders, whalers, colonial administrators, and missionaries, the people of Vanatinai (Sudest Island), the Calvados Chain Islands, Panaeati, and Panapompom continue to make long-distance trading and exchange expeditions of up to hundreds of kilometers using single-outrigger sailing canoes (see figure 2.1).

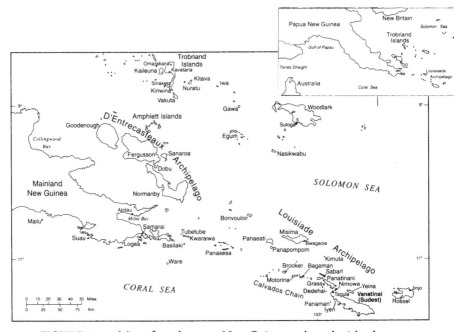

FIGURE 2.1.   Map of southeastern New Guinea and nearby islands.

The persistence of interisland exchange voyages and of feasts honoring the dead that bring together people from many different island communities is no accident. They persist in spite of intense efforts to abolish them by government officers, missionaries, and traders for the last hundred years. Voyaging is key to what Vanatinai people call *taubwaragha* 'the way of the ancestors'. It is a deliberate and consciously articulated resistance to domination by outside political, economic, and religious forces. The sailing canoe and long-distance maritime exchange are key symbols of regional pride, identity, and cultural autonomy.

Louisiade Archipelago islanders, with the exception of the Rossel Islanders, do not perceive themselves as isolated, a word itself derived from the Latin word for island. The sea, though dangerous, is a highway. Social networks of kinship, affinity, trade, and friendship commonly extend hundreds of kilometers, linking exchange partners from four or more linguistic and cultural groups. Louisiade ceremonial exchanges of valuables such as shell-disc necklaces and greenstone axe blades articulate with *kula*, the interisland exchange system of armshells, necklaces, and other goods made famous by pioneering anthropologist Bronislaw Malinowski (1961) in the Trobriand Islands.

Louisiade peoples sail for practical reasons: to reach distant gardens or fishing grounds, to visit relatives, and to barter for foodstuffs and locally manufactured household goods. They sail for religious reasons as well: to request ceremonial valuables for later ritual exchange during mortuary feasts honoring spirits of the dead. People also sail for adventure and romance and to seek fortunes and reputations. They gain wealth and renown through success in exchange; meet lovers and potential spouses; try their luck against treacherous seas, flying witches, and malevolent place spirits; see distant locales; and return to tell their stories to those who stayed behind.

CANOES

Sailing canoes are objects of beauty, pride, and desire. They represent enormous investments of local forms of wealth and the potential for acquiring more valuables. They symbolize the romance of the quest and the potential immortality of an individual's name that comes from regionwide renown for success in exchange. The owner and family have a strong emotional and sentimental attachment to their sailing canoe. I have taken many photographs of people posing by the family canoe, their arms sometimes draped affectionately across its splashboard.

Each canoe has its own name. Many people can identify it from a great distance by its size and shape, by its intricately and uniquely carved splashboards and prows, and sometimes by its paint. The elegant curvilinear designs and stylized bird's head motifs are characteristic of the art forms of the Massim, the name for the islands and adjacent coasts of Eastern Papua for more than a century (e.g., Haddon 1893; Haddon and Hornell 1975).

Sailing and paddling canoes are constructed throughout the archipelago from trees of several species of the genus *Calophyllum*. The preferred species on Panaeati Island is *Calophyllum inophyllum* (Berde 1974:90). These exceptionally hard, dense woods (sometimes called false mahogany) produce distinctively red planks when freshly cut. Sailing canoes are constructed primarily by the men of Panaeati. Building canoes of any type is an exclusively male occupation throughout the archipelago, as is all carving of wood or tortoiseshell.

Panaeati Islanders have had a near monopoly on sailing canoe construction in the Louisiade Archipelago, except for Rossel Island, for at least one hundred years. The monopoly was interrupted at the time David White, an English bêche-de-mer trader and pearler turned gold miner, lived on Vanatinai for five years in the 1880s. The long-delayed annexation of British New Guinea in 1888 was triggered by White and his party's finding gold on Sudest Island, or Vanatinai, which precipitated a rush by Australian miners. White writes that before the rush and the partial colonial pacification that resulted, "nearly all canoes were made at the island of Pannaietti . . . but now they are making them here themselves." Their canoes, he reported, could "carry forty men" and traveled as far as Samarai (White 1893:74).[1] By the early twentieth century, the Panaeati preeminence in sailing canoe manufacture was reestablished. Their specialization in this craft, significantly, is noted in a Vanatinai myth: Rodyo, the creator spirit, instructs a spirit named Bwaileva to build the first canoe, sail it to Panaeati, and tell the islanders that in the future their work will be to make sailing canoes to exchange for ceremonial valuables with other islanders (Lepowsky 1983:470).

Both outrigger sailing canoes and the much smaller paddling canoes are called *waga,* a cognate of the pan-Austronesian term. Sailing canoes are also known today as *sailau,* apparently derived from the English word "sail."[2] The traditional type of sailing canoe is called *waga moli* in the Vanatinai language and *waga hot* in the East Calvados (Saisai) and Misima languages (spoken also on Panaeati and the West Calvados Islands). These "true canoes," as their names literally mean, have not been made since the 1950s. The eight-meter-long single-outriggers, whose planked sides were lashed to the dugout base using bush cord rather than nails, used oval sails of stitched wild pandanus leaf. Their weight made them slow but highly stable. People say the pandanus sails became enormously heavy when they were wet and thus became dangerous in heavy seas and storms. They had superb carving along the keel, prows, splashboards—which had two lobes of different sizes—and bow-pieces (figureheads called *tabura,* a term that connotes spiritual forces, that rose at the bow in front of the splashboard [cf. Macgillivray 1852:I:202]). Bird motifs and curvilinear designs were common. The carvings, *Ovulum* cowries, feathers, and other objects placed on the canoe had magical power as well as aesthetic value. Old people tell me that the sights and sounds of a magnificently carved canoe gliding into harbor, with pandanus streamers fluttering, rows of eggshell cowries hanging down and rattling in the wind, and young men standing on deck blowing the triton-shell trumpet announcing their arrival, were so beautiful as to make one cry.

In the first decade of this century, a Brooker Island man returned from Townsville, Australia, with some innovative ideas for building a different type of sailing canoe. It was not until about the 1930s that his ideas were adopted by the Panaeati Island builders (Berde 1974:96–101). This new type of canoe, the *sailau,* is shorter, lighter, faster, and rides higher in the water but is more likely to capsize,

FIGURE 2.2.   Canoe builders from Panaeati Island take down the sail as they arrive by *sailau* at Grass Island to collect an installment payment. The canoe on the beach was also built at Panaeati.

as island sailors today are well aware. It can be steered by one person, unlike the *waga moli*, which often required one navigator at the stern with the primary steering paddle and a second person sitting on the outrigger platform with a second paddle for greater stability. (I have only seen this once on a *sailau* voyage, when we were heavily laden.) It has a trapezoidal canvas sail, which is more simply rigged than on the *waga moli*. The *sailau* has symmetrical, two-lobed splashboards still magnificently carved, but there is less carving on the prow and keel, no bow-piece, and no more eggshell cowrie decorations. Its mast is centered, unlike that of the *waga moli*, making it easy to tack. A *sailau* is reversible, rerigged while tacking by a sure-footed crew member holding the boom out while walking along the gunwale, as the craft wallows briefly but alarmingly in wind and swell. The old bow becomes the stern, and the outrigger is kept to windward. A *sailau*, like a *waga moli*, is constructed of planks lashed to the dugout hull log and caulked with forest resins. Removable decking covers storage areas in all but the canoe's center near the mast. The outrigger float and platform are constructed like that of a *waga moli* (see figures 2.2 and 2.3).

In contrast to the men of Panaeati, only a few Vanatinai men in any generation have known how to build a sailing canoe, learning from older matrilineal kinsmen. The last one built on Vanatinai was an old-style *waga moli* constructed during the mid-1950s by Gole of Kamerighea, a hamlet near Jelewaga on the south coast. He

FIGURE 2.3.   Young men from Grass Island dressed for a feast on the family sailing canoe. They have just retrieved the mast from the house rafters, where it was stored overnight. This canoe is named Hulmaisena, which means 'Only Child' in the language of Misima and Panaeati Islands.

used this vessel for exchange journeys for over a decade. The men of Panatinani, or Joannet Island, just to the northwest of Vanatinai, built in the mid-1970s a fine, large *sailau* of which they were justifiably proud. They described it as a consumer revolt against the high prices and slow delivery terms characteristic of the Panaeati canoe builders.

Sailing canoes today are still purchased using ceremonial valuables. Prices vary, but a large canoe is worth about five shell-disc necklaces and fifteen polished greenstone axe blades. These are key valuables that circulate as well in *kula* exchanges in the islands north of the Louisiade Archipelago. In addition, the buyer must accumulate and present the builder with ten of the largest pigs, dozens of clay pots full of cooked yams and other vegetables, baskets of yams, and about two hundred bundles of sago starch (Lepowsky 1983:470–71). The only cash involved, ranging from the equivalent of U.S.$75 to $300, reimburses the builder for the money required to purchase canvas for the sail from a trade store and for any store-bought foods, such as rice, he may have used to feed his workers.

Canoe purchases take place on an installment plan, typically lasting over a period of years. The Panaeati people are frequent visitors to the Calvados Islands and

Vanatinai, sailing southeast to solicit installment payments from their sometimes recalcitrant buyers. They are sometimes told upon arrival that their customers do not have the expected necklace or pig. They must sail on (using the canoe for which payment is in arrears) to another island to obtain the valuable from a third party. Sometimes the customers travel to obtain a valuable from an exchange partner elsewhere while the Panaeati canoe sellers wait at the buyer's home. Buyers frequently explain that they must wait for a mortuary feast to take place at which they expect to receive valuables as heirs of the deceased. They will pass these on, they say, to the Panaeati men. Relations between the seller and buyer are cordial on the surface, especially given the threat of retaliatory sorcery or witchcraft, but anger over a reneging exchange partner is often expressed privately by both buyer and seller.

People of the small and infertile Calvados Chain Islands, such as Brooker (Utian), Motorina, and, especially, Grass Island (Wanim), are interisland trade specialists. They often buy new Panaeati canoes and resell them after a year or two of use at a profit of additional shell necklaces, greenstone axe blades, pigs, and so on to the people of Vanatinai farther to the southeast. This saves the people of Vanatinai from the trouble of dealing directly, over months or years, with Panaeati builders over one hundred kilometers distant.

Only a few men know how to make the single-outrigger, unplanked paddling canoes used throughout the archipelago. These canoes are also poled in shallow water by a man or woman (or older child) standing astride the gunwales at the bow. Builders of paddling canoes may become known for their skills beyond their home communities or islands, attracting more distant exchange partners or clients. In one case from the late 1970s, Sale, a Vanatinai man, purchased a well-made paddling canoe with beautifully carved finials from an exchange partner at Sabara (Sabarl Island) in the East Calvados for one fine shell-disc necklace, five large, thin, greenstone axe blades, one large pig, and sixty bundles of sago starch. He could have contracted for a canoe made on Vanatinai but preferred to obtain one from his Sabara exchange partner.

In 1987, Lote, a seventy-year-old man from Jelewaga on Vanatinai, slowly constructed a large paddling canoe in the bush behind his house, with several of his matrilineal kinsmen working under his supervision. He alone did the final carving on the prows. Lote planned to keep the canoe for his own family's use, but some of his neighbors and exchange partners admired it and talked of wanting to purchase it. He was expected to loan his canoe to his neighbors, as there are only a few paddling canoes per Vanatinai settlement, unlike in the Calvados Chain, where most families own a paddling canoe and many also have a sailing canoe. If Lote's neighbors borrowed his canoe to go fishing, he could expect a generous share of the best fish caught. If they borrowed it for a longer trip, he could expect a more substantial gift of sago starch, yams, or, after a major exchange journey, a ceremonial valuable such as a greenstone axe blade. Sailing canoes, too, are often borrowed or rented, depending upon the closeness of the parties, in exchange for substantial gifts of pelagic fish, in the case of an overnight expedition to the barrier reef, or for greenstone axe blades after an exchange journey.

MEN, WOMEN, AND SEA TRAVEL

There is a clear tendency in the Louisiade Archipelago for men to be more heavily involved in traveling by sea than women and for women to be more strongly identified with the land, specifically with yam gardens, which they are said to own in these matrilineal societies. This tendency parallels a pattern familiar in the literature on the Pacific Islands and reported by the other contributors to this volume. In the Pacific, men are almost always symbolically and practically associated with the sea and movement, while women are associated with the land and stability.

However, in contrast with aboriginal Polynesia, where in many societies such as Tahiti and the Marquesas women were forbidden even to travel by canoe, women in the Vanatinai, Calvados Chain, and Panaeati areas of the Louisiade frequently journey long distances by sailing canoe, as they did in ancient times. Both women and men of Vanatinai and the East Calvados crew sailing and paddling canoes. Everyone knows how to paddle and pole, but, unlike East Calvados women, not all Vanatinai women know how to steer and navigate a large sailing canoe. Female sailors are most common in the East Calvados, especially from islands such as Sabarl or Grass, where one must sail across a channel to reach gardens and water sources on larger islands. All-female crews steer, using a large paddle held at the stern as a rudder, navigate, and sail. Some women can sail single-handedly, particularly those from the East Calvados Islands or those from Vanatinai who have lived on tiny nearby islands such as Panaman (cf. Battaglia 1990 for Sabarl).

Throughout the region both sexes sail and paddle to fishing spots on coral patches, to gardens, to favored springs and streams for fetching water, and to other settlements and other islands to visit friends and kinfolk. All-male parties are most likely to make overnight trips to fish on the barrier reef. On family trips for subsistence, exchange, or to attend feasts, both young men and women may serve as crew. The navigator, stationed at the stern with the steering paddle, is usually male, often a middle-aged or older man who is still physically strong. At least one person, often a young woman or man, must bail diligently, using a large, melon-pink bailer shell with two fingerholds punched in it.

Some exchange voyages to Misima or Panaeati have female leaders. This happens somewhere in the region almost every year. A few women from Vanatinai and the East Calvados Islands lead exchange voyages in quest of ceremonial valuables to be used during one of the elaborate mortuary feasts held in a series lasting for years after the death of every individual. They often have a largely male crew consisting of younger kinsmen. On one memorable occasion, I was walking westward with several women from Jelewaga bound for the government station and Vanatinai's one trade store located some thirty kilometers distant. As we prepared to halt for a rest and visit at a small hamlet along the bay, we caught sight of a fine sailing canoe anchored at a break in the mangroves. My friends named the owners of the canoe, strangers to me at that point, who were a married couple. "Is Wona (pseudonym for the husband) on an exchange trip?" I asked. "No," Lemodi said, "Ghayawa is seeking valuables. Wona is following her." Ghayawa, I soon learned, was a big woman, renowned for her prowess in ceremonial exchange and for hosting and contributing generously to mortuary feasts. She was currently seeking shell-disc necklaces, greenstone axe blades, and other valuables for the largest and final feast, which she and her brother would host, in honor of her deceased father. Her husband, also active in exchange, had his own personal partners. He was supporting her, but her reputation and wealth were greater (Lepowsky 1993).

To the women of Vanatinai, Calvados Chain, and Panaeati, the sea is not locally perceived as inherently or exclusively a male domain. Women have the natural right, like men, to go on maritime voyages both for subsistence and for exchange and ritual purposes. Women's mobility and their access to the primary avenue to prestige and renown—the exchange-mortuary ritual complex—mirrors and reinforces the gender egalitarian ethos of the region (Lepowsky 1990a, 1990b, 1993).

JOURNEYS

The people of the small Calvados Chain Islands, Panaeati, Panapompom, and the tiny islands off Vanatinai such as Panaman and Yeina are far more dependent upon sea travel by canoe, even for such daily activities as fetching water and going to gardens. There are significantly fewer sailing and paddling canoes per capita on Vanatinai, which is the largest piece of land for over three hundred kilometers, than on these smaller Louisiade islands. Vanatinai literally means both 'motherland' and 'mainland'. Vanatinai people have traditionally had a pronounced inland orientation, building their hamlets at defensible sites on the slopes of the interior mountain range and, during the early decades of this century, in the interior near the best water sources and most fertile garden lands. The island's coast is largely fringed with mangrove swamp, and sandy beaches and favorable canoe-landing spots are rare. A more marked inland rather than maritime focus is common to high island peoples throughout the Pacific.

Vanatinai canoes often lie on the shore in disrepair, while the East Calvados men quickly repair their broken outrigger platforms, replace the lashings, and caulk the leaks. The local name used on Vanatinai and in the East Calvados for East Calvados people and the inhabitants of Panaman and Yeina is Saisai 'Islands', in contrast to the 'Mainland' (Vanatinai and nearby Panatinani). Saisai people speak their own language, distinct from that of Vanatinai and of Misima, the latter spoken also on Panaeati, Panapompom, and in the West Calvados. The pattern of small island peoples being more active in interisland exchange and trade and owning more sailing canoes is found in other parts of the Pacific as well. For example, in the Caroline Islands it is atoll dwellers, like the people of Puluwat, Satawal, and Lamotrek, who are, or were, the most frequent voyagers, traveling to the high islands of Truk, Yap, and even the Marianas for both ritual and utilitarian trade (Burrows and Spiro 1957; Fischer and Fischer 1957; Alkire 1965; Gladwin 1970).

Daily subsistence, especially on Louisiade islands less favored with fertile garden lands and extensive sago swamps, is based upon food from the sea or upon canoe voyaging in order to trade clay pots, smoked *Tridacna* clam, carved wooden platters, and other goods for vegetable foods such as yams and sago starch. Small island peoples often situate their hamlets on key passages or good harbors to take maximum advantage of opportunities to trade with passing sailors or to launch their own voyages.

In small island households, the first person to awaken goes outside to check the weather and comes inside with a one-word report to the others, consisting of a wind direction such as "southeast." Once the direction of the prevailing wind, and of course the weather, has been ascertained, the day's activities and travels may be intelligently planned. An anticipated trip across the lagoon to a particular garden or stream or a planned fishing expedition to a certain reef or islet may be postponed if gusty winds are blowing in a contrary direction.

The interisland exchange system leads to a higher standard of living on all islands. Each specializes in particular products such as yams, sago, pigs, clay pots, wooden platters, sailing canoes, and shell-disc necklaces. These are redistributed by direct barter or by ceremonial exchange with characteristic *kula*-like delayed return.

As is the case in other parts of the Pacific, ties of maritime trade and exchange serve as a form of disaster insurance for people living on the ecologically marginal, densely populated smaller islands. Even with the presence of trade stores and colonial and national governments over the last century, in times of drought or crop failure, the Calvados Chain Islanders and people of Kimuta and Panaeati Lagoon still sail to the homes of their Vanatinai and Misima exchange partners to request yams and sago to sustain their families. In Micronesia, Alkire (1965) reports a similar pattern involving atolls of the central Caroline Islands and the high island of Yap, almost one thousand kilometers to the west.

People maintain a strong sense of identity with their home island, or district on larger islands like Vanatinai, but their active social universe extends far to include their distant exchange partners. Women and men alike are participants in Louisiade interisland exchange with partners on widely scattered islands who speak several languages and represent foreign cultures. Exchange partners frequently travel to each other's villages and hamlets to participate in local mortuary feasts, contributing food and valuables to their host. They rely on each other to provide shelter, sustenance, and valuables. In former days, especially two generations ago and earlier, exchange partners protected one another from death at the hands of their neighbors when on a journey. They were allies to whom one could flee if pursued by neighbors at home or turn to for help if one's crops failed or the community was attacked.

As a result of interisland exchanges, Louisiade islanders and their Massim neighbors to the north are cosmopolitan in their outlook, accustomed to observing other ways of acting and thinking. They borrow and adapt information, customs, myths, songs, and dances from exchange partners. The most intrepid travelers, those from Grass, Panaeati, Motorina, and Brooker Islands, have occasionally sailed for trading and exchange purposes as far as Ware Island, as well as the Milne Bay region on the New Guinea mainland, Samarai, Normanby Island (Duau), and even, in one recent case, the Trobriand Islands. These communities speak five different languages.

Although Panaeati people often sail all night, most sailors prefer to anchor for the night at an island, uninhabited islet, or sheltered section of reef. Most islanders sail only within sight of land. Given the geography of the archipelago, celestial navigation is generally useful only when leaving Sudest or Deboyne Lagoon (the latter surrounds Panaeati and nearby islands) and traveling northwest, following the long reef that eventually becomes the barrier reef of the south Papuan coast. This very dangerous route, full of coral patches, shifting currents, and whirlpools, leads to the New Guinea mainland and adjacent islands. Panaeati Islanders, who also travel northwest some eighty-five kilometers to the atoll of Panasesa and other barrier reef locales to fish as well as to trade at distant islands like Duau, are among the most knowledgeable and sophisticated sailors in the Louisiade Archipelago. They and skilled sailors from the Calvados Chain have a wide knowledge of star names and star tracks, winds, currents, wave refraction patterns, sea color, and signs of land such as cloud patterns, homing frigate birds, and characteristic greenish tints in the sky.

One of the motivations for sailing canoe owners for a journey to the large, forested island of Duau is to obtain a new outrigger log from a relatively light and buoyant type of wood that does not grow in the Louisiade Archipelago. If not substituted on the canoe immediately, the log is towed home behind it. Voyages to Duau are also stimulated by the need to obtain yams in times of widespread drought or crop failure, when Calvados Chain gardens are devastated and yields are reduced even on the large islands of Vanatinai and Misima. Active exchange links are also maintained between the Calvados Chain, Vanatinai, and Ware Islanders, who commonly attend each other's mortuary feasts (Lepowsky 1983, 1993).

In spite of their marked inland orientation, Vanatinai people value and admire well-built and beautiful canoes. They use both sailing canoes and the more common single-outrigger paddling canoes for transportation to other communities up and down the coast, to travel to garden areas or sago groves separated by swamps or wide bays from their homes, and for exchange journeys and visits to feasts on other islands. Yet, for some trips on their own island, they have the alternative of traveling by foot. It takes from four to five days, however, to walk from one end of the island to the other.

Often a walking trip will include borrowing a poling or paddling canoe to cross large estuaries, like that of the Veora River, the largest on the island, on the north coast. Estuaries can be crossed by wading or swimming, but this can be foolhardy, especially at high tide. They are well known as *walagoi ghabai* 'the place of crocodiles', a prime habitat for the saltwater crocodiles that occasionally kill and eat human beings. The last fatal crocodile attack on the island was in 1985 at Pantava, when a four-year-old boy was taken on the beach just outside his house near a mangrove swamp at flood tide and dragged out to sea before the horrified eyes of his mother and uncle.

Longer journeys on foot frequently involve segments of travel by poling or paddling canoe past extensive swamps or precipitous mountain slopes that plunge to the shore and are impassable by land. Those who live nearby are accustomed to being asked the favor of borrowing a canoe by visiting kinspeople, friends, and exchange partners. The canoe is brought back upon the traveler's return trip. Its owner and the other hamlet residents then get to hear who has been successful in obtaining ceremonial valuables, information they later may use to their advantage.

The women of Brooker Island and, to a lesser extent nowadays, Panaeati Island manufacture clay cooking pots. They sail along with their husbands and brothers as far as Vanatinai, eighty or more kilometers southeast, to trade the cooking pots for baskets of yams and bundles of sago starch. The pots become more valuable the farther to the southeast the traders are willing to travel. At Brooker, a standard-sized pot is worth one two-sided bundle of prepared sago starch. At Grass Island in the East Calvados, it is worth three bundles, and the Brooker people often stop there to trade their pots for food obtained by the Grass Islanders on Vanatinai. On Vanatinai itself, the same pot is worth five double bundles of sago.

Entire families of Brooker Islanders are frequent visitors to Vanatinai, particularly after the yam harvest in July and during the months of January and February. They often trade pots for the privilege of making their own sago from wild palms owned by their exchange partners. The Brooker people, crowded onto a small and barren island, could not support their population without regular recourse to food obtained through trade. I once visited Brooker during a drought. The yam gardens had failed, and people had been living for several months almost entirely on a diet of coconuts and fish. Some had already sailed to Misima and Vanatinai with pots to barter for food (Lepowsky 1983, n.d.).

Journeys to the northwest are travels "down" or "below" *(bodó ko)*. This direction refers to the prevailing southeast trade wind. Louisiade peoples use intercardinal directions. Voyagers, often families plus their friends, neighbors, and exchange partners sailing to distant communities to attend feasts, sail "down" during the last of the southeast trade wind, in October or November. This also is a good time to travel because the new yam crop has already been planted in August or September. They return "up," with luck, on the northwest monsoon, which typically blows from January to April but is more erratic and likely to bring heavy storms with it.

There are still a few sailing canoes in the villages of Misima Island. Misimans are frequently visited by traders and relatives from Panaeati, Panapompom, Motorina, Kimuta, and other small islands. They sail across a deep-water channel with high waves and tricky currents, notorious even to captains of motor vessels, to reach Misima, which is fertile and densely populated. They seek yams, sago, carved hardwood platters, ceremonial valuables, and, nowadays, goods from the island's two trade stores. Misima lacks a barrier or fringing reef except near the principal harbor of Bwagaoia, at the east end, and heavy swells, refracted off its steep submerged mass, produce dangerous sailing conditions.

Misimans have long specialized in intensive yam production and were never as oriented to sea travel as their small island neighbors. The one exception to this inland orientation is the village of Ebora, at the precipitous western tip of Misima, which is completely inaccessible except by sea. Ebora people have closer ties to Panaeati Island than they do to the rest of Misima. Misima friends tell me that, formerly, Misimans sailed to Murua (Woodlark Island) to request *kula* valuables, particularly greenstone axe blades, a major source of which was the quarry at Suloga, on Murua. The quarry has been inactive since about 1870, but the locale is a major source of the finely polished blades still in circulation (Lepowsky 1983; cf. Malinowski 1961). Muruans in the late 1970s occasionally sailed to Misima to obtain valuables from exchange partners and affines. The high island of Murua is, like Misima, much less involved in maritime exchange than it was formerly and far less involved than its small island neighbors from Gawa, Iwa, or Budibud (Lepowsky n.d.; see Munn 1986 for Gawa).

Until 1977 the Mailu Islanders, from a small island off the south Papuan coast, used to sail their enormous, double-hulled canoes 500 kilometers to Vanatinai at the end of the northwest monsoon season. They would dive for *Conus* shell, plentiful in Sudest Lagoon but scarce near the mainland. A plain shell is worth about U.S.$25 in the national capital of Port Moresby and adjacent villages. They are decorated to make armshells, called *toea* in the Motu language and along much of the south Papuan coast, where they are essential for bridewealth. The Mailu used to camp on the Vanatinai beaches for a couple of months, entertaining their hosts with music and dancing. They also brought gifts of the black wild banana seed that grows only on the mainland and that must be used to offset the reddish shell discs in the manufacture of a new *kula*-type necklace. The visitors sailed home on the southeast trade winds (Lepowsky 1983). *Conus* shells are also the raw material used to construct the decorated armshells that circulate in a counterclockwise direction among islands in *kula* exchange, opposite the exchange of necklaces, which travel clockwise. Vanatinai and East Calvados Islanders, who do not exchange armshells themselves, offer *Conus* shells they find on the reef to grateful exchange partners at Panaeati and Ware Islands, who can turn them into *kula* armshells or exchange them further to someone who will.

One of the first acts of the newly formed Milne Bay provincial government in the late 1970s was to ban anyone from outside the province from collecting marine resources. This was directly aimed at the Mailu, who sailed for *Conus* not only to the Louisiade but also to islands near Samarai and as far north as Kiriwina, the largest of the Trobriand Islands. In 1978 I saw an old double-hulled Mailu canoe beached on the estuary of the Veora River on Vanatinai, abandoned there as unseaworthy for the homeward journey by the last party of visiting Mailu sailors.

ROSSEL ISLAND

The remaining island in the Louisiade Archipelago, Rossel, called Yela in its own non-Austronesian language and Rova or Lova by its neighbors to the northwest, is extremely difficult to reach by sailing canoe or small motor vessel. Rossel is surrounded and isolated by its own separate lagoon. It is divided from Sudest Lagoon—one of the world's largest, which encircles Vanatinai and the Calvados Chain—by a treacherous 35-kilometer passage notorious for tricky currents and seven-meter swells even on calm days. Culturally, the people of Yela are quite different from those of the rest of the archipelago, who are all part of the Austronesian-speaking Massim culture area stretching to the mainland and the Trobriand Islands. The people of Yela rarely journeyed to other islands in precontact times.

Rossel was visited for two months in 1920 by anthropologist W. E. Armstrong.

He observed four types of canoes. The first, *nö* 'canoe', also called *pia nö* 'female canoe', was found at the west end. It was a small, unplanked single-outrigger he thought had been introduced from Sudest Island (Vanatinai). Rossel myth recounts that a supernatural snake from Vanatinai brought the first sailing canoe to the island along with the sun, moon, pig, dog, and taro. The other three types, which Armstrong saw as "distinctively Rossel canoes," were all taboo to women, who have a dramatically lower position in the ranked male gerontocracy of Rossel than do women in the neighboring Massim islands. These canoe types were *ma nö* 'male canoe', a paddling canoe found at the east end; *lia nö* 'sailing canoe'; and *para nö*, or *ndap* 'shell-money canoe'. Each of these featured "the decking in of the dug-out for some distance at either end and the building up of the dug-out by one or more planks." They also had prow boards, but these were decorated very differently from other Massim canoes. *Ma nö* and *lia nö* had a sloping platform over the center of the hull extending outward on the opposite side from the outrigger. Armstrong saw only two sailing canoes on the island, both at the west end, plus a "canoe of Sudest, or Panaiati type, which had been made on Rossel under the supervision of a visitor from Sudest. This is, apparently, quite a recent introduction." The *para nö* was a rare, ceremonial canoe, a symbol of rank used only by chiefs, probably to transport shell currency to feasts and for other ritual purposes. A twelve-meter-long paddling canoe with a short single outrigger, it was built for speed in calm lagoon water and used in ceremonial races (Armstrong 1928:21–30).

In 1849 twenty-four-year-old Thomas Huxley, then assistant ship's surgeon and assistant naturalist on HMS *Rattlesnake,* making the first known European contact with the Louisiade islanders, sailed along the northern barrier reef of Rossel Lagoon, observing canoes and islanders. The British could not find a passage and were unable to land, drifting westward to the northern barrier of Sudest Lagoon, where they successfully found the entrance and remained for several weeks engaged in survey work. Huxley, who made several excellent pencil sketches and watercolors of paddling and sailing canoes, wrote in his diary that another canoe "came from the direction of Rossel Id. this morning. It was white with a stage something like the Cape York canoes. It had a regular stand-up mast, supported by rope-stays. And its sail was of matting, oval and neatly woven in one piece. They can hardly have two fashions of canoes in islands scarcely twenty miles apart?" They did. (See Huxley 1935:182, 190–91; cf. Macgillivray 1852:I:205–6.)

Although single-outrigger paddling canoes of the *nö* or *pia nö* type, indistinguishable from others of the Louisiade, are still used by both Rossel men and women, there have been no sailing canoes on Rossel since the 1950s, and the other two types of canoe are extinct. A generation ago people of western Rossel hamlets sailed frequently to Seghe and other hamlets of eastern Vanatinai, where a number of Rossel men and women had married, to attend feasts and for ceremonial exchange. The postpacification colonial period was probably the height of Rossel canoe travel.

In more recent times, Rossel men have built a few small motor vessels of local timbers. The men were trained to build the vessels at Sideia Island, near Samarai, by the Catholic Mission of the Sacred Heart, which has also had a mission at Jinjo, on the north coast of Rossel, since the 1950s. These motor vessels are used to purchase copra and to ship it to Misima, where it is purchased by traders and shipped to Samarai or to Alotau, on the mainland of New Guinea. Locally built motor vessels are also used for travels to Rossel reefs and to reefs near Vanatinai to dive for *Chama pacifica* shell. The reddish rim of the shell of this edible, oysterlike bivalve is used for making the long shell-disc necklaces called *bagi* in most of southern Massim and usually known as *soulava* in Malinowski's time, from 1915 to 1918, in the Trobriand Islands. Rossel, and secondarily Vanatinai and the islands of the East Calvados, are the primary production centers for the necklaces that circulate in the exchange systems of the Massim, including *kula*. Rossel *bagi* mostly reach the rest of the Massim through Vanatinai or East Calvados exchange partners visiting Rossel, or from Rossel people attending Vanatinai mortuary feasts and contributing their necklaces.

Another prized exchange item from Rossel is sandalwood bark, which is used in powerful forms of magic and sorcery. Rossel people are avid to obtain clay cooking pots, which are extremely rare and valuable on this distant island, from Vanatinai exchange partners. Four pots are worth a large pig with tusks. Rossel people will also give a fine shell-disc necklace for one of the green parrots endemic to Vanatinai, a mark of status sometimes seen perched on the bare shoulder of a Rossel big man's wife.

SAILABOUT AND EUROPEANS

Misima Island has had greater exposure to colonial and independent government officers and their policies than any of the other islands of the Louisiade. The government headquarters for the entire archipelago has been at Bwagaoia, Misima, since the early twentieth century. Mission headquarters for what is now called the United Church (formerly the Australasian Methodist Missionary Society) is located several kilometers away by road. For one hundred years, Misima has had more resident white officials, planters, miners, and traders than any other island in the archipelago. (Some islands, including Vanatinai, have had no European residents for years at a time.) Misima has also been the scene of gold mining since 1889, except for the years during World War II. One of the world's largest open-pit gold mines began operations in the mid-1980s on the south coast. All of these enterprises on Misima offer some opportunities for wage labor. Thus, for reasons of geography, traditional orientation, and externally imposed political, religious, and economic pressures, Misimans today are less involved in interisland trade and exchange than most of their neighbors. Similar reasons explain the lesser involvement of Muruans (Woodlark Islanders) in maritime exchange.

Government officials, missionaries, and planters and traders have long been opposed to "sailabout." The term parallels the more widespread Australian expression "walkabout," used originally to describe aboriginal wanderings. There are repeated complaints by the British and then Australian district officers, resident magistrates, and patrol officers in the British New Guinea Annual Reports from 1888 and the

Territory of Papua Annual Reports from 1906 to 1975 about the failure of Sudest Islanders to pay their head taxes or to carry out orders to build rest houses, latrines, or wider paths. Government officers in independent Papua New Guinea make the same complaints. The primary reason, they say, is the islanders' preoccupation with trade, exchange, and mortuary feasts and their resulting frequent absences from their home communities.

Missionaries began extending their influence in the Misima-Panaeati region in 1891 and in the Vanatinai–East Calvados islands in 1947. They agree, whether Methodist or Catholic, that the islanders' preoccupation with sailbout, exchange, and feasting is a waste of time and resources, by men in particular. They believe that the labor and wealth that go into these activities would be better tithed to the church and applied to the care of their wives and children and that they should be at divine services rather than attending feasts on distant islands. Some missionaries explicitly recognize and worry about the religious nature of mortuary feasts and the long exchange voyages, which often precede them, that honor ancestor spirits.

Although there have been Europeans at Misima, there have been no white traders or planters resident on Vanatinai since the early 1970s. These individuals are almost universal, in their writings and conversations, in their dislike of interisland exchange. It competes directly, as they well know, with islanders' availability to perform plantation labor or to produce commodities like copra or trochus shell in exchange for credit at the trade store.

Today, few Europeans with motor vessels visit the islands of the archipelago, with the growing exception of Misima since the construction of the open-pit gold mine. The other Louisiade islands are surrounded by dangerous fringing reefs, coral patches, and barrier reefs with tricky passages. Nautical charts bear the ominous legend, "Unsurveyed. See caution." On the south coast of Vanatinai, motor vessels must anchor up to two kilometers offshore due to the coral reef that emerges from the sea at low tide. Passengers and goods must be loaded by paddling canoe or dinghy. Very little copra is produced, and most people do not bother to dive for blacklip or goldlip pearl shell because trading boats rarely come to buy it. Dangerous sailing conditions, combined with limited commercial opportunities, keep the frequency of boat traffic low.

Until recently, one exception to the infrequency of vessel traffic was the Taiwanese junks, which Vanatinai people accurately describe as banana-shaped, that periodically appeared in the lagoon to poach *Tridacna* clam, cutting out the white muscle meat and dumping the rest in the sea, then returning to a factory ship waiting outside the barrier reef. Meterwide *Tridacna* shells, open and plundered, still dot the reef. The islanders only harvest the smaller and tastier *Tridacna*. They were incensed at the theft of their food, at the waste of resources involved in dumping most of the clam, and at the fouling of the reef. The national government has stopped, or at least greatly reduced, this organized predation, whose end result is eaten in homes and restaurants in Taiwan, Japan, Europe, and the United States.

For two generations a few men from Vanatinai and a larger number from Misima and Panaeati have served as crew and, more rarely nowadays, captains of coastal motor vessels. One sixty-year-old Vanatinai man I knew had spent many years working for a white trader at Misima, once taking the Australian's cutter as far as Cairns, in North Queensland. Provincial government and the Catholic Mission at Nimowa operate small motor vessels, but these are rarely seen. The distant sound of a marine diesel is a rare occurrence, triggering the excited cry, *"Waga laye!" Laye* is a special noun indicating the arrival of a boat; a special verb, *zage*, means to board a boat or (now) a plane. *Waga* is used for motor vessels as well as canoes.

THE SEA, VOYAGING, AND COSMOLOGY

Imagery of the sea, canoes, and voyaging are at the core of Vanatinai religion, philosophy, and cosmology. Good things come from the sea even though the sea is a source of danger and risk. The deep booming of the triton-shell trumpet announces the arrival of an exchange partner by sailing canoe. Many of the most frequently told myths include the motif of a sea voyage that leads to wealth or good fortune, or the loss of it. The rocky outcropping on the shore in a break in the mangroves that constitutes the landing at Jelewaga, the community where I lived, is called "our *waga*" by a leading clan. They say a married couple and the woman's brother sailed in ancient times from the Suau coast of the New Guinea mainland looking for a new home. They stopped first at Ware but then continued up to the unknown southeast, landing on the south coast of Vanatinai. The new land had abundant water, sago, and garden space. While the men were hunting in the bush, the woman set fire to the canoe as it lay on shore so that the men would not be tempted to leave the island. The canoe turned to stone.

Other myths include that of the female snake spirit Bambagho, who traveled by sea from Goodenough Island to Vanatinai seeking a new home and bringing with her the first ceremonial valuables and the magic of exchange. She was chased away by two foolish young men and fled to Rossel Island, favoring her current home with its wealth of valuables. The mythical hero Mankaputaitai, with the magical knowledge and assistance of his mother, slew three monstrous beasts, a giant pig, an octopus, and an eagle, that had been killing and eating the people of an island (some say it is Misima), who had fled in terror. He sent the people a magical signal to return (from Ware, some say) in the form of a model sailing canoe that he cast into the sea. Another mythical culture hero is Alagh, who displeased Rodyo, the snake spirit who owns Mt. Rio, land of the dead, with the noise of his possessions. Alagh loaded one of his wives and his machinery, axes, hammer and nails, chickens, and gold and sailed off in his motor vessel *Buliliti* for the land of Europeans. This is why Europeans have money, machinery, and cargo and why Papuans have only shell valuables. But Alagh comes from Vanatinai, and one day he will sail back to the island with all the cargo that rightfully belongs to it (Lepowsky 1989, 1993).

Each matrilineal clan on Vanatinai has a set of what Charles Seligman (1910) eighty-five years ago described as linked totems. Each clan has one or more species of totem bird, one or more types of fish or marine animal such as a dugong or crocodile, a snake, a tree, and a vine. Elsewhere in the Massim the particular set of totems varies, but fish and other marine totems are common. People have an unspecified kin relationship to their totems. One can catch and eat one's own totem fish, but on Misima one cannot eat one's father's totem fish. Totem animals sometimes communicate with human beings. For example, an old woman from the tiny island of Panaman, a dozen kilometers off the south coast of Vanatinai, first learned a particular style of singing, now widespread in the region, from a shark that appeared out of the lagoon and sang it to her.

In each of the three regional Austronesian languages, the expressions "inland" and "seaward" are used on a daily basis to indicate the location of people and things. The question "Where is Mulia?" usually elicits a response such as "She went inland," meaning that she went to her garden, to forage in the forest, or, perhaps, to visit an inland hamlet. This cognitive orientation is reflected in Polynesian languages as well. Austronesian languages in the Louisiade reflect a preoccupation with the sea in other ways. On Vanatinai fine weather on a sunny day is called *tadi,* which refers to calm seas and an absence of waves. The generic term for 'meat' is *bwarogi,* the ordinary word for 'fish'.

The sea is the domain of powerful supernatural beings, and islanders are well aware that they risk their lives every time they leave land in their fragile craft. Tamudurere, one of two powerful beings who controls the magic of sorcery and warfare, lives in the deep sea. Flying witches may try to drown sailors. These are the same flying witches described by Malinowski (1961) for the Trobriand Islands and by Reo Fortune (1963) for Dobu. In the Louisiade, witches are said to take bodies of their victims to a witches' cannibal exchange feast as a supernatural form of reciprocity. The witches are mostly, but not all, female. Witchcraft may either be inherited from mother to daughter or deliberately learned, sometimes from exchange partners. Witches cut off sailors' lips with a pearl shell so that they will "talk like dogs" and drown, meaning that they will be driven senseless and unable to navigate or save themselves. Witches are also responsible for causing sudden strong winds and storms. On the other hand, witches may choose to protect their own kin from attack by other witches. Motor vessels distantly observed outside the barrier reef are usually thought to be "spirit boats" providing transport to witches. A crocodile that attacks human beings is also the "boat" of a witch (Lepowsky 1993).

Ebora, the lonely hamlet at the western tip of Misima Island reachable only by sea, is the home of witchcraft, according to a widely known myth. But most Louisiade islanders today regard the West Calvados island of Motorina as the place with the most dangerous witches. This belief is formed primarily from the knowledge that the only three sailing canoes in the Louisiade lost at sea in the last forty years were all from Motorina. All were crossing the dangerous deep-sea passage to or from Misima Island, either on exchange journeys or to attend mortuary feasts. In the most recent tragedy, four men sailed for Misima and were caught in a cyclone. The canoe capsized, and three of the men drowned. The fourth man clung to the outrigger float and drifted 170 kilometers north to the island of Nasikwabu near Murua (Woodlark Island), where children playing on the beach found him four days later, nearly dead. He was not blamed for the others' deaths; these were attributed to the witchcraft of their own female kin. The survivor's female cross-cousin, a powerful witch, said publicly that she had been present at the shipwreck and that she told the other witches to save their kin, but they did not listen. Her

Motorina neighbors told me that she saved her kinsman's life. The survivor reported hearing witches whispering when the sailing canoe overturned. When I met him a few months later he was deeply withdrawn and spoke to no one.

Islanders say that powerful place spirits called *silava* inhabit the sea, often at key patches of fringing reef and at passages in the barrier reef or between islands where currents are treacherous, waves are high, and whirlpools common. *Silava* are also found on land, inhabiting cliff faces, rock outcroppings, or sections of stream, and take the form of snakes or birds. *Silava* in the sea assume the shape of giant octopi, fish, or floating logs, and they may try to capsize a canoe and drown its occupants. They must be placated through magical acts such as chewing ginger root while uttering a spell, then spitting charmed saliva on the surface of the sea.

The prudent mariner will only embark on a major journey after learning and performing magic to appeal to ancestor spirits, place spirits, and other supernatural beings for safety from bad weather, *silava,* and attacks by witches (who may themselves be the cause of a sudden storm). Many people perform the magic for calling up favorable winds. The bleached and softened pandanus leaf streamers *(bisila)* tied to the prow, mast, and other parts of the sailing canoe are more than decorations. They are magical aids to help the canoe move quickly, pushed by desired winds.

Some *silava* have specific taboos associated with them, such as a ban on all talking while crossing the area in question, or a ban on speaking in any language other than that of Vanatinai. The penalty might be less drastic than drowning, and it is often said to be the onset of an illness such as sores on the mouth (Lepowsky 1990c, 1993). Since this taboo applies to visitors from other islands who do not speak the language of Vanatinai, it seems to be a supernatural form of protectionism. The most dramatic recent instance of a violation occurred when three Rossel Islanders poled their sailing canoe up an estuary near Jelewaga, which is taboo. They were hunting crocodiles, and they did not ask permission of the clan that owns the area. All three drowned, adding further evidence of the *silava*'s power.

During the period from 1976 to 1979, there were four shipwrecks in the archipelago, an appallingly high number given the relatively few European vessels that enter the lagoons. These included an Australian yacht on the reef near Kimuta Island, a French yacht on the barrier reef north of Nimowa Island, and an American yacht wrecked in a storm off Panawina Island. The fourth shipwreck was a ten-thousand-ton freighter with a Filipino crew out of Sydney bound for Korea with a cargo of beef carcasses and machine oil. Thirty kilometers off course, on autopilot, with a first mate who was on watch but drunk elsewhere on the ship, the freighter ran up on the reef east of Rossel Island, causing a massive oil spill. Bones of cattle picked clean by sharks washed up on the shore at Vanatinai for months afterwards. An elderly neighbor told me with an unmistakable note of satisfaction in his voice, "*Silava* got it."

CONCLUSION

The sea continues to be the primary avenue to wealth and renown and to risk of disappointment and tragedy in the Louisiade Archipelago. Voyaging by sailing and paddling canoes for subsistence, ritual, trade, and pleasure remains central to the lives of most Louisiade peoples. Although colonial and national governments, missionaries, and traders have tried to suppress interisland exchanges, feasting, and visiting for one hundred years, no one has been able to give the people of Vanatinai and their island neighbors to the northwest compelling reasons to give up maritime travel or consistently offer them satisfying alternatives. Maritime exchanges and rituals weave remote communities into webs of social ties that facilitate a higher standard of living, a richer social life, chances at treasure and fame, and the means to honor religious obligations.

A more intense and long-term involvement with the worldwide cash economy and Christian religion has lessened the preoccupation of Misima peoples with mortuary feasting and maritime exchange. But Misimans in precontact times were more likely to receive overseas visitors than to make journeys themselves. In the rest of the Louisiade Archipelago, except for the long-isolated and inwardly focused Rossel Island, interisland exchange remains the core of customary life. The repeated attacks over several generations on interisland voyaging and exchange by outsiders whose motives are held in suspicion by island peoples have made the act of continuing to practice these customs overt signs of resistance to external control. Given the partial availability of alternatives such as cash cropping, wage labor, collecting tropical commodities, eating trade store foods, and practicing Methodism or Catholicism, canoe travel for subsistence or ritual purposes has become more than a practical necessity or rarely questioned religious obligation. Canoe voyaging is a recurring act of assertion and pride that affirms cultural autonomy and personal identity. Islanders who undertake the adventure of a major journey simultaneously demonstrate personal freedom and mobility and social and moral worth. They display courage, resourcefulness, and respect for their kin. They are making a conscious and visible choice, for voyaging and exchange underlie the way of the ancestors.

NOTES

Acknowledgments   The research on which this essay is based was carried out in 1977–1979, 1981, and 1987. I received financial support from the National Science Foundation, the University of California, Berkeley Chancellor's Patent Fund and Department of Anthropology, the National Institute of Child Health and Human Development of the National Institutes of Health, the Wenner-Gren Foundation, and the University of Wisconsin Graduate School. I gratefully acknowledge this support. The map in figure 2.1 was prepared with the assistance of the University of Wisconsin at Madison Cartography Laboratory. Earlier drafts of this essay were presented at the Association for Social Anthropology in Oceania annual meetings in 1990 in Kaua'i, Hawai'i and in 1991 in Victoria, British Columbia. I thank Richard Feinberg, Ward Goodenough, and the participants in the two sessions, "Seamanship in the Modern Pacific" and "Continuity and Change in Oceanic Seafaring," for their comments.

1. Berde (1974:92–94), who questioned people from Panaeati, Misima, and Woodlark (Muyuw) Islands, was told that the original canoe-making area for all of the eastern

Massim was Misima, specifically the north coast around the present-day village of Liak. Misima is also portrayed as the first canoe-building island in Panaeati myths. Other Louisiade peoples besides the Panaeati Islanders exchanged sailing canoes for valuables with distant partners in the early colonial period when warfare was largely but not completely suppressed. Colonial officer G. L. Le Hunte noted in the British New Guinea Annual Reports for 1898–1899 the presence of fine, artistically decorated sea-going canoes at Wari (Ware) Island, near the mainland. "They are made at Utian, or Brooker Island," he said, "and sold for twelve tomahawks" (Le Hunte 1900, cited in Haddon and Hornell 1975:II:253). "Tomahawks" likely refers to the greenstone axe blades for which sailing canoes are still exchanged, and which in the Louisiade today may still be called by the Papuan Pidgin term, "*tamiak ston* (tommy-'awk stone)."

2. Stuart Berde (1974:98), who conducted research on Panaeati Island, credits William Davenport with suggesting that *sailau* (rhymes with "file how") may come from the English nautical expression, "Sail ho!" This works especially well if one imagines a Cockney or Strine (Australian) pronunciation in the English original.

REFERENCES

Alkire, William
   1965   *Lamotrek Atoll and Inter-Island Socioeconomic Ties.* Illinois Studies in Anthropology No. 5. Urbana: University of Illinois Press.
Armstrong, W. E.
   1928   *Rossel Island: An Ethnological Study.* Cambridge: Cambridge University Press.
Battaglia, Debbora
   1990   *On the Bones of the Serpent: Person, Memory, and Mortality in Sabarl Island Society.* Chicago: University of Chicago Press.
Berde, Stuart
   1974   Melanesians as Methodists: Economy and Marriage on a Papua and New Guinea Island. Ph.D. Dissertation, Department of Anthropology, University of Pennsylvania.
Burrows, Edwin, and Melford Spiro
   1957   *An Atoll Culture: Ethnography of Ifaluk in the Central Carolines.* New Haven: Human Relations Area Files.
Fischer, John, and Ann Fischer
   1957   *The Eastern Carolines.* New Haven: Human Relations Area Files.
Fortune, Reo
   1963   *Sorcerers of Dobu.* (1932) New York: E. P. Dutton.
Gladwin, Thomas
   1970   *East Is a Big Bird: Navigation and Logic on Puluwat Atoll.* Cambridge: Harvard University Press.
Haddon, A. C.
   1893   *The Decorative Arts of British New Guinea.* Dublin: Royal Society.
Haddon, A. C., and James Hornell
   1975   *Canoes of Oceania.* (1936–1938) Special Publications Nos. 27–29. Honolulu: Bernice P. Bishop Museum Press.
Huxley, Julian (editor)
   1935   *T. H. Huxley's Diary of the Voyage of H.M.S. Rattlesnake.* London: Chatto and Windus.

Le Hunte, G. L.
1900   Appendix G. *Annual Reports of British New Guinea for 1898–1899.*
Lepowsky, Maria
1983   Sudest Island and the Louisiade Archipelago in Massim exchange. In *The Kula: New Perspectives on Massim Exchange,* edited by Jerry W. Leach and Edmund Leach, pp. 467–501. Cambridge: Cambridge University Press.
1989   Soldiers and spirits: the impact of World War II on a Coral Sea island. In *The Pacific Theater: Island Representations of World War II,* edited by Geoffrey White and Lamont Lindstrom, pp. 205–30. Pacific Islands Monograph Series No. 8. Honolulu: University of Hawai'i Press.
1990a   Gender in an egalitarian society: lessons from a Coral Sea island. In *Beyond the Second Sex: New Directions in the Anthropology of Gender,* edited by Peggy Sanday and Ruth Goodenough, pp. 171–221. Philadelphia: University of Pennsylvania Press.
1990b   Big men, big women, and cultural autonomy. *Ethnology* 29:35–50.
1990c   Sorcery and penicillin: treating illness on a Papua New Guinea island. *Social Science and Medicine* 30:1049–63.
1993   *Fruit of the Motherland: Gender in an Egalitarian Society.* New York: Columbia University Press.
n.d.   Gold dust and kula shells. Manuscript.
Macgillivray, John
1852   *Narrative of the Voyage of H.M.S. Rattlesnake. Commanded by the late Owen Stanley, R.N., F.R.S. and during the years 1846–1850. Including Discoveries and Surveys in New Guinea, the Louisiade Archipelago, etc.* 2 vols. London: T. and W. Boone.
Malinowski, Bronislaw
1961   *Argonauts of the Western Pacific.* (1922) New York: E. P. Dutton.
Munn, Nancy
1986   *The Fame of Gawa: A Symbolic Study of Value Transformation in a Massim (Papua New Guinea) Society.* Cambridge: Cambridge University Press.
Seligman, Charles
1910   *The Melanesians of British New Guinea.* Cambridge: Cambridge University Press.
White, David
1893   Descriptive account, by David L. White, Esquire, of the customs, etc. of the natives of Sudest Island. Appendix U, 73–76. *Annual Reports of British New Guinea.*

KADUWAGA: A TROBRIAND BOAT HARBOR

Susan P. Montague

•   In 1922 Bronislaw Malinowski published *Argonauts of the Western Pacific*, in which he acquainted Westerners with *kula*, an interisland trading system involving the Trobriand Islands and several neighboring groups (cf. Fortune 1932; Powell this volume; Lepowsky this volume). Yet, while Malinowski devoted his famous ethnography to a maritime enterprise, little is known by Westerners about Trobriand maritime activities per se. This essay serves to fill part of that information gap. Most data presented here were gathered at Kaduwaga, a village and boat harbor located on Kaileuna Island (see figure 3.1). Kaduwaga is the only indigenously constructed boat harbor in the northern Trobriands and is one of very few in the Pacific. It has long played a prominent role in Trobriand maritime affairs, making Kaduwaga something of a trade and communication center and serving as a source of income for local villagers.

My essay is divided into three sections. The first describes the Kaduwaga boat harbor; the second depicts the village that is located on the harbor's shore; and the third describes some of the harbor's uses, both by village residents and by other people from the Massim region of Papua New Guinea.

KADUWAGA HARBOR

Kaileuna is the second largest island in the Trobriand atoll series. It lies west of northern Kiriwina, the largest of the Trobriand Islands, and is about five kilometers wide and seventeen kilometers long. Kaduwaga harbor is located on the western, seaward side of Kaileuna Island, about midway between Kaileuna's northern and southern shores. In order to travel by boat from the government center on Kiriwina Island to Kaduwaga, it is necessary to sail across the channel separating the two islands and then to continue around either the northern or southern end of Kaileuna (see figure 3.1). With a good wind, this is a four-hour voyage by outrigger canoe.

Kaduwaga harbor is a natural cove indented into the western coast of Kaileuna Island. The cove is about one kilometer long and one-half kilometer wide. It is

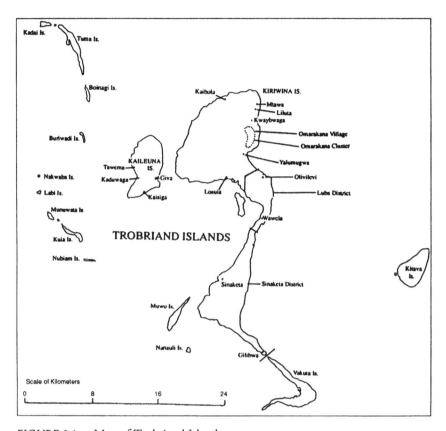

FIGURE 3.1.   Map of Trobriand Islands.

open to the sea, but no waves enter it, as an underwater coral shelf extends out across the cove's mouth for about one-quarter kilometer and acts as a natural break-water. Water depth in the cove varies with the tides. At the mouth it runs between two and four meters; at midway it runs from one-half to two meters; near the shore it measures from zero to just over one meter.

Originally, the shoreline consisted of a beach that sloped down to the water. To-day the water's edge is fronted by a 1.3-meter sea wall built out of coral boulders. The land behind the sea wall is filled in with dirt that is level with the top of the sea wall. The wall is punctuated with two gravel-lined ramps that offer access to the higher ground behind it. During extremely high tides, the higher ground floods to a depth of two to three centimeters. The cove's floor is mostly coral, with a strip of sandy ooze close to the shore. The first time I arrived at Kaduwaga, I stepped out of the boat onto what looked like barely submerged sand and lost both my shoes in a thick layer of clingy muck. The bottom is more easily traversed by Trobrianders, who routinely go barefoot.

The most prominent item of human construction in the harbor is the sea wall. Kaduwagans say that it was built in the 1850s, under the leadership of the Tabalu Guyau people. While the cove was used to shelter boats before that time, the addition of the sea wall made it possible to moor boats close to shore but still in the water, turning it into a "real" harbor. Kaduwagans say their harbor is one of just two constructed under Tabalu Guyau leadership. The other is located at Noagasi on Gumasila Island in the Amphletts. The harbors were constructed to facilitate inter-island *kula*. Fleets sailing south on *kula* voyages from the Trobriands use the Noagasi harbor; fleets sailing northward from the Amphletts use the one at Kaduwaga. Malinowski (1922:274) wrote of Noagasi:

> Here, among the small houses on piles, scattered picturesquely through the maze of little harbors, lagoons and dikes, large groups of people will be seated on mats of plaited coco-nut, each man as a rule under the dwelling of his [kula] partner, chewing betel-nut stolidly, and watching stealthily the pots being brought out to be presented to them, and still more eagerly awaiting the giving of Kula gifts. . . .

Kaduwagans say that, in addition to having a sea wall, the harbor at Noagasi has coral boulder boat slips. These are unnecessary at Kaduwaga because the cove's interior is well sheltered.

KADUWAGA

Malinowski (1922) described Trobriand villages as circles of houses facing a central clearing, but at Kaduwaga the houses are strung out facing each other in two parallel rows along the shore, resembling a street (see figure 3.2). This configuration is typical of shoreline villages in the Trobriands. In contrast, Omarakana, the village from which Malinowski drew his circular prototype, is an inland village. For this reason, his description of economic organization focused on horticultural activities, and he described the populace of each Trobriand village as a gardening team. Although it is not inaccurate to say that the populace of Kaduwaga is a gardening team, one might equally say that Kaduwaga's economy is anchored in fishing. Most Kaduwagan men fish almost every morning, and most Kaduwagan women process fish for consumption almost daily. In terms of labor, the major difference between gardening and fishing is that women work alongside men in the gardens but not on the fishing boats.

When it comes to gardening, the most significant people at Kaduwaga village are the men who own *kwabila* 'large fields'. There are five large fields at Kaduwaga, each capable of feeding the entire village for a year. The fields are gardened in rotation over a five-year cycle. Each large field is owned by one man who determines when his field is to be cultivated. In a cultivation year, the other male Kaduwagans tend one or more plots on the large field as tenant gardeners. This includes the men who own the other four large fields.

For fishing, the most significant people are the men who own *waga masawa* 'amusement boats'. These are large outrigger canoes of which there usually are two

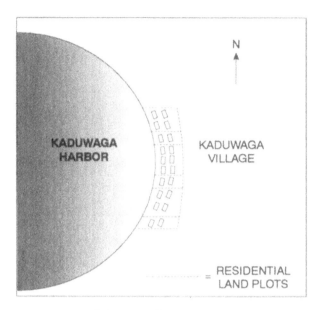

FIGURE 3.2.   Kaduwaga village.

to three at Kaduwaga. Each canoe is owned by one man who has complete authority over its use. Every man who does not own a large canoe serves as a tenant fisherman on one of the other vessels. In addition to the large canoes, there are about
eight small outrigger canoes, called *kalipola* 'fishing craft', at Kaduwaga. Each of
these is also owned by an individual man. The small canoes are used for fishing in
the coastal shallows; the large ones are used in deeper waters offshore. Again, the
owners of the small canoes dictate when they will be used, and other men are tenant fishermen on them.

Men usually build their own small canoes, calling on and paying others for assistance with the heavier labor. By contrast, large canoes are built by specialists. A man
who wants a large canoe contracts with a specialist to build it, usually someone
from the Toliwaga descent line. (*Toliwaga* means 'man who is a source of boats'.)
Although there are boat-building specialists from other descent lines, they are
thought to be less expert than the Toliwaga because they do not possess as much
boat-related magic.

As Powell (this volume) notes, large canoes are expensive items to acquire. Their
mahogany hull logs and balsalike outrigger logs come from exceptionally large trees.
Unlike small canoes, whose hulls are carved out of a single log, large canoes have
compound hulls whose sides are built up out of wooden planks cut from additional
logs. The canoe's future owner must pay for these additional logs and for the labor
required to cut boards from them. Unlike the small canoes, too, the large canoes

have fairly elaborate outrigger platforms, which add to the cost of labor and materials. Moreover, large canoes have elaborately carved prow boards on each end. The prow boards are relief carved with a series of artistic designs. Usually a separate specialist is hired to create these. The wood for them is taken from one of the logs that has already been purchased to furnish hull planks, so it is not an added expense; however, the carving is. A master carver may spend a month producing a single set of prow boards, and skilled master carvers charge a great deal for their work, both for devising a particularly esthetic set of designs and for executing them precisely. Finally, the sail is tailor made to suit the boat. In 1971, when I first visited the Trobriands, sails were plaited from pandanus leaf. Today, most are cut from store-bought cloth. In either case, they are expensive. To plait pandanus sails requires considerable labor, which must be paid for; to purchase large amounts of cotton cloth from trade stores also can be costly.

Most payments are made in the form of yams. Boat builders like to be paid in cash, but most of the men who commission large canoes, although wealthy in Trobriand terms, do not possess much cash. The primary export commodity in the Trobriands is yams, but they cannot be profitably exported to a cash market, as shipping costs are prohibitive. Instead they are exported to noncash markets on neighboring islands in the northern Massim area. It is a chronically annoying feature of local life that Trobrianders participate in one of the wealthiest indigenous economies in all of Papua New Guinea but nonetheless are cash poor.

The cash-poor economy has limited the extent to which Kaduwagans have either adopted Western craft or added motors to their own. With government assistance, Paramount Chief Katubai did obtain a Western boat in the early 1980s—a combination motor-sailing vessel; however, the motor soon gave out. Katubai then sailed it to a shipyard at Alotau for repairs but never could afford to pay for them. So far as he knew in 1988, the boat was still waiting in Alotau; more likely, the shipyard's owner had sold it years ago.

Kaduwagans say that, over the years, several villagers who have children working in Port Moresby have managed to obtain outboard motors, but they have all quickly broken down. Motors do not hold up well in the Trobriands, and there are no local repair facilities. Most owners cannot afford to ship them out for repair, so they are abandoned. For example, in 1988 there was one Western boat at Kaduwaga. It was owned by Sivalolu, a man who had two sons working in Port Moresby. It was an old wooden inboard vessel with, characteristically, a broken motor. Sivalola could not afford to get the motor repaired. Nor could he move the boat to a repair facility, since it was not a sailing vessel. He was looking to sell it but with no success.

For the industry of fishing, boats—the commodity through which fish are accessed—are the items of special significance. For gardening, the item of special significance is the milieu in which crops are produced, namely, land. In contrast with some other islanders' views of their commodities (e.g., for Marovo see Hviding this volume), Kaduwagans say that people own land but not the sea. As a result, Kaduwaga harbor belongs neither to any individual nor to any combination of

Kaduwagans, even if that combination is taken as the entire village. In line with this notion, Kaduwaga harbor is open to free access by any boating parties that choose to sail into it. The village, however, is located on land, and all of the land on Kaileuna Island belongs to specific people. For nonowners to access any piece of land on Kaileuna Island, they must obtain the owner's consent.

The land in the central portion of the harbor's shoreline constitutes the residential portion of the village. It is divided into a series of house plots, called *tumila* 'person transformer', referring to ties with dead ancestors who are thought to reside directly below the houses, on the earth's lower side. Each house plot begins at the water's edge and runs inland, crossing the street (see figure 3.2). Each is sufficiently large to contain several houses.

Both of the ramps that constitute the access openings through the sea wall to the village are situated in the residential area. Both are also located on house plots owned by the village headman, Paramount Chief Katubai. This arrangement means that no boating party can enter the village without his permission. The first order of business upon landing for any non-Kaduwagan boating party is to send word of the reason for its presence to Katubai. The fact that both ramps are located on Katubai's residential land also means that when he tires of the party's presence in the village, it must either leave or become trapped in hostile territory with no access to their boats. As shown in figure 3.2, the residential portion of the village does not span the entire length of Kaduwaga harbor. It is unfeasible, however, to forego use of the access ramps and to come ashore outside of the residential portion of the village. The visitors would be viewed as a raiding party and would be met with physical attack unless they first obtained permission from the owner of the land at the specific place where they came ashore. While anyone may access Kaduwaga harbor as frequently and for as long as he wants, no boating party can possibly remain in the harbor without coming ashore unless it is carrying a sizeable supply of water. At sea, one can obtain some water from raw fish, but, owing to the heavy human traffic, there are few fish in the harbor.

USES OF KADUWAGA HARBOR

The word *Kaduwaga* 'water land place of boats' is the name of both the harbor and the village on its shore. Although there are a number of shoreline villages in the northern Trobriands, Kaduwaga is the only one among them situated by a harbor. This, however, does not mean that Kaduwagans possess very many boats. As noted earlier, there are about three large canoes and eight small ones owned by Kaduwaga villagers. The three large canoes keep the entire village well supplied with deep-sea fish, and they handle local interisland travel demands. The eight small canoes are sufficient to keep the entire village well supplied with shallow-water fish, and they handle the demand for coastal travel. The village populace is around 300, with approximately 75 men. Thus, there is about one boat available for every seven men. Men use boats much more than women do, and the village's boat count always basically reflects men's, rather than women's, usage needs.

Women do not operate canoes at sea. Since the large canoes are used only offshore, this means that women never utilize them except as passengers. Also, since Kaduwagans only paddle small canoes, women never have a chance to operate a sail. They say that it is foolish to sail even very small canoes in the coral shallows, owing to the risk of hitting submerged boulders. At Giva village on the eastern side of Kaileuna Island (see figure 3.1), small canoes are often sailed because they move briefly into deep water as they traverse the narrow channel between Kiriwina and Kaileuna Islands. I have never seen a woman pilot one of them, however. Men's monopoly on sailing corresponds with the common association among Pacific Islanders of men with maritime activity and women with land-based activity. (For a partial exception, see Lepowsky this volume.)

Most Kaduwagan boat utilization centers on fishing. Although the name for the large canoes, *waga masawa* 'amusement craft', refers to their use in the amusing pastime of *kula*, this is a secondary activity. Next to fishing, Kaduwagans use their boats mainly for local traveling, whether intra- or interisland. Most localized travel is for trade, government business, or attendance at mortuary observances. Travel for trade rarely involves trading in fish. The nearest market is at the government center on Kiriwina Island and is too far away to be reached before the fish begin to spoil. Occasionally Kaduwagans smoke their catches and then take them to the market at Losuia, but most Kaduwagans intensely dislike the smell of fish being smoked and, therefore, do not do this often.

Kaduwagans voyage overseas once every several years for purposes of *kula*. They sail in conjunction with people from other villages as part of what they call the Kaileuna *boda* 'enablers'. These are people drawn from villages on Kaileuna, Kuyawa, and Munuwata Islands in the Trobriands and from villages in the Lusancays, a small atoll series to the west of the Trobriands. The boats provided by the Kaileuna 'enablers' add up to a fleet. In *Argonauts of the Western Pacific*, Malinowski spoke of the Kaileuna *kula* fleet and indicated that it consisted of about twenty large canoes (1922:122). When I arrived at Kaduwaga in 1971, I was surprised to discover that there were only two large canoes in the harbor, along with one that was under construction on land. My first thought was that the Kaileuna *kula* fleet had seriously declined in size. I failed to realize that the so-called Kaileuna fleet vessels do not come just from Kaileuna Island. Kaduwagans today say that the Kaileuna fleet is about the same size as it was in Malinowski's day. Kaduwaga village contributes two to three canoes to the fleet. Tauwema, Giva, and Kaisiga villages, all located on Kaileuna Island, contribute two apiece. Kuyawa village, located on Kuyawa Island, contributes another two, and villages in the Lusancays contribute another five or six for a total of eighteen to twenty large canoes.

Malinowski (1922:99–100) said that utilitarian trade is not part of *kula* per se but is secondarily conducted on *kula* voyages. Kaduwagans reiterate this assertion and add that they do not engage in very much utilitarian trade while on *kula* voyages because, since so many people want to sail on those voyages, cargo space is filled with passengers' food and personal effects. Kaduwagans also indicate that more people want to travel on *kula* voyages than there is space available. Large canoes are too expensive to build unless they can pay their way, and they do not pay their way through *kula*. Also, the number of large canoes that can pay their way is smaller than the number that would be required to accommodate all of the people who want to travel on any given *kula* voyage; therefore, some people are left behind. Each canoe owner decides who will be allowed to sail aboard his vessel.

The large canoes generate income primarily through fishing and through fees for local travel, with the bulk of their support coming from the fees paid by tenant fishermen. While the canoes can be hired for overseas trading ventures, this is rarely done because the regional interisland market is tipped in favor of the Trobriands. The primary Trobriand export is yams, the region's staple crop. Yams are abundant in the Trobriands but in short supply elsewhere. The primary Trobriand imports are, by contrast, luxuries, which they do not need nearly as much as their regional trading partners need yams. Trobrianders do not like to engage in any more overseas voyaging than necessary, except in the context of *kula;* instead, they allow their overseas trading partners to come to them.

Kaduwagans are extremely safety-conscious sailors. When Kaduwagans sail their large canoes abroad, whether for *kula* or utilitarian trade, they always sail in fleets. (The same is true of people who sail in from overseas.) Kaduwagans say this practice is a safety measure. Should something go wrong and a canoe become incapacitated, its passengers can be transferred to and spread out among the other vessels in the fleet. Only fools, they say, would sail out of sight of land in parties of fewer than five or six canoes. Similarly, canoe owners refuse to carry any passenger on an offshore voyage who is not a strong swimmer. Each canoe is equipped with a fishing line for each passenger. In rough weather, each passenger ties one end of his line around his waist and the other to the boat. Thus, if a passenger is swept overboard, he is still attached to the boat and can either swim back to it, pulling himself down the line, or can be reeled in by someone still aboard. If the canoe capsizes, both he and the other passengers can pull themselves back and, using the submerged outrigger platform for footing, climb up onto the hull. It is a Kaduwagan maxim that only a fool abandons an overturned canoe in deep water, even if land is in sight and looks to be accessible by swimming. Either the current will push the boat toward shore or it will be too strong to swim against it.

All Kaduwagan boats are outrigger canoes. This is because, whether intended primarily for deep-sea or coastal usage, these vessels must routinely navigate through coral shallows. Outriggers facilitate tracking and enable canoes to resist leeway drift and avoid capsizing, all with minimal draft. The biggest of the large canoes in which I have traveled had a draft of only about fifty centimeters, and Kaduwagans try to avoid making their canoes so large as to have more than about thirty centimeters' draft when empty.

It is possible to construct shallow-draft single-hulled non-outrigger sailing vessels. They must be equipped, however, with centerboards, and if they venture into shallow waters, the centerboards must be retractable. I initially assumed that Kaduwagans shunned such craft because their technology could not handle leakage problems attendant upon the insertion of retractable centerboards into the hulls.

However, they deny that this is the case. They say that all of their boats are maneuvered in shallow waters too frequently to make centerboards desirable. Even under paddle, shallow-draft single-hulled boats are less stable than outrigger canoes unless the hulls are very wide. But if the hulls are very wide, the boats are poorer sailing vessels. Moreover, even if the boats are never sailed, it takes more effort to build wide single-hulled boats than to build narrow-hulled outrigger canoes.

Another seemingly curious feature of Trobriand outrigger canoes is evident in Malinowski's crosscut construction diagram from *Argonauts*, reproduced as figure 3.3. (Malinowski's diagrams show the canoes as having rounded bottoms, while I have yet to see a Trobriand canoe without a deep-V hull. The discrepancy could either reflect a design change between 1918 and 1971, or it could be a drawing error on Malinowski's part.) If the canoe is set on the ground, the platform that attaches the outrigger float to the hull is not level, but slopes upward toward the outrigger float. If the boat is put into the water and loaded with passengers, the hull sinks and the platform's upward slant toward the outrigger increases. Indeed, it takes on such a tilt that the leeward gunwale is barely out of the water. Kaduwagans say the reason for this problematic feature has to do with the ease with which an overturned canoe can be righted in deep water. They assert that a large canoe without a slanting outrigger platform and leaning hull is impossible to right in deep water. In fact, they say that, even with the regular design, it is difficult to right a large canoe in

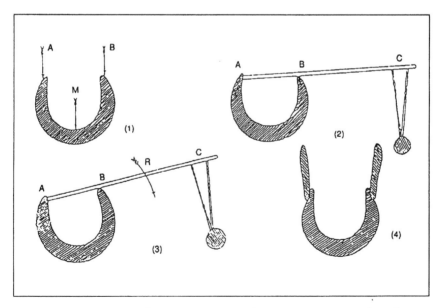

FIGURE 3.3. Diagram showing in transversal section some principles of canoe stability and construction. (Malinowski 1922:109)

deep water and that, more often than not, the passengers wind up sitting upon the overturned hull until assistance comes their way.

The most frequent users of Kaduwaga harbor other than Kaduwagans themselves are Tauwema villagers, followed by Kaibola villagers from the northwestern shore of Kiriwina Island. Both groups trade for Western goods at Kaduwaga's cooperative store. The store is stocked by a Western boat from the provincial capital, Alotau. The store chairman mails stock orders to Alotau on a monthly basis, and every three months or so, the Alotau boat brings supplies. Since national independence, a decline in the Trobriand cash economy has left the arrival of supplies increasingly sporadic, and stocks have dwindled. But Kaduwagans have kept the store going, and it still commands trading voyages from Tauwemans and Kaibolans. Kaduwaga is a good spot for a trade store even though the harbor is too shallow for delivery boats to enter. Instead, the goods are off-loaded onto outrigger canoes and ferried ashore.

Kaibolans sail to Kaduwaga to trade rather than walk south on Kiriwina Island to trade at the government center, Losuia. This is because they trade copra for the Western goods, and copra is heavy and bulky to carry on foot. There are some trucks in northern Kiriwina Island, but they are often unavailable. On the other hand, Kaibolans can count on outrigger canoes, and Kaduwaga is easier to reach by sail than is the Losuia harbor. By contrast, Giva and Kaisiga, whose villages are on the eastern and southern coasts of Kaileuna Island, rarely visit Kaduwaga to trade in Western goods. They can sail to Losuia about as quickly as they can sail to Kaduwaga, and the trade stores at Losuia offer a wider variety of goods, including liquor.

Tauwemans frequently sail to Kaduwaga for funerals. Although many walk the distance, they also usually send some canoes along to carry food and some fiber skirts to be distributed at the mortuary events. In funerary attendance, but not in trade in Western goods, Tauwemans are joined by people from the Kuyawa and Munuwata villages. While Losuia is farther than Kaduwaga from Kuyawa and Munuwata, to sail there does not take much longer. Villagers from Tauwema, Kuyawa, and Munuwata regularly attend Kaduwagan funerals because these are villages into which Kaduwagans marry, and attendance at the funeral of a close relative is almost mandatory. The few Kaduwagans who do not marry endogamously almost always marry someone from these villages, which, like Kaduwaga, are headed by Tabalu people. The concentration of exogamous marriages into these three villages means that many Kaduwagans have close relatives in one or more of them.

Kaduwaga harbor also is used by people from the Lusancays. They trade copra for Western goods at the cooperative store, although, as with Kaibolans and Tawemans, these trips have declined since national independence. More significantly, people from the Lusancays sail to Kaduwaga to trade pigs for yams. The Lusancays are not good for yam production, and many Kaduwagan pigs are farmed out to the

Lusancays to be raised there off wild plant forage. Malinowski (1929) indicated that many Trobrianders cannot eat bush pig. This is because, as pigs eat bush materials, they ingest plants whose consumption by people, through the vehicle of pig flesh, will deleteriously affect the composition of human body substance. Lusancay Islanders weed the dangerous plants out from strips of bush on their islands so the Kaduwagans can eat bush pigs grown there. This is advantageous to Kaduwagans, who do not want to weed those plants out of their own bush, as the plants have uses other than as food. When Lusancay Islanders visit Kaduwaga to trade pigs for yams, Kaduwagans allow them to take home whatever portions they want of any bush plants they desire. The pigs grow in the Lusancays, the bush plants grow in Kaduwaga, and the arrangement works out to everyone's satisfaction as Kaduwagans pay Lusancay Islanders in yams and taro in return for care of the pigs. Lusancay large canoes are larger and heavier than their Trobriand counterparts, and they are equipped with hearths built into the outrigger platform.

Two or three times a year, Kaduwaga harbor is entered by people sailing from the Amphletts to the south. The Amphletts, the small islands lying immediately north of three large islands, Normanby, Fergusson, and Goodenough, are the islands to which the Kaileuna *kula* fleet sails on its overseas voyages. The best known among them to the Western public is Dobu (Fortune 1932; Benedict 1934), which actually is somewhat peripheral to the Amphletts proper. The best known of the Amphlett Islands to Kaduwagans is Gumasila. Amphlett Islanders trade clay pots and rare shells for yams at Kaduwaga, and they also *kula* there.

Another group that sails to Kaduwaga from abroad is the Mailu, who reside on the southeastern coast of New Guinea island. Every two years a Mailu fleet sails into Kaduwaga harbor. The Mailu fleet is an impressive sight: up to twenty huge brown wooden-hulled catamarans with tall rectangular cloth sails, jockeying for space as they maneuver into the harbor. Although Mailu boats are much larger than any locally produced vessels, they have sufficiently shallow draft that they can be brought into the harbor and anchored in protected waters.

On their interisland voyages, the Mailu seek rare shells in return for Western clothing, which they acquire from charitable outlets. The Mailu trade the clothes for shells, trade the shells in the New Guinea highlands for coffee, trade the coffee to Western traders for cash, and spend the cash for desired Western goods. Kaduwagans say that they do not know what the Mailu exchanged for shells before Western clothing was available, but they also say that the trade predates Western contact and that the Mailu have always sought shells from the Trobrianders.

The Mailu fleet I witnessed had been sailing through the Trobriands for a couple of weeks, trading as it went. Its final stop before returning home was Kaduwaga. A neighbor told me that the biennial Mailu trade visits are an old tradition. Her grandmother told her about eagerly waiting for the Mailu visits as a young child and of being told by *her* grandmother about the same thing. My neighbor told me that this Mailu fleet would stay for a few days to trade with Kaduwagans, then depart; but days went by, and the boats remained. At length, I heard that the departure was held up by hull repairs on two of the vessels. A major virtue of Kaduwaga harbor is the fact that wooden boats need not be dry-docked in order to do major repair work. The harbor is shallow enough that boats can be worked on while either still in the water or raised slightly above it on a wooden platform. In the latter instance, water is immediately at hand to keep the hulls wet.

Kaduwagans have two ways of caulking their canoes. The first is for "dry-sailing." The hull boards are dry when caulked, and canoes are only sailed short distances and then removed from the water. The other is for "wet-sailing." The hull boards are wet when caulked, the canoes are sailed longer distances, and then kept in the water. Should one dry-dock vessels that are caulked for wet-sailing, the boards shrink and the caulk falls out. Then the boards must be resoaked and re-caulked before the canoes can put back out to sea. Kaduwagans say that all of the native craft in the Milne Bay region that are sailed long distances are caulked for wet-sailing and that it is desirable to make hull repairs on them without putting them into dry-dock.

As I learned about hull repairs in the context of the Mailu visit, I discovered that Amphlett Islanders also make Kaduwaga harbor their last stop before beginning the voyage home. They too use Kaduwaga harbor to repair their boats before once again setting out to sea in them. In turn, the Kaileuna *kula* fleet uses the comparable harbor next to the Noagasi village on Gumasila Island in the Amphletts for refurbishing and repairing its vessels before embarking on its voyage home. Kaduwagans profit from providing repair and maintenance services to the visiting fleets as well as supplies for the home voyage. They charge captains for material and labor for repairs and maintenance, and for food needed for the journey.

The last group of non-Kaduwagans who use the harbor is Westerners. Most Western vessels have too much draft to be able to enter the harbor. Instead, they are forced to anchor at the outer edge of the underwater coral shelf. Occasionally a Western vessel stays overnight if the weather is good, but most captains prefer to find safer anchorage. Today, such anchorage is available at Losuia harbor. It should be noted, however, that Losuia harbor only became available to Western vessels after the channel leading into it was dredged. When this was done is not clear, but informants say that in the nineteenth century most ships anchored at the outer edge of Kaduwaga's reef because it was the safest anchorage in the northern Trobriands.

CONCLUSION

When I first arrived at Kaduwaga, I saw that the village was situated on the shore of a large cove, but I did not realize that Kaduwaga's cove was a boat harbor. This was probably because I did not see outrigger canoes as needing harborage. At the other shoreline villages I had visited on Kiriwina Island, local craft are "moored" by dragging them up onto the beach, and I assumed that this was all that there was to the matter. It was only as I traveled on large Kaduwagan canoes that I came to understand the distinct nuisance of needing to beach those vessels at other villages. Small dry-caulked canoes are light and easy to beach, and they are moored on land, even at Kaduwaga. But the large canoes, which are wet-caulked, are heavy, difficult to beach, and when beached, require onerous labor if their hulls are to be kept wet.

As I came to recognize that Kaduwaga is a boat harbor, I thought about the size of the village on its shore. With a populace of around 300, Kaduwaga is among the largest villages in the Trobriands. Certainly it is the largest in the northern Trobriands that is not located on Kiriwina Island. The village's size, I discovered, is directly linked to its location on a fine natural boat harbor.

The harbor's importance may be seen in the fact that traffic remains heavy despite the considerable rerouting of trade through Losuia. Although most canoes that come into the Trobriands from abroad now stop and trade at Losuia, they still aim for Kaduwaga—the place where sailors can repair and refurbish their vessels for the voyage home. The wharf at Losuia, although on the lagoon, is not well protected, and in rough weather, most of the canoes moored there must be brought ashore. Moreover, even in calm weather, currents frequently run too strongly for craftsmen to stand and work in the water. At Kaduwaga, the chop remains minimal even in very rough weather, and, while there is tidal pull, the effect is minimal to a person standing in the water and working on a boat hull.

Kaduwaga harbor is a highly significant feature of the northern Trobriand landscape. Although the residents of the village on its shore are primarily engaged in horticulture and fishing, they also profit from the harbor. They profit from the ease with which it enables them to maintain their own small fleet of large canoes. They profit from the fact that the harbor facilitates both local and overseas trade. And they profit from the fact that incoming fleets pay for maintenance and repair services and to obtain supplies for their return voyages. Small wonder that most Trobrianders immediately commented upon learning that I resided at Kaduwaga, "Oh, that's such a wealthy place!" It surely is, what with good garden lands, good fishing, and a fine boat harbor.

NOTE

Acknowledgments   Fieldwork was conducted in the Trobriand Islands from June 1971 to September 1972, in June and July 1980, June and July 1981, and June 1988. I am grateful to the National Institute of Mental Health, the National Endowment for the Humanities, and Northern Illinois University for making the fieldwork possible.

REFERENCES

Benedict, Ruth
1934   *Patterns of Culture*. Boston: Houghton Mifflin.
Fortune, Reo
1932   *Sorcerers of Dobu: The Social Anthropology of the Dobu Islanders of the Western Pacific*. New York: E. P. Dutton.
Malinowski, Bronislaw
1922   *Argonauts of the Western Pacific: An Account of Native Enterprise and Adventure in the Archipelagoes of Melanesian New Guinea*. London: Routledge and Kegan Paul.
1929   *The Sexual Life of Savages*. New York: Harcourt Brace and World.

SEAMANSHIP AND POLITICS IN NORTHERN KIRIWINA

Harry A. Powell

• This essay explores the relationships of seamanship and seafaring to the political organization of Kiriwina, the main island of the Trobriand group, which lies off the southeast coast of New Guinea (see figures 2.1 and 3.1). It focuses on the connections between rank in Kiriwina and the seamanship of followers of the Tabalu chiefs of Omarakana village, its traditionally dominant leaders. It is argued that the unique status of these chiefs may be related to the anomalous geographical position of the communities of northeast Kiriwina in the *kula* ring of ceremonial exchange, the local form of interisland conventional competition. Coupled with the limitations of the Kiriwinans' seafaring capabilities, this geographical position makes it worth their while to support a powerful leader under whom they can unite to gain entry into the *kula* circuit, in olden times by force, if necessary. This essay postulates further that the integral complex of traditional rank, seamanship, and *kula* is likely to continue until northern Kiriwinan social institutions so develop as to enable the islanders to participate fully in global, as well as local, conventional competitive activities.

The Trobrianders had intermittent contact with foreign whalers, missionaries and traders, and government officials for three generations or more before representatives of all three categories became resident on Kiriwina around the turn of the century. Malinowski commented on their destructive influences in his books and predicted that "complete disorganisation is sure to take place . . . , followed by a gradual disintegration of the culture and extinction of the race" (1932:115; see also Young 1979). Fortunately, his books have helped to falsify his prophecy (but cf. Saville 1974:28, 72), and in 1950 and 1951, I recorded a resurgence of the indigenous culture.

Under Sir Hubert Murray's paternalistic regime as lieutenant governor of Papua between the world wars, indigenous leaders were appointed village councillors or policemen and given insignia of office. This helped mitigate earlier policies, which had undermined chiefly power. After his predecessor's death in 1930, Mitakata, the paramount chief in my time, received a monthly government allowance of two pounds of trade tobacco, at that time the local currency, in respect of his services as the senior councillor. The Methodist Mission's attacks on polygynous marriage and lax sexual mores, for which, together with wood carving and cricket, the Trobriands are famous, were moderated. The Trobriands were treated as a reserve of indigenous culture and were shielded from much of the social change that affected the rest of Papua, to the extent that Trobrianders could not be recruited for plantation labor away from home.

Murray's policies were mediated in the Trobriands by able and sympathetic resident administrators (cf. Austen 1945), who were left there long enough to begin to learn the local language and, aided by Malinowski's books, to understand the culture. The changes in government policy partly reflected shifts in the indigenous power structure resulting from the trade in sea products, notably pearls, which was controlled by the lagoon villages. This trade opened a way to wealth for those not qualified by descent to claim the rights of chiefs. Some of these rights had been broken by decree, and the chiefs' control of magic had been attacked to the extent that Mitakata's predecessor was imprisoned for sorcery; but the right of chiefs to polygynous marriage was no longer opposed, and Mitakata was able to marry as many wives as his predecessor.

The Trobrianders' culture is remarkably tolerant and, therefore, the more resistant to change, and they have been well able to adopt and adapt foreign concepts and institutions to their own. Government and missions were given their dues, but their laws and teachings did not replace those of tradition; rather, they were integrated with it as much as possible and otherwise were paid lip service. Relationships with Europeans became additional avenues to prestige in the indigenous power hierarchies. The wealth accruing from pearl fishing and copra production, until the markets collapsed in the thirties, was used in the same ways as the surplus yams: in traditional ceremonial exchanges and displays, or "feasts of merit." But the most spectacular example of Trobriand cultural resilience is perhaps their adaptation of cricket as a surrogate for traditional warfare (kabilia), which was forbidden (Powell 1952, 1960; J. Leach 1975, 1983:137).

By the time of the outbreak of the Japanese war, pearl fishing had virtually ended and copra prices had dropped so much that the Trobrianders were hard-pressed to meet government taxes and mission collections. There were no funds available to invest in the technologies of production and transport needed to convert the surplus yams into a reliable cash crop (cf. Howard this volume). The abrupt withdrawal of all the resident Europeans in 1941 and 1942 was followed by a resurgence of traditional institutions and political intrigues, including warfare. But this resurgence was aborted ·by the arrival of Sergeant Gordon Saville of the wartime Australian New Guinea Administrative Unit, who gives a lively account of Kiriwina at war in his book, *King of Kiriwina* (1974). The occupation of Kiriwina was part of the Allied campaign to recover the Solomons. By mid-1945, some 50,000 troops, mainly American, had passed through it. Few Japanese impinged upon the islanders directly, and their air raids did little physical damage, though according to Saville they intensified the trauma caused by the occupation. As in the rest of Papua New Guinea, local men were drafted to work in the military installations, which completely disrupted indigenous life in northern Kiriwina, including interisland *kula*.

It was the *kula* system of ceremonial exchange of shell valuables between overseas partners, as described by Malinowski in his *Argonauts of the Western Pacific*, that put the Trobriands on the ethnographic map. The primary concern of my visit to Kiriwina from 1950 to 1951 was to study the culture changes since Malinowski's time, but I found it necessary first to clarify the indigenous political system. In addition, in early 1951 I was planning to accompany the first postwar *uvalaku* 'fleet sailing' to obtain armshells from Kitava (cf. Malinowski 1922:chapter 20). I hoped to study canoe building, sailing, and the *kula* on the expedition, but it was delayed until I finally had to leave Kiriwina, so my observations of seamanship were limited to its preparations, as were Malinowski's (1922:479).

Overseas *kula* was not entirely precluded by the Allied military occupation of 1943–1945 (Mair 1948:chapter 10; Powell 1956:557ff), but it became impracticable for northern Kiriwinan fleets. They had kept up some inland *kula* for necklaces with the lagoon villagers who obtained them from Vakuta and the Amphletts, and there were a few voyages for armshells to Kitava from Sinaketa despite the threat from the Japanese and the restrictions imposed by the Allies. The northeasterners' prewar canoes had long since rotted, so the whole fleet had to be rebuilt. This made the project that I witnessed the first postwar, if not the first ever, canoe building in northern Kiriwina on such a scale. The enterprise reflected both a swing back to tradition after the occupation and the Kiriwinans' conviction that the Sinaketans and Vakutans would preempt their *kula* partnerships in Kitava unless the northeasterners were strong enough to prevent them. Mitakata, as paramount chief, had more than once asked the government of Papua for help to prevent this 'theft' *(veilau)*, as he saw it, of the northerners' rightful valuables, since its law forbade him to use his traditional sanctions of magic and warfare on his followers' behalf.

CANOE BUILDING

I lacked enough film stock to cover the entire canoe-building process, but my film records some of the major transactions it involved in 1951 in the neighborhood of Omarakana. They included payments for goods and services, like that from the men of Tilakaiwa to Mitakata for the tree he provided for their new canoe hull. Mitakata in turn used this payment to reward Banasi, the canoe magician, for his services. A *paka* 'feast of merit' at the *vayola* 'public display' of the new canoes on April 3 attracted visitors to witness the *kula* status of the owners and crews and to advertise it to the rest of the population. Malinowski does not mention 'public displays' as such, but his account of *tasasoria* 'trial sails' (1922:146) includes elements of them.

I saw no *kabigidoya* 'ceremonial visits' of new canoes such as Malinowski reports (1922:163–66; cf. Tambiah 1983:183, 189); few were made in 1951, perhaps because of the number of canoes being built. In a normal year no more than one or

FIGURE 4.1. Mitakata of Omarakana and his senior wife Geumwara in his new hangar *(bunatogu)* with his new canoe, named according to Tabalu tradition *Nigada Bu'a* 'Seeker of Betel Nut'—one of the prestations expected when new canoes are taken on the *kabigidoya* ceremonial visits (cf. Malinowski 1922:plates 21, 40, 41). These open-sided sheds with thatched roofs must be big enough to house the canoes with room for their builders to work. Chief Mitakata's hangar has high open sides; hangars of lower-ranking canoe owners have eaves almost to the ground. Note that the outrigger platform is level in the canoe hangar, but the hull is set higher than the outrigger float. Since the outrigger uprights and the hull are roughly parallel vertically, the hull will heel away from the outrigger when afloat so that freeboard will be reduced, and more so when loaded. Montague (this volume) asks whether the hull could be canted toward the outrigger to keep it more upright and the platform level afloat, a question worthy of a field *kula* voyage from Kilivila to Kitava.

two canoes are likely to be replaced in a given fleet. If an *uvalaku* 'fleet sailing' is planned, a collective 'display' may be held after refitting; otherwise those going to Kitava might hold individual 'displays'. As all the northeastern fleets were being reestablished, a collective display conserved energy and resources; but canoe owners decided individually whether to make 'ceremonial visits'. *Nigada Bu'a*, Mitakata's canoe (figure 4.1), went for reasons of prestige, though it sailed without him; most other owners made do with the 'public display' and 'feast of merit'.

Five canoes were built in the Omarakana cluster of villages: Mitakata's, which he shared with Waibadi of Kasanai, his second successor-to-be; two in Tilakaiwa, one of which I co-owned with my subclan 'brothers'; and one each in Youlawotu and Wakailua. Waibadi and his mother's brother Vanoi, who was Mitakata's sister's son and his first successor-to-be, had planned to build a canoe of their own with a crew from Kasanai but could not because they were at Losuia most of their time, learning government procedures in the district office. Elsewhere in Kilivila, one canoe was built at Liluta for Chief Yobukwau, Mitakata's traditional rival in rank (see Malinowski 1932; Powell 1960:141ff); one at Kwaybwaga for Chief Tonuwabu; one at Yalumugwa for Nalibutau, one of the Toliwaga military rivals of the Omarakana Tabalu chiefs (Powell 1960:141–43, 1976; cf. J. Leach 1983:133, map 6; Nesbitt 1975); and one each for commoner owners at Kwaymwata and Mtawa. In Luba district, two canoes were built at Oburaku and one at Okaiboma by supporters of Nalibutau.

The *kula* participants of Osapola were to sail in the Liluta canoes, the men of Moligilagi and a second Kwaybwaga crew were to borrow canoes from Kaileuna, and the Olivilevi contingent was to be transported by the trader Ralph Lumley in his boat, *La Belle*, a plan that fell through because of his illness. In Sinaketa, where overseas *kula* had already been resumed, one canoe was being built at Kumilabwaga. The total of sixteen canoes from Kiriwina district, excluding the Olivilevi men, thus outnumbered the eleven Kiriwinan canoe crews recorded by Malinowski (1922:122). The Kilivila fleet comprised subfleets led by Mitakata, by Yobukwau of Liluta, and by Nalibutau of Yalumugwa.

Malinowski's account (1922:105–45) is comprehensive on the social organization and magic (cf. Tambiah 1983:189–92) of canoe building and sailing, which remained much the same in 1951, but it is less thorough on the technology. My own observations and discussions with my 'brother' and partner, Daibuna, and the members of our crew produced the following outline of the building stages. Preparations began months in advance of building with finding and negotiating for suitable trees (cf. Feinberg; Howard; Ammarell, all this volume).

To build the new canoes and store them when not in use, houses or hangars *(bunatogu)* had first to be constructed (see Malinowski 1922:plate 22; Powell 1952:section on *kula*). Figure 4.1 shows Chief Mitakata's new canoe in its hangar; figures 4.2 and 4.3 depict a *masawa* canoe modeled by a Kwaybwaga craftsman, illustrating the following parts:

1. The *waga* 'hull' log is roughly shaped where it is felled in the bush and finished in its hangar on the beach. The outrigger *(lamila)* is fully shaped in the builder's village from a light balsalike wood.

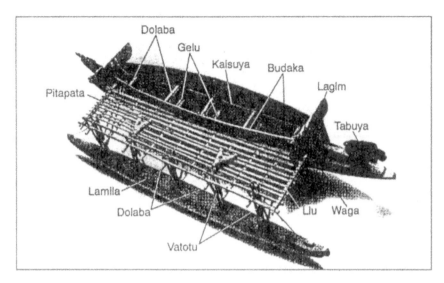

FIGURE 4.2. Model canoe showing interior structure. The parts are described in the text. The model is 66.6 cm long overall with 20.3 cm beam and 11.44 cm depth. Its cross-sectional construction is in scale, but the model should be longer by two hull bays and three outrigger poles *(dolaba)*.

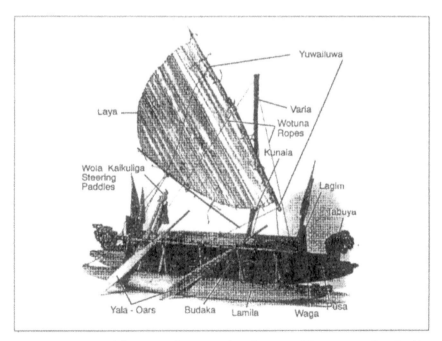

FIGURE 4.3. Model canoe with mast, sail, and rigging. The parts are described in the text. The mast, sail, rigging, and other gear are not to scale.

2. *Gelu,* pairs of half 'frames', are fitted to the hull log after it has been hollowed, to hold the planks (strakes) that form the canoe's topsides.

3. *Kaisuya,* a 'strength stick' as long as the hollow part of the log, is fitted on each side through holes drilled in the middle of the vertical arm of each half frame so as to link it to its neighbors. These sticks are tied down to the hull log between each 'frame' pair. They are called *kala peula waga* 'strength of the canoe', as the frames will part and the canoe will disintegrate if they fail.

4. *Budaka,* the 'strakes' (planks) that give the hull its depth, are shaped next to fit the 'frames' and the hull log. A *masawa* seagoing canoe has one deep strake on the main frames and a narrower second one above it fitted to light vertical extensions of alternate frames; this feature and the 'strength stick' distinguish *masawa* from *kalipoulo* 'fishing canoes' (cf. Malinowski 1922:111, figure 2).

5. The *tabuya* 'prow boards' and their *lagim* 'cutwater buttresses' are fitted while the strakes are bent apart to generate enough thrust to push their ends into slots cut into the inboard sides of the 'prow boards'. This presses the boards against the 'buttresses', which slot into their outer faces and into the solid ends of the hull log. The prow boards are lashed down to eye holes in the hull log to prevent their being dislodged upward. The outward bend of the strakes shapes the canoe's topsides so as to optimize the load-carrying volume enclosed by the prow boards.

6. *Liu* sticks are lashed along the strakes under the poles (*dolaba,* see no. 8) that form the basis of the outrigger 'platform', so that they cannot be pushed back into the canoe hull. No such sticks are fitted to the model, but the end of one can be discerned in figure 4.2. The term *liu* may refer to the sticks lashed above and below the ends of the platform sticks, and below them between the poles that hold the outrigger to the hull. These butt onto the main strake, so they counter any forces tending to push the outrigger assembly toward the hull. In either case, the *liu* sticks could hardly be fitted before the other outrigger components had been assembled.

7. *Lamila,* the 'outrigger log', or float, is carefully set and supported in relation to the hull so that it will be in the intended position when the canoe is afloat and properly loaded.

8. *Dolaba* 'outrigger poles'—up to eight poles are fitted through holes in the main strakes on the outrigger side of the hull and lashed across it to the tops of the main 'frames' to form the outrigger mounting.

9. *Vatotu,* 'stand up' sticks, are fitted to hold the outrigger log at the proper depth below the eight poles. A single upright stick is driven into the outrigger float and lashed to the end of each pole to act as the main bearer of the weight and to fix the height of the platform above the floating outrigger log. On either side of this upright, a pair of crossed sticks is driven into the float and lashed to the pole and the upright, so as to limit the float's fore-and-aft movement in relation to the hull.

10. *Toraba,* pairs of curved struts, are fitted from the *dolaba* poles where they pierce the top strake to each side of the *vatotu* sticks where they enter the outrigger log (cf. figure 4.2). They are called *kala peula lamila* 'strength of the outrigger', because they keep the float at the proper angle to the hull under stress.

11. *Pitapata,* longitudinal sticks, are lashed fore and aft across the *dolaba* outrig-

ger poles and the *liu* sticks between them to form the outrigger platform.

12. *Pusa,* traditional magic patterns, are carved on the ends of the hull into which the *tabuya* and *lagim* boards are slotted.

13. *Laya,* the 'sail', and *yuwaiyoluwa,* its 'running rigging', are assembled in the village to match the canoe's size and its carrying power.

14. *Varia,* the 'mast', and *kunaia,* its 'standing rigging', including the curved strut *(kaina'ila)* that supports it above its foot, must be matched to the hull and sail.

Vayola, the final lashing together and magic of the canoe, are done in the canoe hangars while visitors witness the event and admire its results (see Powell 1952). There follows *kaibasi* 'caulking', which is done by scraping the soft roots of a tree called *kaitawola* into a coconut dish with a mussel shell and dribbling and kneading seawater into the scrapings until they form a rough paste. This is worked into the joints of the canoe and any faults in the wood. Both the caulking procedure and the prepared material are called *kaibasi.* *Pwaka* and *mulaka* (not shown), white and red paints, are applied to the finished canoe, which is further embellished with cowrie shells *(buna)* and sticks bearing pandanus streamers *(bisila)* (figure 4.1 and Powell 1952). The building is now completed, and *tasasoria* and *usagelu* 'trial sails' and 'congratulatory gifts' follow the first launching of the new canoes, which may sail to other beaches for display and to receive *usagelu* from the crews of other fleets.

The Hull

Like the foregoing, the information that follows derives from discussions with informants in the light of my experience of sailing rather than from my limited observations of the *masawa* in action. The seagoing hulls are built with distinct or even pronounced "rocker"; that is, the bottom of the hull curves downward from the ends to the middle (see figure 4.1). Both ends of the hull are grooved for the prow and buttress boards and are distinctly V-sectioned. Either end serves equally well as the bow, and the V-section continues along the bottom of the rest of the hull. The asymmetry of the hull is not exploited intentionally to reduce leeway, but the depth of rocker affords some lateral resistance under sail, fair directional stability when paddled, and a pivot point that helps steering, especially of longer hulls.

The outrigger float is almost as long as the hull and heavy enough when kept to windward to counteract the capsizing moment of the wind on the sail, but because it is solid, it loses most of its buoyancy and will sink if weight on the outrigger platform submerges it. There is no balancing platform on the other side of the hull, so no load can be placed there to offset weight on the outrigger side (cf. Dodd 1972:129ff; Lewis 1972:260 on some Polynesian and Micronesian single-outriggers). Cargo and passengers are carried in the middle sections of the hull *(gebobo)* (Malinowski 1922:204), which is up to 1.7 meters deep and 1.3 meters wide amidships. The *masawa* canoe is twelve or more meters long overall, with a beam between the outboard sides of the hull and outrigger assembly of about one-quarter of its length; but its carrying capacity is less than these dimensions may suggest because of the lack of reserve buoyancy in the outrigger log.

In a deep-hulled *masawa,* lateral resistance under sail is reasonable when leeway is minimal with the wind more or less abeam, but it is hardly enough for efficient beating to windward, except perhaps in sheltered water. My informants showed no knowledge of the use of center- or leeboards, though the big steering paddles, thrust down at the aft end of the platform through reinforced gaps between its poles, could have provided models for either. Outrigger drag tends to turn the canoe into the wind but may be offset when working to windward by so trimming the sail as to bring its center of effort over the canoe's center of lateral resistance, which eases steering but increases leeway, as does pitching into oncoming waves (but cf. Lewis 1972:268–72). Thus, under sail, except when headed directly downwind, a canoe must steer a course well upwind of its destination.

The northern Kiriwinan seamen are aware of these limitations and are reluctant to sail if they cannot lay a direct course to their destination, unless the wind would be dead aft. This is the most dangerous point of sailing for most craft because waves from astern tend to make any vessel "broach to" by pushing its stern against the rudder so that it lies across the wind. A clipper ship broached to and "taken aback" by the wind shifting to the lee side of her sails would become unmanageable and might be dismasted or sunk. If the wind takes a canoe's sail on the lee side, its pressure may submerge the outrigger float and capsize the canoe. Thus, the seagoing canoe must be so rigged and handled as to minimize this risk while enabling it to sail in safety as fast as the wind, sea, and its course permit.

The Rig

J. Leach (1983:429, plate 2) shows the shape of the sail *(laya)*, and my film (Powell 1952) shows its construction. The shape is powerful and efficient with the wind on or abaft the beam, but it becomes less so as the apparent wind (the product of the canoe's passage through the true wind) draws ahead, and to windward it is inefficient. Unlike a lateen sail, which it resembles in shape, the *laya* cannot be "peaked up," that is, have its leading point or tack hauled back toward the mast so that the top edge or luff of the sail becomes more upright and efficient upwind. However, as the hull shape is not efficient to windward anyway, this is no great handicap. Since the *masawa* must be sailed with the outrigger to windward, it cannot be steered "through the wind's eye" to reverse its direction, as can such fore-and-aft-rigged craft as dhows, junks, and yachts; so it matters less that its rig cannot be tacked in this way than that it should be efficient off the wind (cf. Feinberg, this volume, on Nukumanu canoes and Lepowsky, this volume, on Louisiade canoes; contrast Ammarell, this volume, on Bugis vessels).

The mast *(varia)* is a single spar with a natural upper fork. This serves as the masthead lead for the halyard rope by which the sail is set, which is belayed at the foot of the mast. An artificial fork at the foot, roughly at right angles to that at the masthead, supports the mast inside the hull on an outrigger spar. There a loop of rope from the frame on the outrigger side of the hull holds it in place. In an eight-spar canoe, the mast would be stepped on the spar at the after end of the first compartment of the hull in the direction in which the canoe is to sail. The mast is stepped with its inner curve toward the outrigger, with the sail set inside this curve on the outrigger side. As the outrigger is always to windward of the hull, the sail is always to windward of the mast, whichever way the canoe is heading.

As well as bending toward the outrigger, the mast is canted over its platform but is prevented from falling onto it by the curved strut (kaina'ila), which is so lashed to the mast that its height above platform level can be varied to adjust the cant of the mast. Its foot rests in a socket on the outrigger platform above the pole on which the mast is stepped. The strut is needed since, with the foot of the mast in the hull, there is not enough "drift" between it and the side of the canoe away from the outrigger for it to be held up by a rope on that side, as it is supported by ropes from its head to points on the hull and outrigger platform. Under sail, wind coming over the outrigger takes the weight of the sail and mast off the strut. The ropes then prevent their being blown to leeward. They serve both as "shrouds" to adjust the sideways cant and as "stays" to trim the fore-and-aft rake of the mast.

When set, the sail is trimmed by ropes from its tack, from the yard from which it hangs, and from the after end of the boom, the spar to which its lower edge or foot is attached. More ropes may be added to help vary the sail's shape to suit the wind strength and direction. The ropes from the yard correspond to the braces of a square sail or to the vangs from the gaff of a fore-and-aft sail, which trim the sails about the midline of the hull. The upper spar on which a *laya* is set is properly termed a yard because it crosses the mast, whereas a gaff butts onto it. The fore end of the yard with the tack of the sail is bowsed down by ropes to the fore ends of the hull and of the outrigger platform so that its height and angle can be varied. The halyard is tied to the yard about one-quarter of its length back from the tack of the sail and raises the yard and sail against the pull of the tack ropes. The fore end of the lower spar is left free, with one or more ropes attached to it so as to control the curvature of the foot of the sail as well as its angle to the hull. The curve of the well-rounded after end of the sail, its leech, can also be varied. The ropes from the boom, the lower spar, which also is a yard because it does not butt onto the mast, correspond to the sheets that control the angle of the foot of the sail to the hull in fore-and-aft-rigged yachts.

SEAMANSHIP

As far as I know, the *masawa* canoes of Kiriwina district (Malinowski 1922:112; cf. Tambiah 1983:187) were normally used only for voyages to Kitava during the favorable northwesterly winds but had to be extensively refitted each season. For the remaining eight to nine months, they were not kept in use but were brought out from their hangars for and rehoused after any outings (cf. Malinowski 1922:chapter 20). The crews had few opportunities to practice sailing their *masawa* canoes other than the trial sails after building or refitting them in preparation for the actual *kula* voyages. Few of the men had much opportunity to handle other canoes either, since no canoe fishing was done from the coast of Kilivila (J. Leach 1983:130–32, map 5), as the east coast of Kiriwina south of Mtawa is too exposed to the southeasterly trade winds, and its currents are too tricky. By contrast, the canoes of the lagoon villages of northern Kiriwina, and of Sinaketa, Vakuta (Campbell 1983) and Kaileuna

(Montague this volume) can be used for traveling and fishing all year round. The material return to the northeasterners from *kula* with Kitava hardly seems to justify their investments of labor and resources in the canoes.

These investments continue while the *masawa* canoes are in use for *kula*, since a numerous crew is needed to handle them ashore and to man them for such maneuvers as changing tack. As the outrigger must be kept to windward, the canoe must bear away across the wind and stop while the sail is lowered, bundled on its spars and end-for-ended, and the mast must be unshipped, restepped, and rerigged at the new bow. The sail must then be reset and trimmed, and the steering paddle, or paddles, must be reshipped before the canoe can get under way in the new direction. Unless each crew member carries out his part of the procedure efficiently, the maneuver is easily bungled so that control of the canoe is lost. Even when carried out efficiently, the maneuver takes minutes rather than the seconds needed to tack a modern yacht through the wind. By contrast, some Polynesian and Micronesian craft go about like the *masawa* but need only to reverse the rake of the mast and sail that are stepped amidships (cf. Dodd 1972:138; Lewis 1972:261–72).

On a yacht, the sheets vary the angle of the boom and sail to the hull in the vertical plane so as to obtain maximum drive from the wind. The sail is trimmed in toward the midline of the hull to the most efficient angle of attack if the wind is from ahead and is let out with the wind from further aft. In gusts it can be let out to "spill" wind and reduce heeling, but when it is incorrectly trimmed or eased too far, it will flog. In the *masawa*, the scope for letting out the sail is limited by its being set on the windward side of the mast and by its inability to stand flogging. The traditional sail is strong enough unless it is allowed to flap; then, especially when wet, the fore-and-aft strips of pandanus and their cross stitching soon begin to come apart. So the *laya* sail can be eased off in the vertical plane only to a limited extent without risking its loss. Instead, it can be dropped until the squall passes and then reset; or according to my informants, if the wind stays strong and the crew feel competent, they can readjust the rigging so that the mast is canted further down over the outrigger platform. This reduces the sail's angle of attack and the area it presents to the wind, as does easing the sheets, but in the horizontal, rather than the vertical, plane. The sail's center of effort is lowered and the heeling moment on the hull reduced, as if it were reefed. This technique would allow boat speed to be kept up, but the horizontal trim of the sail might tend to make it "kite" and lift the outrigger from the water, with the risk of capsizing to leeward. Easing the sheets still further would reduce the sail's lift and the risk of capsizing but might make it flog.

The helmsmen and rigging trimmers are normally stationed on the outrigger platform, onto which the whole crew can move as ballast in an emergency. In general, however, crew and passengers should try to stay put and not panic, for if the wind were to drop suddenly, extra weight on the platform might submerge the outrigger and capsize the canoe to windward. If the wind still rises, all that can be done is to stow both sail and mast to reduce windage and to set all hands to bailing. The risk then, unless the canoe breaks up at sea, is of being blown to leeward and being unable to make a safe landing. Thus, sailing a *masawa* canoe safely requires skill, discipline, nerve, and practice.

The Kilivilan crews' relative lack of practice at seamanship as much as the unhandiness of their canoes may have made them reluctant to undertake upwind passages. Kitava, their *kula* target, lies to windward of northern Kiriwina during the southeasterly trade winds *(bwailima)*, from May to September. In 1951 the southeasterlies were not fully superseded by the northwesterly monsoon *(yavata)*, which should prevail from about December to March (cf. Malinowski 1935:50–51). Between these periods, doldrumlike conditions occur with variable winds. A northeasterly wind *(bomatu)* gives a beam reach from Kaulukuba beach to Kitava, but it is unreliable and stormy, and it put in no appearance that year.

Nevertheless, there were days between the 'trial sail' and the fleet's eventual departure for Kitava when a passage south could have been made as it finally began, under paddles. But as I was told more than once, while Mitakata's predecessor, To'uluwa (cf. Malinowski 1922:478ff), was as keen on canoes as on *kula*, Mitakata was much less addicted to the former. So the Argonauts of Kilivila sat in their villages or on Kaulukuba beach, whence Kitava is visible on the southeastern horizon, because the master of the fleet *(toliuvalaku)* (Malinowski 1922:208) was so reluctant to sail in his own canoe that he tried for weeks to obtain passage on a European boat. That his fleet did not sail without Mitakata suggests that its master's importance was less nautical than political.

KIRIWINAN POLITICS

In 1950 the Trobrianders were still recovering from the traumas of the occupation. They called it a period of 'famine' *(molu)* (cf. Malinowski 1935:160) not because of food shortages, which were averted by the issue of U.S. Army rations to the local work force, but because the disruption of gardening left them without the yams needed for the ceremonial exchanges of their institutions of conventional competition, notably those of marriage and the *kula*. I argued in my article on competitive leadership (1960) that Trobriand politics is a variant of the Big Man pattern typical of mainland New Guinea. Aspiring leaders accumulate wealth in the form of pigs and shell ornaments to present to their rivals in fulfillment of their existing obligations and to place the recipients under even heavier obligation to themselves. Polygynous marriage is instrumental in the accumulation of pigs since a man's wives play a key role in raising them, and he depends upon his pigs for his trade and ceremonial exchange partnerships, through which he acquires other valuables. Communities that would otherwise be feuding or at war are less destructively linked in conventional competition through the Big Men's exchange transactions.

In the Trobriands this pattern is varied by an institution of hereditary rank that divides the matrilineal descent groups *(dala, Malinowski's 'subclans')* into *guyau* 'chief' and *tokay* 'commoner'. 'Chiefly' rank legitimizes the wealth and power that the senior men of a subclan may acquire by the exercise of traditional privileges. In pre-European times, a commoner who broke the leaders' virtual local monopoly of coconut and areca palms, pigs, imported cooking pots, and greenstone axe blades

would have been attacked by jealous commoners as well as chiefs because he had no
"right" to do so; but the most important chiefly privilege for present purposes is
polygynous marriage. The men of a woman's descent group and village must produce annual crops of yams *(urigubu)* (Powell 1960, 1969a, 1969b) for her husband,
and they owe him other services. By exploiting these services, an able chief of
Omarakana could sometimes command enough wealth and support from his
affines to dominate all of Kiriwina and even beyond (Powell 1960) and to ensure
entry into overseas *kula* for himself and his followers.

Most northern Kiriwinan villages are grouped in clusters, each village being
owned by one or more, usually commoner, subclans, with the leader of a higher
ranking subclan as the de facto cluster leader, or 'chief'. Malinowski, like most Europeans resident in the Trobriands, called the Tabalu 'chief' of Omarakana the
paramount chief. There was, however, no office of head of an indigenous bureau-
cratic hierarchy. Although subclan membership is matrilineal, secular power is exer-
cised by men; but birth into a 'chiefly' subclan does not in itself make even its most
senior male an effective leader. He must exploit his privileges, initially by making
advantageous marriages. With his immediate cluster followers, the men of his wives'
subclans and villages form a body of supporters of their sisters' husband in the
'feasts of merit' at which his accumulated wealth is redistributed so as to place others under obligation to him. When he is strong enough in his own district, he can
demand wives from leaders of more distant communities by threatening to attack.
If the senior man of a chiefly subclan fails to validate his position, another member
who ousts him by political maneuver or eliminates him by ambush, sorcery, or poison has a legitimate claim to the leadership.

The rank of the subclans is enshrined in myths of origin *(liliu)* that narrate the
emergence of their first ancestors from Tuma, the underworld, announcing their
rights to territory, names, ornaments, taboos, and magic. Most of the 'chiefly' subclans are credited with some special magical power, often of gardening or fishing,
and sometimes of sorcery. There are two special cases. The Toliwaga 'subclan' is
'commoner' but has the most potent war skills and magic; and the chief of the Tabalu of Omarakana, the highest ranking of the 'chiefly' subclans, controls the most
powerful of all systems of magic, the *to'urikuna* magic of sun and rain. With it he
can cause famine or plenty *(malia)* (Malinowski 1935:160) throughout the
archipelago without leaving Omarakana. By contrast, his rival, the Toliwaga leader,
must exercise his power as warrior in person. The ritual status associated with the
Omarakana Tabalu chief's control of the weather is held to legitimize his claims to
polygynous marriage and to the political power that it underwrites.

The persistence of rank in the Trobriands, whether it was an indigenous development or an alien introduction, suggests that it is ecologically advantageous. This
may have to do with regulating competition. Kiriwina is about fifty kilometers long
and no more than seven kilometers wide. Population density in the 1950s was
about 130 people per square mile in northern Kiriwina, where the institutions and
effects of rank are fully developed. It may have been twice as high in pre-European
times and has risen again since 1950.

Unlike the populations of mainland New Guinea, the Kiriwinans had no other territory to which to flee from famine if unbridled competition for power resulted in the mass destruction of crops. The institution of rank does not eliminate competition but does restrict it to legitimate rivals. A possible explanation of the role of the Toliwaga warrior leader is that it offered a check to prevent the power of the Tabalu chiefs from becoming so great as to crystallize their position into that of a hereditary regime entitled to eliminate competition. This check would constitute a mechanism for restoring the balance of competitiveness and so maintaining the system. If the competing units had been wider or had the Trobriands been in conflict with other islands, the advantages of larger scale political integration might have pushed the rank system toward a static rather than the dynamic, fluctuating equilibrium of its indigenous form. In 1950 *kula* was regaining its significance as a conventional competitive source of prestige and power in both intra- and interisland politics, which is why the northeastern Kiriwinans rebuilt their fleet.

SEAMANSHIP AND POLITICS

The Kilivilan crews' frustration of waiting to sail for Kitava was exacerbated by reports that a Kitavan fleet had brought home many armshells from Iwo and Gawa, where some of the Kilivilans had hoped to go. As the southeasterlies persisted, alternative routes to Kitava were mooted. The shorter, but nautically more risky, route was to paddle south, as far as possible inshore of the fringing reef for shelter from onshore seas, and sail eastward for Kitava from Luba district with the wind abeam. The longer, but less exposed, route was to round Kiriwina Island by the north shore and the lagoon and sail from Gilibwa to Kitava.

The crews, however, were reluctant to embark on either course, especially on the latter since the fleet would have had to traverse the waters of a number of lagoon villages. In pre-European times, these villages would have either opposed the northerners' passage as enemies or welcomed and entertained them as friends or allies. Such entertainment would have imposed a major strain on the host villagers' resources, which their guests would have to reciprocate in due course. In any case, the northern fleets could be sure of hospitable receptions only if they were strong enough to force a passage should they be opposed anywhere on the way to Gilibwa (see J. Leach 1983:135–38).

The Sinaketans and Vakutans, on the other hand, could have monopolized *kula* to Kitava altogether had they been numerous enough to withstand pressure from the other Trobriand communities, which seems unlikely. The Omarakana Tabalu and their followers would have had no difficulty in dominating them if they could have reached their territory without traversing that of their nearer rivals; as they could not, they had as a last resort to dominate the latter also. In 1951 the government would have punished their using force, which is why Mitakata felt entitled to its help in securing his followers' *kula* 'paths' *(keda)*, or partnerships (Campbell 1983:202). Still, the host villages were honor bound to match their hospitality to the visitors' prestige, which the latter would have to validate by even greater generosity to their rivals in their turn.

Mitakata's repeated postponements of sailing delayed the fleet until those of its leaders who were village councillors and policemen had to attend the government Anzac Day parade at Losuia on April 25. By then, calms had set in, and on April 24 I saw most of the canoes paddling south past the Okaiboma village beach to Wawela. There I recorded the *mwayola* 'public display' and the redistribution among their owners of forty-eight armshells brought from Kitava by the twenty-man crew of the headman's canoe, who were associated with the fleet led by the Toliwaga Nalibutau of Yalumugwa (see Powell 1952:part 4, note 16; cf. Malinowski 1922:503). This 'public display' suggested what the delays might have cost the northeasterners in armshells.

Mitakata had gone early to Losuia in a final attempt to obtain a passage in the government's recently acquired launch, but it had been out of action since its arrival. His crew and those of the other leaders waited at Wawela until their captains could join them on April 26 and then paddled on to Kitava. Mitakata's followers were well aware that, if the uncertain end to the trade winds had not been compounded by his procrastinations, the fleet could have reached Kitava in time to intercept some of the shells that went to Sinaketa and then returned, albeit reluctantly, for the Anzac Day parade. I never learned what spoils the fleet succeeded in bringing back from Kitava in 1951, but if the delay prevented my participant observation of local seamanship, it highlighted the implications of its limitations and of the geographical position of northern Kiriwina in the *kula*.

In view of these considerations, I proposed (Powell 1978) that the preeminence of the Tabalu among the high-rank *(guyau)* subclans of Kiriwina might have to do with the peculiar situation of its northeastern villages in relation to overseas *kula*. These villages have the richest garden lands in the Trobriands, and Omarakana, the seat of the dominant leader of that subclan, is one of them: other villages dominated by its "cadet" branches control less productive garden land of the rest of northern Kiriwina and the lagoon villages. I argued (1960) that rank served to restrain competition in a relatively confined and densely populated environment; but this did not explain the traditional preeminence of the dominant Tabalu among the other 'chiefs'.

Irwin (1983:51) rejected my hypothesis as "unnecessary now that it has been established that the northern leaders had an independent basis for their power." This conclusion derives from his analysis of the congruence of the villages of the highest-ranked leaders with the most favored sites in his models of relative centrality in the communication network of northern Kiriwina (1983:30ff). His models are not all equally congruent with the data on the distribution of power in relation to resources, and Irwin explicitly weights some demographic, social, and geographic factors so as to obtain closer agreement with the models he prefers.

His explanation of rank and the location of the leaders' villages seems compatible with my account of Trobriand social organization as a variant of the Big Man system in which hereditary rank restricts the right to compete for power (Powell 1960, 1969a:601; cf. Irwin 1983:51). I characterized the social system as one of fluctuating equilibrium in which the leaders built up their power until, through age or unpopularity they lost their capacity to maintain it. Then the foci of power might change temporarily, though the structure of social relationships within and between local populations remained stable, except in times of famine, when basic survival became the overriding aim.

Irwin (1983:30) mistakenly attributes to me the assertion "that all those [sub-clans] which supplied cluster leaders were *guyau* . . ." (1983:30). There are village clusters (e.g., Irwin 1983:33, map 1, nos. 30–35) without effective 'chiefly' leaders, and the Toliwaga were *tokay* 'commoners' (Powell 1978:13), which is why they were not ritually qualified to displace the Tabalu when they beat them in formal warfare (cf. Irwin 1983:51–52; J. Leach 1983:135–38). Yet, as I noted (Powell 1978; cf. Irwin 1983:52), had it not been for European intervention, the Toliwaga might have been in line for elevation to *guyau* rank. Irwin remarks that his "theory does not explain all that is characteristic of the Tabalu . . ." and that "Among dala of guyau rank the Tabalu appear to be different in kind as well as degree" (1983:52, 53). If, as he argues, the general form of Trobriand rank and leadership is partly at-tributable to factors in the local ecology, it should be possible to relate the unique status of the Tabalu chief of Omarakana, as well as the distribution and varying roles of the Tabalu and other chiefs, to coordinate factors in their demographic and geographical situations. One such set of factors has to do with the Omarakana Ta-balu chief's role in overseas *kula*.

It is not clear to me whether Irwin's application of weightings in analyzing re-gional *kula* routes (1983:54ff, map 7) takes account of such nautical factors as sea-manship as well as spatial distances. He (1983:49ff) rightly rejects Brunton's (1975) hypothesis that Tabalu rank resulted from their entry into *kula* by giving wives in the past to the Kitavan *kula* leaders, which would have subordinated the Tabalu as tributary affines to the Kitavans and weakened them in the Trobriand arena (see Powell 1960, 1969a, 1969b, 1978:170). Rather, Irwin's analysis (1983:52) en-dorses Uberoi's (1962) and my view that, for *kula*, eminence derives from rather than generates status at home, though there is feedback between them (cf. Camp-bell 1983:203).

Yet, Irwin (1983:49) appears to accept Brunton's contention that Kiriwina could be bypassed in the *kula* network. Brunton (1975:548) points out that the "natural" *kula* route between the Kitavan and Dobuan "bottlenecks" is via Sinaketa and Vakuta, bypassing the other Trobriand communities altogether. My argument goes further than this; it is not merely that "Kiriwina could expect more adverse winds . . ." or that it could be bypassed, as Irwin notes (1983:49). It is that, given the limitations of their seamanship, the northeastern Kiriwinans were effectively out of overseas *kula* for most of the year.

Any map of the *kula* region shows that the northern Kiriwinan communities are the only ones all of whose possible overseas partners are upwind of them during the southeasterly trade wind season. This is the time of the harvest and ceremonial distribution of the main garden crop. It culminates in the *milamala* season of feasts of merit, of dancing, and nowadays of cricket and ends in the ritual *yoba* expulsion (Malinowski 1935:110) back to the underworld, Tuma, of the spirits of the dead ancestors who attend the festivities. The inauguration of the next year's ceremonial gardens follows (cf. Powell 1952:parts 2 and 5).

Local demography is also significant in the context of overseas *kula*. The more than ninety men who crewed the five canoes of the Omarakana village cluster in 1951 comprised nearly all its warriors, in whose absence on a fleet visit to Kitava the villages would be undefended. The taboos on outsiders described by Malinowski (1922:484) would have protected the villages to an extent, and in the case of Omarakana would have been reinforced by fear of its chief's control of weather magic and sorcery, which both justified the military potential of his marital alliances and reinforced the taboos. But, while some individuals may be able to go away on *kula* via Sinaketa during the southeasterlies, not even Omarakana can do without its manpower for more than a few days. Thus, crews of canoes, let alone of a fleet, cannot normally take advantage of breaks in the winds to sail their own vessels to Kitava but must wait for the slack period of gardening when the northwesterlies should have set in. If the Kilivilans do not go then, however, their *kula* roads become vulnerable to rivals.

By Irwin's weighted criteria (1983:55, map 7, 59, figure 1) the relationship between Kitava and Kilivila is fairly central in the Trobriand local communications network. But his criteria do not take into account that Kilivila is the only district in the *kula* with no overseas partners who can be reached by sailing with, rather than against, the southeasterly trade winds. By contrast, Kitavan canoes or fleets can sail downwind to northern Kiriwina during the southeasterlies (Malinowski 1929: chapter 20), and direct passages either way between Kitava and Sinaketa or Vakuta are possible all year round with any wind other than the northeaster, while the southeasterlies are optimal for either passage.

The northern Kiriwinans' downwind position would have been a disadvantage even if, as Malinowski reports (1922:144–45), they had in earlier times built and sailed the larger and more weatherly *nagega* canoes of the eastern *kula* ring. But my informants doubted whether the deep-draft *nagega* could have sailed from the northeastern beaches because of the lack of such a haven as Kaduwaga (Montague this volume) in which to keep them afloat. If for any reason the northeastern Kiriwinans had to use the *masawa* canoes while their competitors sailed the *nagega*, the latter would have had an even greater nautical advantage.

Irwin's models confirm the conclusion that the natural route into the island from the south and east is via Gilibwa and the lagoon. From the north and west, landings are possible on the beach of Kaibola during the southeasterly winds, and the USAF aerial survey maps from which my sketch maps (1960) were made show a trawler anchorage off Olivilevi for the northwester season, though its beach and reef are too exposed during the southeasterlies. No Kitavan fleets had sailed to the northeastern beaches of Kiriwina since the occupation, as they did before it (Malinowski 1922:479), but individual canoes often sailed to one of the Kiriwinan lagoon villages, whence their crews walked overland to visit their partners. One such party came to Omarkana in 1951 on a *kula* visit to Mitakata, which took him by surprise and was over by the time I heard of it.

Irwin's analysis, moreover, explains the association between rank in Kiriwina and control of local natural resources and the commodities imported from other islands. Omarakana shares with other 'chiefly' village sites the communications advantages described by Irwin, though in his unweighted models it is not the most 'central' site in the local network. Omarakana is a focus of the most productive garden land in Kiriwina, which is why its leaders' ability to claim wives from the widest area they could dominate was so effective a source of power. Irwin (1983:48) rightly infers that "at harvest times there were a lot of yams on Trobriand roads, travelling especially to chiefs . . ."; but intercluster ceremonial gifts were predominantly to the Tabalu.

Yet, the ritual status that endorses this prerogative, by crediting the Omarakana Tabalu with magical control of sun and rain, reflects the vulnerability of the garden lands to drought. In pre-European times, it was the lagoon villagers, dominated by the Tabalu cadet branches, who controlled the more reliable resources of the sea. Under European government, this control shifted the balance of power toward them as long as pearl fishing and wider trade prospered. As the ritual status of the Tabalu was as much the rationale as the source of their power, its equivalent might, if the trend had lasted long enough, have been ascribed to any lagoon subclan able to dislodge them permanently.

The conventions of rank were ecologically advantageous in that they inhibited rivals from seeking to usurp Tabalu status. My informants held that when internecine struggles for control of 'chiefly' communities got out of hand in pre-European times the resultant political instability disrupted gardening to the point of widespread starvation. Without the restraint of rank in general as a qualification for competition for leadership, such a degree of instability might have been the usual state of Trobriand politics.

The dominance within northern Kiriwina of the Tabalu chiefs ensured their followers' control of or access to the lagoon imports and products. In normal times this was structured through the various forms of exchange, including inland *kula* with the lagoon communities, which are congruous with Irwin's 'centrality' models. Even when garden produce was in short supply so that normal exchanges were restricted, the potential military strength of the Omarakana Tabalu chief's marital and other local alliances ensured such access to his Kilivilan followers. But these considerations do not explain his preeminence throughout not only the Trobriand group but beyond it to much of the northeastern *kula* circuit. It is the technological problem of communication posed by the geographical relationships of Omarakana village and Kilivila district to the rest of the Trobriands and to the *kula* ring that offers such an explanation.

Brunton argues and Irwin recognizes that they are off the direct *kula* routes and are easily bypassed; but their people's access to overseas *kula* is further restricted by the limits imposed on their seamanship by the characteristics of their canoes and by the limited opportunities for sailing afforded by the northeastern coast of Kiriwina, where they are based. At the same time, delay or failure of the onset of the northwesterly season into the time of the villages' greatest need of their manpower may restrict the Kilivilans' chances of making use of the favorable winds.

Yet, in 1951 these considerations need not have precluded the fleet sailing for Kitava without Mitakata when the winds permitted. In retrospect, it is surprising that, after all the trouble and costs of the canoe-building, the fleet reduced its chances of acquiring the best armshells by deferring a twenty-mile voyage to a visible destination because of Mitakata's reluctance to sail in his own *masawa* canoe. His political followers could hardly have taken advantage of preceding him to preempt his *kula* partners, though rivals such as Yobukwau of Liluta might have tried to do so. Granted his aversion to canoe sailing, Mitakata's attempts to find a berth in a European vessel may also have had to do with his wish to appear to have European support for his and his followers' *kula* claims. But the critical factor seems to have been that, if the fleet had left him behind, his political and ritual status, upon which ultimately depended his and his followers' access to overseas *kula*, would have been diminished.

But why did the Omarakana Tabalu and his followers bother with overseas *kula* at all? It may be inferred from Irwin's models that they could have obtained as much material advantage from their exchanges with the lagoon villages, without the costs of canoe building and maintenance. Brunton's argument that 'chiefly' rank was derived ultimately from control of trade, for example in stone axe blades *(beku)*, is contradicted by my informants' assertions that, until steel axes became readily available, the great majority of northern villagers had to rely upon local shell blades and fire for their garden needs, as there were never enough stone blades for all. Moreover, most people had to cook in seashells, except on ceremonial occasions, when they borrowed Amphlett *kulia* cooking pots, the other major item in pre-European trade, from their leaders.

Entry into overseas *kula* was necessary because it was the idiom of conventional competition between members of communities too far apart for the intracommunity exchange idioms to be practical, inasmuch as they involve the transportation of large amounts of bulky foodstuffs. These idioms include the exchange relationships of kinship, rank and polygynous marriage, mortuary prestations, and the *paka* displays of wealth and power in feasts of merit, which focused traditionally on dancing and nowadays on cricket, the modern surrogate for traditional formal warfare *(kabilia)*. Not to have *kula* partners overseas would have left the Omarakana Tabalu with the same status as other local leaders, while if they entered the overseas *kula* ring at all they had to do so with enough success to sustain and enhance their status overseas as well as at home. But to enter the overseas *kula* ring, they had to break into the natural route, unlike those whose territories were part of it.

CONCLUSION: CONTINUITY AND CHANGE

A more centralized form of political leadership than that of mainland Papua New Guinea was advantageous to Kiriwinans because it limited the potential of ecologically destructive conflict by substituting more constructive forms of conventional competition for uncontrolled warfare. *Kula* provided the means of carrying on interisland conventional competitive gift exchange where the intraisland exchanges of bulk commodities could not be maintained. The northeastern Kiriwinans were motivated to support the dominance of the Tabalu chief of Omarakana as the leader of a body strong enough to gain entry into the *kula* ring by force if necessary, since, given their nautical technologies and the geographical location of northern Kiriwina, the natural route for voyages between the Trobriands and Kitava bypassed them. Their motivation was political rather than economic; in order to dominate intraisland conventional competition, they needed to compete effectively in the interisland arena. They had, therefore, to maintain and man their own fleet of *masawa* seagoing canoes, and this preserved the indigenous traditions of *masawa* canoe building and sailing in northeastern Kiriwina.

The resurgence of these activities, which I observed in 1951, was in part a reaction to the traumas of the military occupation from 1941 to 1945. If increased use of European technology has affected Kiriwina as it has other parts of Oceania, I may have taken part in the last major traditional canoe building in that part of the *kula* ring. J. Leach's (1975) account of cricket and Kabisawali in Kiriwinan politics confirms my impression that Kiriwinans have been capable adaptors of alien institutions to their own culture, but recent developments may penetrate its defenses. *Kabisawali* (Nesbitt 1975; Powell 1976; cf. Young 1979:17–20), a political movement led by Nalibutau's Australian-educated sister's son, his heir, ostensibly to modernize Trobriand economics and politics, failed. This was partly because of the strength of the traditional institutions, but it was equally because Nalibutau and other Toliwaga leaders sought to use Kabisawali to oust the Tabalu rather than to overturn the system that sustained them.

That some Kiriwinans have gained and lost preeminence in the politics of postindependence Papua New Guinea may have both reinforced and weakened traditional leadership patterns in their home islands. In Weiner's film (1990), Puliasi and Nalibutau, successors of the Toliwaga and Tabalu leaders of 1950, carry on their traditional rivalry using trucks and money, and Puliasi attains another wife and more tributary affines (cf. Powell 1976). A fundamentalist Christian mission has been established in the Omarakana neighborhood, but the islanders may be able to reconcile its teachings with or dissociate them from their own cosmology and social institutions as they have done with those of the Methodists and Catholics. In 1950 and 1951 the full range of canoe magic was performed, and in Tilakaiwa of Omarakana village cluster, the full sequence of garden magic (Powell 1952:part 2) was carried out for the first time since the Japanese war because mission prayers, on which the villagers had relied, had yielded poor harvests. My nominally Methodist informants had "given up" magic on their conversion; but in Weiner's film the Kwaybwaga village leader gives her his magic to preserve because he and his successors had become "born again" Christians, which may present a greater threat to its survival than did the Methodists or Catholics.

Perhaps more significantly, Weiner's film also shows Nalibutau's university graduate daughter running a trade store on Kiriwina and another Kiriwinan woman who owns a supermarket on the mainland. They both use trade goods and money to take part in women's ceremonial exchanges as well as traditional "women's wealth," which the latter woman cannot accumulate herself. Nalibutau says on camera that in ten years there will be two kinds of Kiriwinans, village and "educated," but maintains that the position of the chiefs will be the same; but his daughter says that people are no longer satisfied with growing and exchanging yams as a way of life and increasingly want to work for money.

Growing Kiriwinan involvement in national trade, and perhaps a revival of tourism, coupled with wider participation in national politics, could provide the Trobrianders with new arenas of conventional competition. This would open the way to the radical changes in Kiriwinan politics that the Kabisawali movement with its cooperative bank failed to produce because of the demands of traditional kinship and rank. If both men and women can obtain modern wealth, so that the yam gardens cease to be the ultimate source of power, the status of those who exercise magical and secular control over them must be eroded.

Even with some such erosion, the chiefs, especially the Tabalu of Omarakana, might be able to exploit their ritual preeminence so as to retain their entrepreneurial centrality in northeastern Kiriwina through polygynous marriage. But if both marriage and *kula* are replaced by other idioms of conventional competition, the advantage to the northeastern Kiriwinans of the unique status of the Omarakana Tabalu chief as political leader and ritual figurehead, behind whom they could unite to break into overseas *kula*, may well be lost and with it such traditions of canoe building and seamanship, as I was able to record. Not that this loss of tradition in itself would necessarily mean the end of some form of overseas *kula* or of the northeastern Kiriwinans' part in it. My 'brothers' often said that for them *kula* is "like going on holiday for you Dimdim [Europeans]." If they no longer need to be able to enter the *kula* ring by force and if their standard of living rises, Kiriwinans might, like Mitakata, prefer to travel on *kula* as passengers on modern tourist vessels rather than in their own *masawa* canoes.

REFERENCES

Austen, Leo
  1945   Cultural changes in Kiriwina. *Oceania* 16:16–60.
Brunton, Ron
  1975   Why do the Trobriands have chiefs? *Man,* N.S., 10:544–58.
Campbell, Shirley F.
  1983   Kula in Vakuta. . . . In *The Kula,* edited by Jerry W. Leach and Edmund Leach, pp. 201–27. Cambridge: Cambridge University Press.
Dodd, Edward H.
  1972   *Polynesian Seafaring.* Lymington, U.K.: Nautical Publishing Company and George G. Harrap and Co.
Irwin, Geoffrey J.
  1983   Chieftainship, kula, and trade in Massim prehistory. In *The Kula,* edited by Jerry W. Leach and Edmund Leach, pp. 29–72. Cambridge: Cambridge University Press.
Leach, Jerry W.
  1975   *Trobriand Cricket.* 16 mm film. U.K.: R.A.I. Film Library.

1983   Trobriand territorial categories. In *The Kula,* edited by Jerry W. Leach and Edmund Leach, pp. 121–46. Cambridge: Cambridge University Press.

Leach, Jerry W., and Edmund Leach (editors)
1983   *The Kula.* Cambridge: Cambridge University Press.

Lewis, David
1972   *We, the Navigators.* Canberra: Australian National University Press.

Mair, Lucy P.
1948   *Australia in New Guinea.* London: Christophers.

Malinowski, Bronislaw
1922   *Argonauts of the Western Pacific: An Account of Native Enterprise and Adventure in the Archipelagoes of Melanesian New Guinea.* London: Routledge and Kegan Paul.
1932   *The Sexual Life of Savages.* 3rd edition. (1929) London: Routledge and Kegan Paul.
1935   *Coral Gardens and their Magic,* Vol. 1. London: Allen and Unwin.

Nesbitt, Alec
1975   *The Trobriand Experiment.* 16mm film. BBC *Horizon* Series.

Powell, Henry A.
1952   *The Trobriand Islanders.* 16 mm film and video. U.K.: R.A.I. Film Library.
1956   An analysis of present day social structure in the Trobriand Islands. Unpublished Ph.D. Dissertation. London: University Senate House Library.
1960   Competitive leadership in Trobriand political organisation. *Journal of the Royal Anthropological Institute* 90:118–45.
1969a   Territory, hierarchy and kinship in Kiriwina. *Man,* N.S., 4:580–604.
1969b   Genealogy residence and kinship in Kiriwina. *Man,* N.S., 4:178–202.
1976   Review of film *The Trobriand Experiment. R.A.I. News* 13:3–6.
1978   The Kula in Trobriand Politics . . . ? Unpublished manuscript for first Kula Conference. Cambridge, U.K.

Saville, Gordon, with John Austin
1974   *King of Kiriwina.* London: Leo Cooper.

Tambiah, Stanley J.
1983   On female witches. . . . In *The Kula,* edited by Jerry W. Leach and Edmund Leach, pp. 171–200. Cambridge: Cambridge University Press.

Uberoi, J. P. Singh
1962   *Politics of the Kula Ring.* Manchester, U.K.: Manchester University Press.

Weiner, Annette B.
1990   *The Trobriand Islanders of Papua New Guinea. Disappearing World* Series. Video: Granada Television Ltd., Manchester, U.K.

Young, Michael
1979   *The Ethnography of Malinowski.* London, Boston, and Henley: Routledge and Kegan Paul.

MARITIME TRAVEL, PRESENT AND PAST, IN MAROVO, WESTERN SOLOMON ISLANDS

Edvard Hviding

• Although a considerable body of literature about traditional material culture of the Solomon Islands, mainly with reference to the late nineteenth and early twentieth centuries (cf. Edridge 1985), contains much information on canoes and fishing gear, there is almost nothing in print dealing with the role of more recent, introduced technology such as outboard motors and their influence on maritime travel.[1]

In this essay, I attempt to fill part of this information gap in Melanesian ethnography by providing a detailed account of maritime travel in a strongly sea-oriented society of the western Solomons, namely, that of Marovo Lagoon in the New Georgia archipelago (see figure 5.1). In other accounts, I have documented and analyzed customary marine tenure, traditional fishing practices, and knowledge of the marine environment in Marovo, with particular emphasis on contemporary sociopolitical contexts and on the role of the sea in cultural identity (see Hviding 1988, 1989, 1990, 1996; Hviding and Baines 1994). In the present account, I focus specifically on Marovo people's travel at sea, within the Marovo area and its spectacular lagoon, throughout the New Georgia Group of islands, and beyond. My main emphasis is on contemporary seafaring and its associated skills, technologies, and sociocultural contexts—themes that also prominently embrace fishing. For reasons that will become evident, I emphasize the contemporary maritime technology that centers on large dugout canoes with outboard motors.

The historical importance of maritime travel among New Georgians also figures in the following essay, largely because of the Marovo people's own conscious maintenance of strong links with their maritime past. These links are not limited to local appreciation of former generations' considerable practical skills in canoe building and seafaring, including long-distance voyaging. They are equally based upon a grounding of Marovo cultural identity in a history embedded in the seascape in the form of sacred sites and deeply meaningful place names with associated stories and legends. This emphasis on the symbolic significance of an intimately known and classified seascape is of considerable ethnographic interest and will be examined in some detail in the final sections of this essay (cf. Hviding 1996).

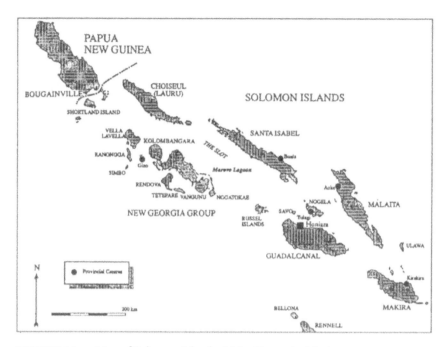

FIGURE 5.1. Map of Solomon Islands, Main Group Archipelago.

I begin the essay by focusing attention on the regional backdrop of Marovo sea-faring: the blue, turquoise, and green reef-fringed rain forest world of the New Georgia Group, where each of the numerous languages, as is common throughout Oceania, applies a single term to all those endlessly shifting nuances of color displayed by forest, lagoon, reefs, and ocean. In the Marovo language, the term *buma* represents the spectrum of shades in the land- and seascape, ranging from the dark green of the dense forest to the deep blue of the open sea. When moving through this blue-green space, New Georgia people generally have few options other than to use the sea as their main road.

MARITIME TRAVEL IN THE NEW GEORGIA GROUP

The New Georgia Group, located in the western part of the Solomon Islands, consists of a fairly compact cluster of high, volcanic islands, arranged like stepping-stones on a northwest to southeast axis (figure 5.2). The west and southeast sides of the main island of New Georgia are fringed by the raised barrier reefs that form the Roviana and Marovo Lagoons, respectively. The latter also embraces the volcanic islands of Vangunu and Gatokae and is known as one of the world's largest coastal reef-and-lagoon complexes. Historically, the minor expanses of open sea between most of the lagoon clusters and larger islands have linked, rather than separated, the inhabitants of the different parts of the archipelago. The people of the New Georgia Group were, and remain, frequent interisland travelers, whether in the large,

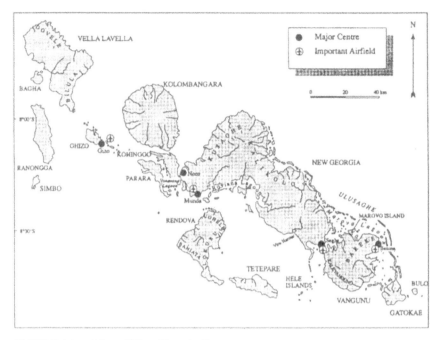

FIGURE 5.2.   Map of New Georgia Group.

paddle-propelled, ornamented plank canoes of former times or in today's brightly painted dugout or fiberglass canoes powered by outboard motors.

Early European observers, including the ethnographer A. M. Hocart (e.g., 1931, 1935, 1937), who wrote on the small outlying island of Simbo (formerly Eddystone); the British naval officer Somerville (1897) in his ethnographic notes, mainly from Marovo; and a number of traders, travelers, colonists, and missionaries (e.g., Cheyne 1971; Burnett 1911; Woodford 1888, 1890, 1909; Goldie 1909) were alternately fascinated by the superior maritime technology represented in New Georgia's war canoes and horrified by the far-ranging head-hunting expeditions carried out in such canoes by the coastal dwellers of most of the western Solomons. The people of the Roviana and Marovo Lagoons, and of Simbo, Vella Lavella, Rendova, and other islands, went raiding and trading within the group and also further afield, across the ocean to Isabel, Choiseul, the Russell Islands, Savo, Guadalcanal, and other remote destinations, possibly even to Malaita (Hviding 1996; McKinnon 1975; Findlay 1877:773).

Because of their history as voyagers, the people of present-day New Georgia retain kinship links within and beyond the archipelago. Cognatic descent, prevailing in Marovo and Roviana, contributes to the maintenance of bilateral kin connections that are often traced to captives taken generations earlier. The connections are maintained today by frequent visiting and intermarriage, which also work to bolster land claims. A high level of spatial mobility continues to characterize life in the New Georgia islands. Modern infrastructure is dispersed. The steep and rugged volcanic topography of these islands inhibits ground transport; and air travel, although fairly well developed, is prohibitively expensive. Maritime travel thus remains the all-important means of transport throughout the New Georgia Group.

THE MAROVO LAGOON AND ITS PEOPLE

The people of Marovo retain close links with the sea. Their lagoon is the cornerstone of economic life and spatial mobility, and it plays a crucial role in history and the formation and maintenance of cultural identity (see Hviding 1996). The Marovo reef-and-lagoon complex, the core of existence for its village populations, stretches from the village of Kolobaghea, near the northern tip of New Georgia, southeast for more than one hundred kilometers to the island of Gatokae (figure

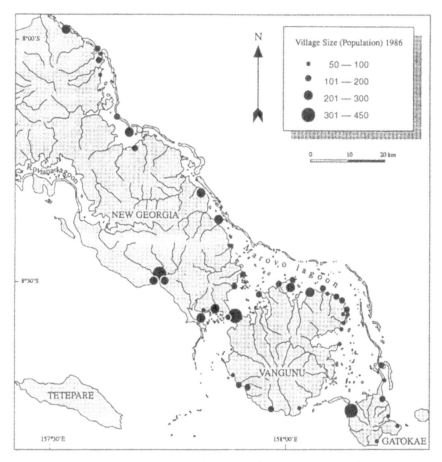

FIGURE 5.3. Map of Marovo area showing settlement pattern as of 1986.

5.3). The long and winding lagoon formed by the row of raised, forested barrier reef islands running parallel to the coasts of the New Georgia and Vangunu "mainland" covers an area of about seven hundred square kilometers (Stoddart 1969). In the main lagoon area, in smaller adjacent lagoons, and on the weather coasts of the main islands lives a Melanesian population of around ten thousand (1994 estimate based on 1986 census [SIG 1989]). These people are associated with a culture complex that is generally termed "Marovo" both by themselves and by other groups throughout the Solomons, and they are contrasted with the culturally related Roviana area of west and southwest New Georgia.[2]

The Marovo area has an abundant and diverse marine and terrestrial resource base and, so far, relatively low population densities. In many parts of Marovo, the natural environment retains an almost pristine quality, but the area as a whole faces future prospects that include rapid population growth (at an annual rate exceeding 3.5 percent) and an increase of commercial ventures in fishing, mining, logging, and tourism. The abundance and diversity of resources underpin a varied household-based subsistence production centered on shifting agriculture and fishing. Hunting (mainly of feral pigs) and gathering of shellfish and *Canarium* (or *"ngali"*) nuts provide important dietary supplements. The contemporary village economy includes a growing and diversifying cash sector, with income in recent years from such sources as wood carving and other handicraft; the sale of trochus, pearl shell, bêche-de-mer, and other marine products; the marketing of garden produce and fish; the sale of logs to a local sawmill run by the Seventh-Day Adventist church; and the production of cash crops, including cocoa and copra.

The Marovo climate is hot and humid throughout the year, with major changes only in wind directions and tidal cycles. From April to October, the southeasterly trade winds prevail, while the more irregular and wet northwest monsoons dominate the period from December to March. The time of the southeast trades *(hecha)* coincides with the seasonal occurrence of low tide at daytime *(mati rane)*, and the time of the northwest monsoons *(mohu* 'wet') coincides with low tide at nighttime *(mati ipu)*. This recurring pattern is important for the yearly cycles of fishing and maritime travel and is connected with local knowledge about a number of other cyclical events in the environment.

A traditional dichotomy in Marovo society between 'people of the coast' *(tinoni pa sera)* and 'people of the bush' *(tinoni pa goana)*, categorizations that most importantly apply to localized, corporate groups, remains culturally and politically important.[3] Since the end of warfare and the advent of colonial power and missions early in the twentieth century, however, all villages gradually came to be situated on the mainland coasts or on small islands in the lagoon (see figures 5.3 and 5.4). This settlement pattern, with groups of both 'bush' and 'coastal' identities all residing in coastal villages (though still separately), makes maritime travel and the utilization of marine resources universal phenomena in which every Marovo villager participates. The contemporary pattern sharply contrasts with that from precolonial times, when constant enmity between coastal and bush dwellers, and the military superiority of

FIGURE 5.4.   Partial view of a typical village shore in the central part of the Marovo Lagoon.

the former, forced the latter to stay inland (cf. Somerville 1897).

Throughout the Marovo area there is a heavy reliance on the sea for virtually all transport and communication purposes. There are no land paths at all between most villages, separated as they are by extensive mangrove swamps. The weather coast areas are an exception; there, the exposure of the seashore to surf and heavy swells severely inhibits canoe launching and travel, while an absence of extensive mangrove swamps allows intervillage travel along coastal footpaths.

GROUPS AND RESOURCES: LAND, SEA, AND THE WIDER WORLD

The resources of land and sea in Marovo are controlled by corporate kin groups, largely through customary law. Marovo society is divided into more than twenty named, largely corporate and localized, descent-based groups *(butubutu)*. Each controls a defined area of land and (in most cases) sea, termed *puava*. This term literally means 'earth' or 'soil', but in the context of corporate territorial holdings, it applies to terrestrial and submerged areas alike (see Hviding 1996). Whereas the *puava* of 'bush' *butubutu* generally contain only dry land and cover most of the main islands, the *puava* of 'coastal' *butubutu* consist mainly of lagoon and barrier reef areas and only strips of coastal land. Reciprocal agreements on limited use rights give bush groups access to marine resources and vice versa. Control over, and allocation of, resources is carried out through an authority structure where each *butubutu*'s affairs are managed by a senior male leader with a number of associate leaders, all recruited from a core of people permanently resident in the *butubutu*'s area. Succession to senior leadership positions has a strong genealogical element, usually going from father to son.

From the 1970s, the traditional resource management system of Marovo has been challenged by an increasing number of outside parties wishing to exploit the resources of lagoon and forest on a large-scale commercial basis. These parties are mainly transnational logging, fishing, and mining enterprises. Strong and successful local resistance to such initiatives has been the rule rather than the exception (Hviding 1996; Hviding and Baines 1994).

MARITIME TRAVEL: SEASONAL ACTIVITY PATTERNS

Maritime travel around Marovo, as elsewhere in the Solomons, has a definite peak period from late November to late January, owing to the high level of intervillage and interisland visiting associated with the Christmas and New Year celebrations. Most wage laborers in Honiara and Gizo return to their home village by early December for at least one month's holiday, and many weddings are held in this holiday period in order to maximize attendance. This further increases intercommunity and interisland travel, as many Methodists of Marovo go to the Methodist-dominated Roviana, Vonavona, and Gizo areas of western New Georgia, and many Seventh-Day Adventists visit their counterparts in Viru Harbour, Ranongga, Vella Lavella, and Kolobangara.

This peak period of contemporary travel by Marovo people coincides with the most intensive period of interisland raiding and head-hunting of precolonial times. The period from November to December is generally the calmest time of the year, coming in between the seasons of *hecha* 'trade winds' and *mohu* 'monsoons'. It was during this period of calm seas that raids to faraway destinations could be most easily executed without the risk of sudden squalls or strong head winds. The weather conditions, which in former times facilitated paddling on head-hunting raids, now allow extensive long-distance travel in heavily loaded dugout canoes powered by outboard motors. These canoes sometimes transport almost an entire village population to weddings and other celebrations in locations more than two hundred kilometers distant.

The more mundane maritime travel that takes place outside the peak period also has clear patterns. The southeasterly trade winds of April to October, which blow most continuously during the middle months of the season, tend to limit long-distance travel and may virtually prohibit sea access to villages on the weather coasts for weeks. Most fishing during this season focuses on fishermen's "home reefs". These are barrier reef areas directly adjacent to one's village, with little distance to be covered between fishing sites. During the 'wet' season of the more erratic northwesterly monsoons, travel—whether for purposes of fishing or visiting—is more often of a long-range nature. This is because of the many intermittent spells of fine weather. Furthermore, pelagic fish, including the much-prized skipjack tuna *(Katsu-*

wonus pelamis), appear in abundant, predictable schools off the barrier reef. From December to March, an emphasis on highly mobile trolling techniques encourages fishermen to range beyond their home reefs. Petrol consumption rises considerably, and many canoes may at times be seen out in the open sea.

In addition to these seasonal patterns, Marovo people's maritime travel is influenced by a number of monthly, weekly, and daily cycles. Fishing is guided by sophisticated traditional knowledge of spatiotemporal regularities in fish behavior, and fishing activities have definite peaks around new and full moons. The weekly run of activities in all Marovo villages is strongly influenced by church obligations, particularly by the prescribed days of worship and rest. The Seventh-Day Adventists have their most intensive day of fishing on Fridays, obtaining food for their Sabbath on Saturdays, whereas the early and late hours of the Sabbath itself are characterized by much organized intervillage travel by church functionaries and song groups. A similar pattern applies to the Methodist villages for Saturday and Sunday, respectively.

Finally, the daily patterns of maritime activity are influenced by a general desire to be back home by nightfall. This desire does not arise from fear of spirits so much as from other hazards of negotiating a pitch-dark lagoon. Particularly during the monsoon season, when tides are low at night, mazes of shallow reefs pose a danger to outboard motors. Throughout the year, floating debris does the same. Moreover, it is nowadays increasingly commented that after dusk, especially when there is no moonlight, the number of fast, motorized canoes out traveling makes the lagoon unsafe for people in small, black paddling canoes.

MARITIME TRAVEL: SPATIAL AND SOCIAL CONTEXTS

Marovo's complex and dynamic customary marine tenure system provides a spatial context for maritime activities. Marine tenure defines the lagoon and barrier reef areas as composed of discrete units to which corporate groups lay recognized claims through ancestral title. Elsewhere, I provide detailed documentation and analysis of this system (see Hviding 1988, 1989, 1990, 1996). It will suffice here to say that customary marine tenure in Marovo is based on exclusive territorial holdings and on the flexible situational activation of specific limitations on the use of different fishing methods and on the harvest of different target species. So far the holders of customary authority over Marovo's reefs and seas have proved to be highly capable of dealing with the increasing commercialization of local fisheries. They have also succeeded in imposing tight restrictions on industrial tuna-fishing boats' access to the lagoon for bait-fishing purposes.

Travel by small craft as well as interisland passenger ships is generally free through any part of the Marovo Lagoon, including passages through the barrier reef to the open sea beyond, as long as intensive fishing is not attempted. In fact, the concept of free canoe movement throughout Marovo and New Georgia is a much-appreciated basic right enjoyed by all residents. In political terms, this right is the antithesis of limitations on intervillage travel and long-term visiting imposed by the British colonial government as one means of enforcing the detested head tax system.

The only major exception to the rule of free maritime movement applies to foreign yachts, which regularly pass through the lagoon for their crews to enjoy the scenery and to buy wood carvings and other handicrafts from villagers. Several of Marovo's *butubutu* habitually refuse to allow yachts to anchor in their sections of the lagoon, referring to past experiences when yacht crews have disturbed traditionally sacred reef areas, dived for rare and precious shells, or otherwise shown disrespect to the customary holders of reefs and sea space. Finally, despite eighty years of mission influence, many Marovo villagers retain a belief in localized malevolent spiritual powers. Since spirits often inflict sickness on alien travelers, that is, villagers unrelated to the *butubutu* associated with the residential spiritual powers, Marovo people are frequently reluctant to travel through stretches of sea space traditionally known to be particularly dangerous (cf. Lepowsky, Feinberg this volume).

Marovo society is characterized by strong intervillage kinship ties. Maintaining a wide variety of such ties through interpersonal and intergroup networks is seen as vitally important by Marovo people at most stages in life, not just for the sake of socializing in itself but also for the role accorded to the proper maintenance of kin ties in supporting claims to and rights in land and reefs. Thus, it comes as no surprise that intervillage travel in order to visit and spend time with relatives figures prominently in daily life throughout the Marovo area. This type of travel (*ene butubutu*, literally 'kindred travel') is, except on the weather coasts, always done by canoe.

CANOES OF MAROVO: CHANGE AND CONTINUITY

> The canoes of New Georgia are built, as in the rest of the Solomon Islands, on the Malay model, with high prow and stern post. Nothing can exceed the beauty of their lines, and carefulness of build—considering the means at disposal—or their swiftness when properly propelled. They are a most astonishing revelation of scientific art in a people little removed from complete savagery. (Somerville 1897:369)

The British naval lieutenant B. T. Somerville visited the New Georgia islands during an extensive surveying trip in 1893 and 1894 on board the HMS *Penguin*, which had extended stays around the Marovo Lagoon. Somerville learned some of the language and, in several writings, reported in some detail on his experiences there. These writings are the first published reports that concentrate specifically on Marovo. Like other early observers, Somerville was impressed by the New Georgians' advanced canoe-building skills. His remarks quoted above clearly apply to the *magoru*, more commonly known in the literature by its Roviana language name, *tomoko*. These large, richly ornamented plank canoes (see figure 5.5) were sometimes more than six to seven fathoms long. They held up to thirty men, were outriggerless, propelled exclusively by paddling, and were built and used for interisland raiding and warfare (see Woodford 1909; Waite 1990). This canoe type, once built throughout the New Georgia islands and representing the utmost achievement in maritime technology, today survives only in the form of a few scattered specimens in metropolitan museums.[4]

FIGURE 5.5.   A replica of a Marovo war canoe *(magoru)* built between 1986 and 1991 at Chubikopi village, Marovo Island, central Marovo.

However, the plank-built war canoe still looms large in the consciousness of New Georgia villagers. In an atmosphere of cultural revival, noteworthy in this region of heavy Protestant mission influence, several attempts have been made in recent years to build replicas of war canoes under the supervision of those few remaining elders who possess the construction skills. Full-size replicas have been built at Choiseul and Vella Lavella, the former now deposited at the Solomon Islands National Museum and the latter having been presented at exhibitions in Australia. In Marovo a nearly full-scale *magoru* was launched in August 1991 after five years of construction under the guidance of the old master canoe builder Simon Tuni at the Chubikopi village on Marovo Island in the central lagoon. This small volcanic peak was one of the original strongholds of Marovo's nineteenth-century maritime raiding groups and was also an early focus of European trading, in the course of which its name came to be applied to the entire lagoon area on the first charts made (Somerville 1897). The sense of cultural revival in connection with the Chubikopi *magoru*-building project has been strong, and the activities received support from the University of the South Pacific and the Western Provincial Government.[5]

To the New Georgians of today, the traditional war canoe is an icon of ethnic pride. The transmission of war canoe–building skills has become a powerful symbol of renewed ties with a maritime tradition that was long suppressed by the steadily more indigenized missions, ostensibly because of its violent and "heathen" aspects.

FIGURE 5.6.   A recent replica of a late-nineteenth-century *toto isu* figurehead from Marovo Island in the central Marovo Lagoon. The original is still kept by the lineage chief.

A related source of powerful present-day symbolism is the *toto isu,* a war canoe prow ornament, more commonly known by its Roviana name, *nguzunguzu* (see figure 5.6). This ornament is a small, black humanlike image, often also with doglike features, carved from wood and inlaid with patterns of nautilus shell, and depicted as holding either a seabird (for navigational aid) or a human head (for success in head-hunting) in its hands. Its wide open, staring eyes were supposed to ward off any troublesome sea spirits. A *toto isu* was lashed to the prow of every departing New Georgia war canoe to ensure safe passage and efficacy in warfare. Originally carved from light wood and stained black, such figureheads are now produced for the tourist market by modern village carvers working in ebony or other exclusive woods; some exhibit dazzling inlay patterns. Like the canoe to which it was attached, this former spiritual helper of navigators and headhunters has become a national symbol for the Solomon Islands, reaching beyond its western Solomons origins. While the New Georgia war canoe is a central element in the design of the Solomon Islands coat of arms, *toto isu* images are now encountered in all kinds of advertising logos, including those of the national airline and of the telecommunications company.

After the end of head-hunting around the turn of the century, New Georgia war canoes rapidly fell into disuse. Some of the last remaining ones were confiscated by the colonial government (see Woodford 1909 for an account of such an incident in central Marovo) and ended up in museums. Others ended their days as missionaries' preferred means of lagoon travel, well into the 1920s.

The term *mola,* which formerly denoted smaller plank canoes for everyday use (cf. Feinberg this volume), distinct from the *magoru,* was gradually transformed to its present meaning as a generic term for 'canoe'—nowadays even including fiberglass ones. Dugout canoes do not appear to have been part of precolonial maritime technology, probably owing to the unavailability of steel tools and to the emphasis given to functional design and seaworthiness. The traveler Eugen Paravicini, however, reports from his visit to Marovo in the mid-1920s that dugout canoes *(chore)* (see next section) were already well established and in increasingly common use for inshore fishing, while the plank-built *mola,* still distinctly named, was used for open-sea travel (Paravicini 1931:178).[6] Right after World War II, the British colonial officer Tom Russell reported that

> The *mola* is fast disappearing due to the superiority of technology required in its manufacture and the continual maintenance which is necessary to keep it in seaworthy condition. . . . The dug-out is by far the most popular craft. . . . The war-canoe . . . has all but disappeared from Marovo. (Russell 1948:312–13)

In 1984 and 1985 the Solomon Islands Statistics Office conducted a survey of village resources in, among other areas, Marovo (SIG 1985). The survey shows that among 985 Marovo households in a total of ninety-three settlements (of which fifty-six were proper villages with five households or more), there were 1,496 canoes. Allowing for some underreporting (almost certain because of the regular use of canoes away from home) and based on a total population estimate calculated from the subsequent 1986 census, there was one canoe for every four persons, or nearly two canoes per standard household. Survey figures give no breakdown as to types of canoe, but judging from my own quantitative material from representative villages, it can be assumed that around 20 percent, or at least three hundred canoes, are large ones of the so-called "dinghy" type, intended for use with an outboard motor (cf. Sikaiana in Donner this volume). Most of these craft are dugout canoes that measure at least three and one-half to four fathoms long. (The 'fathom' [*ngava*], measured by the span of the builder's arms, remains the universal Marovo unit for canoe measurement.) They have a squared-off stern, reinforced with particularly tough wood, and are termed *mola gete* 'large canoe', *chore gete* 'large dugout', or *digi* (from English dinghy). Normal-size wooden 'dinghies' carry up to five or six adults, whereas the largest ones may reach eight or nine fathoms in length and carry at least twenty adults.

Judging from my own quantitative material and subjective impressions, at least 10 percent of these 'dinghies' are fiberglass canoes. Several Honiara-based manufacturers produce a variety of such canoes, from eighteen to twenty-three feet long and with a carrying capacity of about six adults. They typically cost at least S.I.$3,000, the equivalent of more than two years' wages for an unskilled urban worker.[7] A fiberglass canoe thus represents a substantial investment that usually derives from a civil servant's or urban businessman's obligations to his village; a *butubutu*'s joint income from bait-fishing royalties paid by the tuna-fishing industry; or from the pooling by a number of villagers of combined savings from the sale of wood carvings, cash crops, or marine shells. In the Marovo language, fiberglass canoes are generally referred to by nonindigenous terms: either the directly derived *digi* or the slightly more adapted term *faeba*, from *fiber*glass. Apart from these nationally manufactured 'dinghies', there are few nonlocal craft in Marovo, most of which are possessed by the small Australian-owned tourist resort in the central lagoon.

DUGOUTS AND TREES: CANOE MANUFACTURE AND OWNERSHIP

An overwhelming proportion of canoes in Marovo villages are locally manufactured dugout canoes. Among them were, in 1986, an estimated 1,250 or more paddle craft, ranging in size from one to four fathoms and carrying from one child to six or seven adults. The Marovo term for 'dugout canoe' *(chore)*, refers literally to the act of 'digging out'. Almost without exception, these craft are made from the trunk of the *goliti* tree *(Gmelina moluccana)*, used throughout the high islands of Melanesia for canoes and known widely in the Solomons by its Kwara'ae (Malaita) name, *arakoko*.[8] *Goliti* trees grow in lowland, little-disturbed rain forest (cf. Henderson and Hancock 1988:218) and are often left standing when these areas are cleared for gardens. Such trees are closely guarded possessions in Marovo. Generally each known tree is claimed by an individual person or a family and left untouched until its owner or owners decide that it is time to use it. Individual *goliti* trees are usually inherited, often from father to son, and may also be transferred to persons beyond the immediate kinship circle through purchase, gift, or in return for services rendered.

When a decision has been made to build a canoe, a suitable *goliti* tree is felled and the building of the canoe is commenced on the spot, usually in forest above garden clearings. If the tree is particularly large, two (or even three) canoes may be built simultaneously, with several builders cooperating in the effort. Working quickly with an axe and heavy adze, the builder hollows out the trunk and shapes the outside of the hull. The roughly shaped hull is then pulled down through the forest and gardens to the nearest seashore. As this is a heavy task, taking a full day and involving the mobilization of a group of male relatives and fellow villagers, a feast is subsequently hosted by the owner of the canoe. At the seashore (or in the village, if paddling the roughly shaped canoe home is feasible), the builder uses smaller adzes to carve the inside and outside of the hull as thinly as possible without sacrificing strength. If this has not already been done, the canoe is at this stage paddled to the village of the owner, whereupon final testing and shaping are carried out to ensure that it floats properly and "cuts the waves" in the required manner. On larger canoes or on any canoe whose hull has been made exceptionally thin, ribs and knees are fashioned—usually from already bent sections of mangrove wood—and lashed to protruding points left along the inside of the hull. All cracks and minor faults in the completed hull are then carefully caulked with a putty obtained by grating nut kernels of the *tita* tree *(Parinari glaberrima)*. The canoe is then left on the shore for a week or two, sheltered from the sun by coconut leaves, to allow the caulking to dry. The entire building process may take from one week to several months, depending upon the intensity of work. Today chain saws are sometimes used for the initial shaping of the *goliti* log, minimizing the time spent working in the bush.

Dugout canoes are manufactured in every Marovo village, most often by the men of a household in need of a new canoe. The same applies to paddles, which are usually made from the plank buttress roots of forest trees, especially the *vasara (Vitex cofassus)*. There are also a number of specialized canoe builders around Marovo, who spend much of their time on the manufacture of dugouts and paddles of various sizes. These craftsmen often work according to individual orders, where time of completion and conditions of payment have been agreed upon. As of 1992, the prices asked for new dugout canoes typically followed a norm of forty to fifty Solomon Islands dollars per fathom of hull length, with the largest craft costing much more per fathom than small ones.

Canoes of all types, whether owned individually, by a family, or by a wider group, are frequently borrowed for single trips. When borrowing canoes for fishing, it is considered proper to provide a small share of the catch to the owner or even, in the case of fishing that leads to marketing of the catch, to pay the owner a dollar or two. When canoes are borrowed for nonfishing purposes, a nominal fee may be paid in cash or in kind. The act of borrowing, however, is more commonly regarded simply as an element of ongoing reciprocity in relations of kinship or friendship. Within the highly capital-intensive realm of motorized travel, involving fiberglass canoes, outboard motors, and expensive petrol, economic practice and symbolic relations take on a sharper character.

CHARACTERISTICS OF MOTORIZED TRAVEL

The prestige item of modern maritime technology in the Solomons is the outboard motor, which costs S.I.$3,000 or more and involves running expenses of more than S.I.$5 per gallon of petrol.[9] My own conservative estimate indicates that as of 1992 there were at least two hundred outboard motors owned by Marovo villagers. The scale of capital investment in maritime transport by villagers in the New Georgia Group is evidenced most strikingly on market days in the provincial capital, Gizo, when the harbor is congested by large dugout and fiberglass canoes, nearly all with outboard motors.

Petrol is sold in most villages of the Marovo Lagoon, by trade stores or by villagers who run a small petrol business. A typical all-day trip for fishing or visiting purposes costs at least S.I.$25 in petrol alone. It is even more expensive in the more remote parts of northern New Georgia, where fewer trade stores stock petrol, and those that do have to pay extra freight to obtain their three or four 44-gallon drums. When used by people other than the owner, or owners, motorized canoes are not borrowed but are subject to rental. Little money may be charged for a wooden dinghy, but for a fiberglass canoe S.I.$5 is typically required, in addition to the normal daily fee of at least S.I.$5 for the engine. Clearly, a notion of return on heavy cash investments runs strongly among present-day canoe and engine owners, although this may be more relaxed in circumstances where the engine or canoe is under more communal ownership.

The large motorized dugout canoes of today parallel the old war canoes in several ways, not least in their role as markers of local identity in regional contexts. Motorized dugouts dominate group travel since their size makes them suitable for open-sea and interisland journeys, and since there are only few such craft in each village, the largest or most seaworthy of them is often identified with the community as such. Most large motorized dugouts of Marovo are individually named and well known throughout the area, as were the *magoru* war canoes. When a 'dinghy' passes by or approaches, people watching it from a distance generally speak of it as "the people of village so-and-so," referring to the canoe as a representation of that specific community. In a nonlocal context, regional identity is also signaled by the style and shape of the large dugouts. When such craft travel beyond their home island to other parts of the New Georgia Group, their place of origin may be readily identified by such characteristics as build and color. For example, the weather coast people of Gatokae, Rendova, and Vella Lavella are known for their large, high, heavy oceangoing canoes, often painted in dark colors, whereas the people of the Roviana and Vonavona Lagoons in western New Georgia are known for their brightly painted canoes, whose light, sleek hulls are built up in "Roviana-style," with a plank and gunwale along each side.

The increasingly numerous fiberglass canoes do not display such singular markers of local identity. And, as they are considerably smaller than the largest dugouts, they figure less prominently in interisland group travel. Having superior stability and sheltered cargo stowage, but limited passenger capacity, fiberglass canoes are first and foremost working tools for intensive and heavy fishing—such as open-sea tuna trolling or shark fishing—and for fast ocean travel with only a few persons. Local-level government officers have such canoes at their disposal for touring the villages of their area.

Like their dugout counterparts, fiberglass canoes are associated with large 15- or 25-horsepower outboard motors, preferably of the latest Japanese "heavy duty" model. Like other New Georgians, Marovo people strongly prefer Yamaha outboard motors and, to a lesser degree, those by Tohatsu, Suzuki, and Mariner. Non-Japanese products, like those of Evinrude, Johnson, and Mercury, are considered inferior, unreliable, noisy, and "weak."[10] Like the old war canoes, fiberglass canoes and engines are definite objects of prestige in their own right, since the expense of buying one makes them out of reach for a majority of villagers.

Large motorized canoes are frequently handled by their drivers with tough, determined, and often macholike attitudes. Indeed, maritime "driving" is invariably men's work, since very few Marovo women operate motorized canoes. (The few who do are young, assertive women who, it is often said, drive the canoe as if "crazy.") As noted earlier, people who paddle small canoes on the lagoon after dark frequently express concern over the dangers posed by fast-running craft with "rough" drivers. A number of canoe collisions in recent years (none, surprisingly, with a fatal outcome) have prompted many owners of motorized dugouts to paint the gunwales and upper sides of their craft in white or other light colors "so that paddlers can see us approaching and get out of the way," as some of them say. A historical parallel to such rather brusque ways of acknowledging weaker parties' fear of onrushing danger can be drawn to the high ornamented prows of the New Georgia war canoes. From dawn to dusk, and sometimes even in moonlight, an approaching war party could be spotted from shore as the prow emerged on the horizon. Nowadays, the tall prows of the *magoru* are said (somewhat jokingly) to have functioned as an announcement of impending doom to the unfortunate shore dwellers of other islands. It was held that, with assistance obtained from formidable war spirits and oracles, the New Georgia headhunters would be able to find their victims, even if the latter did their best to hide from the approaching raiders.

SAFETY AT SEA: NAVIGATION AND CANOE HANDLING

Though presenting itself as a benign and beautiful environment, the seas of Marovo are regarded with respect by those who travel on them and depend upon their resources. Still, considering the scale and multitude of maritime activities carried out daily around Marovo and the number of people they involve, the sea can by no means be considered a particularly dangerous world. Marovo seafarers, young and old, quite confidently handle most types of trouble.

Those aspects of the environment perceived as dangerous to seafarers, particularly weather forces, are not generally regarded as potentially fatal. Most deaths at sea, according to Marovo informants, have been caused by shark attacks during underwater spearfishing; three or four such fatal accidents have occurred since the 1960s. There are two recalled instances—one of them recent—where lone paddlers on the lagoon were struck and killed by lightning. In addition, there are a few cases in which people simply disappeared while fishing on their own, and their bodies were never found. These incidents have most often been attributed to a shark attack or suicide.

It is interesting that drowning without additional causes does not figure in the Marovo repertoire of fatal accidents. It is taken for granted in this sea-oriented society that all, including small children, are able swimmers; there are no known instances where the capsizing of a canoe has resulted in anyone drowning. Falling into the sea is not in itself considered a particularly dangerous mishap by Marovo people, who often jump into the lagoon waters to warm up when rain and wind make a fishing trip a cold experience. The only safety rule pertaining to swimming in Marovo is that no one should swim in the deep, open sea, nor should people swim or dive in the deeper waters of the lagoon without having a canoe nearby. Both these rules serve to minimize the danger of a shark attack, since the sharks of the open ocean are considered to be "wild," aggressive, and of another type than the generally predictable lagoon and reef sharks, while even the latter ones may become daring and aggressive if they find a diver alone without a canoe. Most types of shark are not regarded as dangerous as long as they are met with in a context where their behavior is predictable.[11]

The Marovo Lagoon's wide expanse of inshore water is often disturbed by choppy waves, sharp, foaming, and closely spaced. Marovo seafarers comment on the striking difference between aggressive lagoon waves and the much taller, but also much more gentle, ocean swells, saying that the former are confined by the barrier reefs and therefore have no room to stretch out. Occasionally, canoes capsize during the frequent squalls of the monsoon season, even within the lagoon, particularly in conditions of big waves and strong undertows. Colliding currents and whirlpools sometimes create dangerous conditions in and around passages through the barrier reef and along the outer reef edges; the open weather coast areas are sometimes avoided altogether, except by experienced men from the weather coast villages themselves. But even expert seafarers may experience the capsizing of a canoe, and since such mishaps may lead to the loss of cargo, of a valuable canoe, and of an exceedingly valuable outboard motor, most canoe drivers do their utmost to maximize safety and avoid potential dangers.

In practical navigation, ensuring safety on the sea means utilizing one's knowledge of waves, currents, and other environmental forces so as to obtain as smooth a passage as possible. This also involves knowledge of practical magic for counteracting forces like waves, squalls, thunder, and lightning. In general, the mark of an expert driver (see figure 5.7) is said to be that he knows the paths of travel and handles the canoe and engine in a such a manner that not only a safe, but also a comfortable, passage is obtained. Although never attaining the dignified position and composed behavior described for navigators elsewhere in Oceania (cf., for example, Gladwin 1970), expert canoe drivers of present-day Marovo nevertheless command considerable respect in their own communities and beyond.

FIGURE 5.7.   Two experienced drivers handling one of the largest dugout canoes of Marovo.

The use of stars as navigational aids, well documented from other parts of the Pacific, including the eastern Solomons (Lewis 1972; Gladwin 1970), was among the vital skills possessed by travelers of head-hunting times. Today this knowledge is only vaguely remembered by a small handful of old Marovo men, none of whom have extensive firsthand experience. The most renowned of these old expert seafarers, a Gatokae man born just before the turn of the century, has undertaken the long open-sea crossing to the Russell Islands numerous times, paddling for days alone in a small dugout canoe. Certain other techniques for open-sea navigation and land finding remain among experienced interisland canoe drivers of present-day Marovo. People of the northern lagoon sometimes travel across some eighty kilometers of open sea to Choiseul, and on these occasions they make use of cloud patterns and reflections in the sky not only to determine the general direction but also, further assisted by gradually emerging mountain features on the horizon, to reach land at the chosen destination. This is no less important when returning to Marovo with the intention of reaching one's own home entrance through the barrier reef. Similarly, people of central Marovo have on occasion traveled to Isabel, a distance of at least one hundred kilometers, using the same techniques. The weather coast people of Gatokae remain intrepid open-sea travelers, and occasionally canoes from there may go all the way to Honiara, 230 kilometers distant. Navigation on these journeys is facilitated by several uninhabited islands that mark the route to the Russell Islands group, from which there is but a short open-sea trip across to Guadalcanal. Carrying enough petrol (normally one 44-gallon drum) and keeping the engine running are the main concerns of these modern open-sea navigators.

A number of experienced Marovo seafarers possess detailed knowledge about rhythms and sequences in wave patterns. This permits safe launching and landing of canoes even in heavy surf by counting waves and exploiting predictable calm intervals. In rough-weather travel along outer reefs or weather coasts, it is important to know how to predict currents, swells, and breakers and how to keep clear of the reef edges and rocky shores. When traveling on the lagoon under adverse conditions, experienced drivers utilize their knowledge of how islands, islets, and shallow reef patches deflect wave patterns and create calmer stretches of sea. "Jumping" from island to island within the lagoon, thereby minimizing exposure to the prevailing southeasterly or northwesterly winds and associated currents, is important in such rough-weather travel, in both motorized craft and small paddled canoes. When paddling under calm conditions, people also utilize their knowledge about currents. Men, women, and children are adept at locating their canoes in the middle of one of several tidal currents known to move in pairs along the lagoon, parallel to the mainland and barrier reef, respectively. Paddlers, thereby, avoid countercurrents and increase their speed by moving with the other current.

SYMBOLISM OF THE SEASCAPE: ENCOUNTERING HISTORY

It has been noted that for Marovo people the sea space of lagoon and ocean is a cornerstone not just of material production and spatial mobility; it also plays a crucial role in mediating history as well as forming and maintaining group identity

(Hviding 1990, n.d.). Maritime travel involves repeated and sequential encounters with places whose names and associations invoke local history and cultural identity, thereby infusing the process with symbolic significance.

In the oral traditions of Marovo, historical and mythical events are usually described with reference to detailed sequences of named places. The sequential occurrence of such place names in well-known oral tradition gives added meaning to *butubutu* members' daily encounters with their environment. Similar processes whereby the place names and landscape features invoke history through their association with named ancestors, narratives of past events, and mythology are well known from Australian aboriginal societies (cf. Berndt 1970 and Davis 1984 for documentation relating to coastal and marine areas) and from Melanesia, although mostly from inland peoples (e.g., see Feld 1982 on the Kaluli of the Papuan Plateau; Keesing 1982 on the Kwaio of the Solomon Islands; Bonnemaison 1985 on Vanuatu societies). Malinowski, in his description of the *kula* routes between the Trobriand and D'Entrecasteaux archipelagoes, draws attention to a maritime context and to relations between history, mythology, and places along the sea route from Dobu to Kiriwina:

> Here is the land and sea where the magically inspired sailors and heroes of the dim past performed feats of daring and power. . . . Here the narrow gorge has been broken through by a magic canoe flying in the air. There the two rocks standing in the sea are the petrified bodies of two mythological heroes. . . . Here again, a land-locked lagoon has been a port of refuge to a mythical crew. . . . And in the past these lands and seas must have been the scene of migrations and fights, of tribal invasions, and of gradual infiltrations of peoples and cultures. (Malinowski 1922:40)

These aspects of Massim history and mythology echo the Marovo people's emphasis on recalling ancestors' dangerous paths of travel to places beyond the horizon. Like the Dobu-to-Kiriwina route, traditional Marovo canoe paths are represented as sequences of places encountered by the travelers, each place in turn associated with certain stories and important historical events (Hviding 1996).

Marovo tales about heroic overseas deeds of warrior ancestors and about their less warlike trading activities contain abundant references to sea routes or 'paths' *(huana)*, represented as sequences of named places of historical significance. Certain legends, classified as different from "real" hero tales and emphasized by narrators to be from the extremely distant past, tell of travels through remote parts of the Solomons archipelago, indicating wide spatial horizons and far-ranging known paths during the time of only vaguely remembered ancestors. Marovo oral tradition tells of warfare and conquest, but also of more peaceful travel for the purposes of exchange and visiting far-off relatives. An essential feature of such stories is their way of linking important ancestors of today's groups with regular travel along 'paths' marked by islands within and beyond the *puava*.

Linking the social groups and physical territories of Marovo, thus, are symbolic relations, embodied in the natural and cultural environment in and beyond the *puava* to the members of the associated *butubutu*. Key meanings are mediated in everyday experience through sets of signs, mainly named places, that communicate key aspects of history and identity. In daily life, by using the land, reefs, and sea of their primary *butubutu* and by participating in the management of the resources of the territorial estate, persons come to know the *puava* and its history and, thereby, their own association with a culturally, socially, and spatially distinct unit.

In Marovo the most fundamental symbolic associations of sea and barrier reefs relate to a history of outward orientation. The sea is historically associated with departure and arrival, and with meeting others, both violently and nonviolently (cf. Donner this volume). Most significant, the deep entrances to the Marovo Lagoon, places traditionally guarded by formidable shark spirits, connote a history of travel, warfare, and cross-cultural meetings between island peoples and between Marovo people and Europeans. This rich and complex cultural history is evoked through the place names in and around the barrier reef entrances.

From a background with local and regional history and cultural identity deeply embedded in the seascape as well as the landscape, and with the seascape, in particular, pointing to intergroup contact, maritime travel remains a deeply meaningful component of Marovo people's practical life (cf. Bloch 1977; Bourdieu 1977). Seafaring is an activity that fulfills economic purposes; creates, transforms, and maintains social relations; and communicates and reinforces important aspects of Marovo identity by linking the present to the past.

NOTES

Acknowledgments   I wish to thank Harold Jimuru and Vincent Vaguni for training me thoroughly in the practical life of Marovo seafaring, and the people of the Chea village, particularly Kata R. Ragoso and the late D. K. Jimuru, for education and kind hospitality. I am also grateful to the Marovo Area Council, the Western Provincial Government, the Ministry of Education, and the Ministry of Natural Resources for permission to carry out this work. The field research was generously funded by the Research Council of Norway, the Institute for Comparative Cultural Studies, and the University of Bergen. I gratefully acknowledge this support.

This essay is based on twenty-seven months of field research carried out in the Marovo area during three periods: 1986–1987, 1989, and 1991–1992. These stays included visits to other parts of the New Georgia Group as well as brief stays in Honiara during which studies were made in archives. During my residence in Marovo, I traveled to most villages of the area and to other islands of New Georgia, in many instances handling my own dugout canoe and outboard motor. I also spent a considerable proportion of the overall research period at sea, fishing with my Marovo coworkers. Thus, the information contained herein is strongly based on personal experience of maritime travel.

1. Among the few exceptions to this statement are the brief descriptions by Bayliss-Smith (1978, 1986) of changes in sea transport in Ontong Java Atoll, a Polynesian outlier.

2. Five languages, all related and belonging to the northwestern and central Solomons Austronesian family (Tryon and Hackman 1983), are spoken in the Marovo area today. These are Marovo, Vangunu, Bareke, Hoava, and Kusaghe, the first being the language of

the 'coastal people' (often termed "Ulusaghe language" within the New Georgia Group). The other four are spoken by groups of 'bush people'. Present-day linguistic patterns are influenced by the two dominant church denominations of Marovo: the United church (Methodist), present since 1912 and now followed by 33 percent of the population, and the Seventh-day Adventist (SDA) church, present since 1915 and now followed by 59 percent of the population. The remaining 8 percent are followers of the Christian Fellowship church, an indigenous movement that started in the 1950s as a breakaway from the Methodist church. Whereas Marovo retains a status as the lingua franca of the Seventh-Day Adventist church in the New Georgia Group and beyond, Roviana is the lingua franca of the Methodists in the western Solomons, including many of those living in Marovo.

3. The Marovo dichotomy between 'coastal people' and 'bush people' represents a widespread pattern in coastal Melanesia, although the term "saltwater people" is more often used for the former. For historical and ethnographic material on such dichotomies and their implications, see Ivens (1927) and Bennett (1987) for the Solomons, and Rodman (1987:16–17) for Vanuatu. For a New Guinea river basin example of the complex relations between coastal and inland groups, see Gewertz (1983).

4. A well-preserved and very large New Georgian war canoe from Kuava in southern Vella Lavella is in storage at the Museum of Mankind in London.

5. The Chubikopi war canoe project has indeed received much recognition beyond Marovo. Notably, the Chubikopi community was recently invited through the Solomon Islands National Museum to send a team of *magoru* builders to the Viking Ship Museum at Roskilde, near Copenhagen, Denmark, to construct a *magoru* as part of a running ethnographic program of documenting traditional boat building from around the world. A four-fathom war canoe replica was duly built by four Chubikopi men in Denmark during April 1993 from materials brought from Marovo.

6. It is also worthy of note that Waterhouses's Roviana dictionary (1928), based on fieldwork before 1920, states that dugout canoes (*hore* in Roviana) were common and were increasingly replacing plank-built *mola*.

7. The value of the Solomon Islands dollar (S.I.$) has plummeted in recent years. By early 1993 the exchange rate was approximately S.I.$1 = U.S.$0.30.

8. In the Solomons, *Gmelina moluccana* is preferred for dugout canoes for a number of reasons. It can easily be worked without cracking, it is lightweight and floats well, and it can withstand continuous soaking and drying out (see Henderson and Hancock 1988:218–19). Another major contributing factor is that it is a very straight-growing, tall tree with sufficient girth for even the largest canoe. The sole dependence upon *goliti* in Marovo must also be attributed to the continuing relative abundance of this tree in the area. Only on rare occasion are other woods—usually the swamp tree *rigi (Pterocarpus indicus,* trade names "Rosewood" and "Amboyna")—used for dugout canoes in Marovo. This contrasts with less well-endowed parts of the Solomons; in the dry and seriously deforested Sandfly Islands of Gela, Central Province, I even observed dugouts being made from the crucially important *Canarium* nut trees in 1991.

9. The Imperial Gallon remains the dominant measure for petrol in Solomon Islands village-level trading, despite recent official efforts to introduce metric standards. As one village trade-store owner in Marovo expressed it in terms eminently compatible with global consumerism, "I only quote prices per liter when I want it to sound cheaper. Somehow, $1.50 per liter sounds less than $6 per gallon!" The gallon is important in another sense: distances in and around Marovo are invariably measured in "gallons of petrol spent." When asked about how far it is from one village to another, experienced canoe travelers invariably reply by stating how much petrol a normal outboard motor can be expected to consume on

that one-way trip. Thus, the distance from Seghe to Batuna (see figure 5.2) is "three gallons" *(ka hike galoni)*.

10. "Johnson" survives as a common term in Solomon Islands Pijin and vernaculars for larger outboard motors; smaller ones are referred to as "Seagull," also a manufacturer's name. These terms are mainly used by older people; younger speakers prefer the generic term *ijini*, from engine.

11. One notable exception to this rule is the tiger shark *(Galeocerdo cuvier),* most often encountered in the lagoon and sometimes in the shallows or even near village shores. In Marovo, the saltwater crocodile *(Crocodylus porosus)* and the tiger shark are both considered highly dangerous to swimmers or divers and are classified as "wild," uncontrollable, and relentlessly aggressive toward humans.

REFERENCES

Bayliss-Smith, Tim
1978   Changing pattern of inter-island mobility in Ontong Java atoll. *Archaeology and Physical Anthropology in Oceania* 13:408–73.
1986   Ontong Java atoll: population, economy and society, 1970–1986. Occasional Paper 9. South Pacific Smallholder Project, University of New England, Armidale, N.S.W., Australia.

Bennett, Judith A.
1987   *Wealth of the Solomons: A History of a Pacific Archipelago, 1800–1978.* Pacific Islands Monograph Series No. 3. Honolulu: University of Hawai'i Press.

Berndt, Ronald M.
1970   *The Sacred Site: The Western Arnhem Land Example.* Canberra: Australian Aboriginal Studies No. 29.

Bloch, Maurice
1977   The past and the present in the present. *Man,* N.S., 12:278–92.

Bonnemaison, Joel
1985   The tree and the canoe: roots and mobility in Vanuatu societies. *Pacific Viewpoint* 26:30–62.

Bourdieu, Pierre
1977   *Outline of a Theory of Practice.* Cambridge: Cambridge University Press.

Burnett, Frank
1911   *Through Polynesia and Papua.* London: Francis Griffiths.

Cheyne, Andrew
1971   *The Trading Voyages of Andrew Cheyne, 1841–1844,* edited by Dorothy Shineberg. Canberra: Australian National University Press.

Davis, Stephen
1984   Aboriginal claims to coastal waters in North Eastern Arnhem Land, Northern Australia. In *Maritime Institutions in the Western Pacific,* edited by K. Ruddle and T. Akimichi, pp. 231–52. Senri Ethnological Studies No. 17. Osaka: National Museum of Ethnology.

Edridge, Sally
1985   *Solomon Islands Bibliography to 1980.* Suva: Institute of Pacific Studies, University of the South Pacific.

Feld, Steven
1982   *Sound and Sentiment: Birds, Weeping, Poetics and Song in Kaluli Expression.* Philadelphia: University of Pennsylvania Press.

Findlay, Alexander George
1877   *A Directory for the Navigation of the South Pacific Ocean, with Descriptions of Its Coasts, Islands, etc., from the Strait of Magalhaens to Panama, and those of New Zealand, Australia, etc. Its Winds, Currents and Passages.* 4th edition. London: Published for Richard Holmes Laurie.
Gewertz, Deborah
1983   *Sepik River Societies: A Historical Ethnography of the Chambri and Their Neighbors.* New Haven: Yale University Press.
Gladwin, Thomas
1970   *East Is a Big Bird: Navigation and Logic on Puluwat Atoll.* Cambridge: Harvard University Press.
Goldie, John Francis
1909   The people of New Georgia, manners, customs and religious beliefs. Royal Geographical Society of Queensland, *Proceedings* 22:23–30.
Henderson, C. P., and I. R. Hancock
1988   *A Guide to the Useful Plants of Solomon Islands.* Honiara: Research Department, Ministry of Agriculture and Lands.
Hocart, A. M.
1931   Warfare in Eddystone of the Solomon Islands. *Journal of the Royal Anthropological Institute of Great Britain and Ireland* 61:301–24.
1935   The canoe and the bonito in Eddystone Island. *Journal of the Royal Anthropological Institute of Great Britain and Ireland* 65:97–111.
1937   Fishing in Eddystone Island. *Journal of the Royal Anthropological Institute of Great Britain and Ireland* 67:33–41.
Hviding, Edvard
1988   *Marine Tenure and Resource Development in Marovo Lagoon, Solomon Islands.* FFA Report No. 88/35. Honiara: Forum Fisheries Agency.
1989   'All Things in Our Sea': The Dynamics of Customary Marine Tenure, Marovo Lagoon, Solomon Islands. Special Publications No. 13. Boroko, Papua New Guinea: National Research Institute.
1990   Keeping the sea: aspects of marine tenure in Marovo Lagoon, Solomon Islands. In *Traditional Marine Resource Management in the Pacific Basin: An Anthology*, edited by K. Ruddle and R. E. Johannes, pp. 7–44. Jakarta: UNESCO/ROSTSEA.
1996   *Guardians of Marovo Lagoon: Practice, Place, and Politics in Maritime Melanesia.* Pacific Islands Monograph Series No. 14. Honolulu: University of Hawai'i Press. In press.
Hviding, Edvard, and Graham B. K. Baines
1994   Community-based fisheries management, tradition and the challenges of development in Marovo, Solomon Islands. *Development and Change* 25:13–39.
Ivens, Walter G.
1927   *Melanesians of the South-east Solomon Islands.* London: Kegan Paul, Trench, Trubner.
Jackson, K. B.
1978   Tie hokara, tie vaka: black man, white man. A Study of the New Georgia Group to 1930. Ph.D. Dissertation, Australian National University, Canberra.
Keesing, Roger M.
1982   *Kwaio Religion: The Living and the Dead in a Solomon Island Society.* New York: Columbia University Press.

Lewis, David
1972   *We the Navigators: The Ancient Art of Landfinding in the Pacific.* Honolulu: University of Hawai'i Press.
McKinnon, John M.
1975   Tomahawks, turtles and traders: A reconstruction in the circular causation of warfare in the New Georgia Group. *Oceania* 45:290–307.
Malinowski, Bronislaw
1922   *Argonauts of the Western Pacific: An Account of Native Enterprise and Adventure in the Archipelagoes of Melanesian New Guinea.* London: Routledge and Kegan Paul.
Paravicini, Eugen
1931   *Reisen in den Britischen Salomonen.* Frauenfeld: Leipzig, Huber.
Rodman, Margaret C.
1987   *Masters of Tradition: Consequences of Customary Land Tenure in Longana, Vanuatu.* Vancouver: University of British Columbia Press.
Russell, Tom
1948   The culture of Marovo, British Solomon Islands. *Journal of the Polynesian Society* 57:306–29.
SIG (Solomon Islands Government)
1985   *Village Resources Survey, 1984–85.* Honiara: Statistics Office.
1989   *Report on the Census of Population 1986.* Honiara: Statistics Office.
Somerville, Boyle T.
1897   Ethnographical notes in New Georgia, Solomon Islands. *Journal of the Royal Anthropological Institute of Great Britain and Ireland* 26:357–413.
Stoddart, David R.
1969   Geomorphology of the Marovo elevated barrier reef, New Georgia. *Philosophical Transactions of the Royal Society* B 255:388–402.
Tryon, Darrell, and Brian Hackman
1983   *Solomon Islands Languages: An Internal Classification.* Pacific Linguistics C–72. Canberra: Australian National University.
Waite, Deborah
1990   *Mon* canoes of the Western Solomon Islands. In *Art and Identity in Oceania,* edited by A. Hanson and L. Hanson, pp. 44–66. Honolulu: University of Hawai'i Press.
Waterhouse, J. H. L.
1928   *A Roviana and English Dictionary, with English-Roviana Index and List of Natural History Objects.* Guadalcanar: Melanesian Mission Press.
Woodford, Charles M.
1888   Exploration of the Solomon Islands. Royal Geographical Society of Queensland, *Proceedings* 10:351–76.
1890   Further explorations in the Solomon Islands. Royal Geographical Society of Queensland, *Proceedings* 12:393–418.
1909   The canoes of the British Solomon Islands. *Journal of the Royal Anthropological Institute of Great Britain and Ireland* 39:506–16.

ROTUMAN SEAFARING IN HISTORICAL PERSPECTIVE

Alan Howard

• Rotuma is one of the more isolated islands in western Polynesia. It is located at 12°30′ S, 177° E, some 465 kilometers northwest of Cikobia, the northernmost island in the Fiji group (Woodhall 1987). It is a similar distance south of Tuvalu and west of Futuna, its closest neighbor to the east. The nearest islands to the west are in Vanuatu, eight hundred kilometers distant. Legends suggest that Rotuma had intermittent contact with Samoa, Tonga, Futuna, and Fiji (Churchward 1939) prior to European intrusion. Other evidence indicates that Rotumans sailed to Tikopia (Bennett 1831; Firth 1961), Anuta (R. Feinberg, personal communication), Kosrae (J. Tobin, personal communication), and possibly even to Raiatea in the Society Islands (Anonymous 1938). Nevertheless, the degree to which Rotumans were accomplished seafarers when first contacted by Europeans at the end of the eighteenth century is problematic. Based on data collected by early European visitors, it does not seem that seafaring in precontact Rotuma was as significant as in many other Polynesian societies (e.g., for Nukumanu see Feinberg this volume; for Sikiana see Donner this volume).

Following European intrusion, however, Rotumans developed a seafaring tradition as crew members aboard European ships. Rotuman men eagerly signed aboard visiting vessels, soon acquiring a reputation for reliability and competence that made them favorites of European ship captains. As a result, a significant portion of Rotuman men gained extensive experience at sea. This had, and continues to have, a distinct effect on the culture and economy of the island. Sailors have been a major source of information about the outside world, thereby introducing and legitimating cultural changes, and have contributed considerably to a standard of living that is extraordinarily high for an isolated Pacific island.

Since we are dealing with a heritage transformed from an earlier, precontact formation to one that has been shaped by European seafaring traditions, it is necessary to approach our subject historically. I begin by presenting background information on Rotuma and its environs; then I describe seafaring technology and traditions

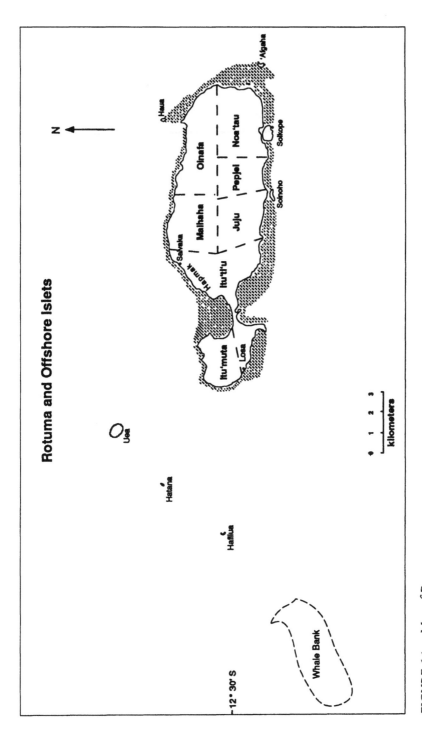

FIGURE 6.1.   Map of Rotuma.

shortly after contact. Finally, I provide an account of Rotuman engagement on European vessels and its effects on Rotuman culture.

BACKGROUND INFORMATION

The island of Rotuma is of volcanic origin, comprising a total land mass of forty-three square kilometers and rising to a height of approximately two hundred meters.[1] It is surrounded by a fringing coral reef that attains a maximum width of 1.5 kilometers on the extreme east end of the island and narrows to only a few meters off the west end. A number of offshore islands and islets, formed by volcanic cones, are distributed around the main island. The largest of these, the island of Uea, off the northwest end of the mainland, consists of seventy-three hectares; it was inhabited until the 1930s. Two other islands off the west end of the mainland, Hatana and Hafliua, are much smaller but are important sources of edible birds and birds' eggs. These islands lie several kilometers away and require journeys across open sea. Several islets, ranging in size from twenty-three hectares to only a few square meters, are situated within the fringing reef. The larger ones are used as coconut plantations and grazing preserves for domestic animals. They can be reached by walking across the reef at low tide or by canoe, punt, and launch when the tide is high.

Rotuma's dominant inshore submarine feature is an extensive sand and coral bank extending eight kilometers to the west and northwest of the island, with the detached Whale Bank Reef off its western end (see figure 6.1). Whale Bank Reef is approximately 5 by 1.6 kilometers, with an average depth of seventeen to eighteen fathoms. A current, setting west-southwest at speeds of less than one knot, occurs most of the year (Fisheries Division n.d.:3).

Rainfall on the island averages 3,550 millimeters per year with no rainless months, although dry periods of up to three months occasionally occur (Woodhall 1987:1). The soil is very fertile, giving Rotuma a reputation for growing coconuts and other produce of exceptional size and quality. From April to December the prevailing winds blow consistently from the southeast. From December to April, winds are variable, sometimes blowing hard from the northwest. Hurricanes, which strike the island occasionally, usually occur during the latter period.

The island's resident population is approximately twenty-seven hundred individuals, but over six thousand Rotumans now live in Fiji, which has political jurisdiction over Rotuma, and perhaps an additional one thousand to two thousand Rotumans live in Australia, New Zealand, North America, and Europe.

ROTUMAN SEAMANSHIP AT CONTACT AND IN THE
EARLY NINETEENTH CENTURY

Rotuma was "discovered" in 1791 by Captain Edward Edwards of the HMS *Pandora* while he was searching for the *Bounty* mutineers. Edwards remarked on the great number of paddling canoes coming out to meet his vessel. He wrote that although Rotumans knew of Tonga (the "Friendly Islands") "their canoes were not so delicately formed nor so well finished as at the Friendly Islands, but more resemble those of the Duke of York's, the Duke of Clarence's and the Navigators' Islands" (Thompson 1915:65).

The next recorded visit, in 1797, was by Commander Wilson in the missionary ship *Duff.* Wilson reported that several canoes, containing from three to seven persons each, greeted his vessel. He commented, "Their single canoes (for we saw no double ones) were nearly the same in all respects as at the Friendly Islands, being of the same shape, sewed together on the inside, and decorated in the same manner [but they] seemed not so neat and well finished" (Wilson 1799:292).

In the next two decades, a great many whaling ships stopped at Rotuma for provisions. Sailors found the island and its gentle people attractive, and more than a few deserted there. Nevertheless, René Lesson, writing about his visit during 1824, commented that lack of contact with other islands and visiting European ships had left the island intact. He remarked that Rotumans welcomed Europeans who settled on the island with "extraordinary eagerness" (Lesson 1838–1839:415). Lesson opined that the islanders must be skilled fishermen because of the huge nets they used, which he estimated at more than forty feet long. He made the following remarks about Rotuman canoes:

> The canoes *(vaka)* used by these islanders have a roughly carved outrigger. They are enclosed and pointed fore and aft, and driven by oval paddles which are also carved without much taste. We saw only one small double canoe *(aoe)* which came in the evening. The mast was notched and set up on a piece of wood which linked the two canoes. It held up a sail of very coarse matting. The canoes were covered by a platform which prevented sea water from getting into the hull and which supported a shelter consisting of an awning of flexible branches. On the whole, it was a poorly designed vessel, and long-distance navigation was probably undertaken in larger canoes. (Lesson 1838–1839:431, translated from the French by Ella Wiswell)

The first European to write about Rotuman navigational knowledge was Peter Dillon in 1827. He reported that Rotumans knew of several islands in their "neighborhood," including the islands of "Vythuboo" [Vaitupu] and "Newy" [Nui], in what is now Tuvalu. He stated that Vaitupu abounded with white shells much in demand on Rotuma and that Rotumans made frequent voyages there for the purpose of obtaining them. Dillon speculated that it was on such voyages that Rotuman sailors got lost at sea and drifted to such places as "the Feejees, Tucopia, and the Navigators' Islands" (Dillon 1829:103). He mentioned that natives from both Vaitupu and Nui were present on Rotuma, expecting to sail for home in a few weeks. He was unable to obtain information concerning wind, weather, and tides from his informants—two renegade sailors—but assumed that westerly winds prevailed at certain times of the year, enabling Rotumans to sail to Tonga and the Navigators' Isles. He based his assumption on the fact that he met a Rotuman in Tonga whom he returned home (Dillon 1829:103–4).

Robert Jarman arrived on Rotuma in 1832 aboard the whaler *Japan*. His account suggests that although Rotumans built large double canoes they were not especially capable seamen:

> In many huts we observed canoes of immense size and length, or more properly double canoes, about eight feet apart, and secured together by upright and cross pieces strongly bound with lashings made of the cocoa-nut husk. I should suppose these canoes capable of carrying from one hundred and fifty to two hundred men; and are from sixty to ninety feet in length. I was led to enquire for what purpose the natives had constructed them, apparently so unwieldy and useless, as they must have cost them with the tools they possess, such infinite time and labor.
>
> They are formed of a single tree of immense size, hollowed out, and partly decked over from the stem aft. Curiosity or a spirit of enterprise seems to have prompted them. Soon after the island was discovered, the natives were puzzled to ascertain how a ship could come there. Consultations were held by the chiefs, and it occurred to them, that there must be something in the horizon, through which the ship entered; therefore it was resolved to fit out many canoes, and send them in search, as the only method of discovering it. Many were accordingly sent to sea upon this strange expedition, and so soon as they lost sight of their native land, were driven by the wind to the neighbouring islands; many undoubtedly perished, some reached the Fejee Islands, and others were driven as far to the westward as Santa Cruz, where their descendants are still living with the inhabitants. Since Mr. Emery [an English deserter who took up residence circa 1827] has resided among them, many have put to sea, and no trace of them have [sic] ever been discovered. (Jarman 1838:183–84)

George Cheever, who kept a log of the whaling ship *Emerald*, which visited Rotuma in 1835, also reported that Rotuman canoes were rough concerns, displaying little in the way of ornamentation. He mentioned one large double canoe, about one hundred feet long, which was presumably the largest on the island (Cheever 1834–1835). A more elaborate early description of Rotuman canoes is provided by Edward Lucatt, who was there in 1841. He wrote:

> The native canoes are of peculiar construction. They have no trees high enough of the proper wood to form the main body of the canoe, like the New Zealanders; they are therefore built out of several pieces, which are sewed together with a sort of twine, of their own manufacture, made from the husks of the cocoa-nut. They are deep and narrow, somewhat angularly formed; the thwarts for the pullers to sit upon are made fast to the gunwales, and, to prevent the canoe from capsizing, they have an outrigger attached. They are unsightly-looking things, wanting altogether the lightness and grace of a New Zealand canoe; their paddles, too, are clumsy and heavy, and lack the symmetry and grace of the New Zealanders. There are several large double canoes on the Island, connected together by a strong platform; and in former times, when the population of the country exceeded the means of support, or it was feared that it would do so, oracles were consulted, and at their instigation a party would start off in one of these canoes in search of fresh land: sometimes failing in their object, they would find their way back again in a most miserable plight; but the result of the generality of such expeditions was never known. Of late years, there have been no adven-

tures of the kind, and these ship-canoes from their long disuse are fast falling to decay; there are seventeen or eighteen of them upon the Island, carefully built over to protect them from the weather. These ship-canoes are no two of the same length; the longer one will be from eighty to ninety feet, while the smaller, answering the purpose of an outrigger, would not exceed fifty or sixty feet: each canoe has from four to five feet beam, but they have no floor; and, looked at separately, without their stem and stern pieces, they would be taken for troughs. They are kept about six feet asunder by cross beams lashed and otherwise made fast to the gunwales of both canoes; the beams are planked over, which furnishes a deck of from fourteen to sixteen feet in breadth. Both canoes are entirely covered in, and there are small hatchways with sliding covers. When a party has determined upon an exploring expedition, they build a house upon the main deck and stow their provisions, &c. in the holds of the canoes. Their sails are made of a species of rush marled together: in form they resemble the New Zealanders, being when set like an inverted triangle. (Lucatt 1851:177–78)

C. F. Wood, visiting Rotuma on a yachting cruise some thirty years later, confirmed the disuse into which double canoes had fallen. He reported seeing large double canoes, similar to those he had seen in Fiji and Tonga, lying in sheds on the beach. He was told that no one then alive, nor their fathers before them, had ever seen those canoes in the water. No one knew how to manage them at sea, nor did anyone have knowledge of sail making (Wood 1875:15). An old chief told Wood that in the past such canoes would sail off, loaded with men, never to be heard of again. Wood commented that he knew of canoes from Rotuma landing on the northern coast of Vanua Levu, where half-breed descendants could be found. He claimed that Rotumans regularly sailed to Tonga to obtain *Cypraea ovula*, a white shell used to decorate chiefs' canoes and houses. "They did not buy these from the natives of Tonga," Wood wrote, "but they themselves fished for them on outlying reefs" (Wood 1875:25–26).[2]

Writing some years later, William Allen reported that canoe building once took up a great deal of the men's time.[3] He suggested that double canoes took many years to build, as many as eight or ten (Allen 1895). During his visit in 1896, however, J. Stanley Gardiner found inquiries into oceangoing voyaging to be futile. Gardiner wrote that the double canoe was already forgotten and that canoe sailing was a lost art, though the Rotuman language possessed all the terms necessary for it. He also mentioned his finding a steer oar belonging to a canoe he estimated to have been sixty feet in length (Gardiner 1898:459). Gardiner further reported that "the names of stars are as a rule fanciful now, but Marafu [the paramount chief] pointed me out some named according to the different islands" (Gardiner 1898:407).[4]

ROTUMAN CANOES IN DETAIL

The most extensive information recorded about Rotuman canoes is contained in Gardiner's account and in the field notes of Bishop Museum ethnologist Gordon MacGregor, who visited Rotuma in 1932. Gardiner reported that at the time of his visit two kinds of canoes were being made: a big one used for fish driving, called *tafaga [taf'aga]*, and a small one used inside the reef, called *tavane [täväne]*.[5]

Taf'aga varied from twenty-five to thirty-five feet in length, took from eight to twelve paddlers, and could carry up to twenty people. Regarding canoe construction, Gardiner wrote:

> A suitable tree is selected, cut down, and roughly shaped. It is then properly allowed to lie for a few months, after which it is dragged down to the hanua noho (village) which is going to build it. It is then hollowed out to the desired shape, the ends being left solid and the walls up to 2 inches thick. In the centre the sides would not be strong enough to bear the strain, and so are removed, fresh planks being fitted into their place. These are fixed by sinnet, holes for the lashings being bored through the planks; wedges are then driven in between from the inside to make the whole watertight. The sinnet makes the holes watertight, but pieces of sponge from the reef are driven in to ensure it. There is a distinct bow and stern, the former sharp and pointed up, the latter blunter and curved downwards. The first three feet of the deck at each end is covered. The breadth along the whole centre is about the same: 1 1/2–2 feet. The side towards the outrigger, or sama, is slightly straighter [figure 6.2C] than the other. The outrigger is about 5 feet or rather less away; it is not quite half as long as the whole canoe. It lies usually on the right, or starboard side, and consists of a post of light wood slightly pointed at one end. This is supported by two hard wood beams, driven into it, lashed across the canoe itself; the bend at right angles, which is necessary, is cut out, but can be, and was, frequently induced in the growth of the timber. Another beam runs just above the bend between these; to it rods of hard wood are lashed, previously driven into the post underneath [figure 6.2B]. A platform is generally made to take the paddles and carry the nets between the canoe and the outrigger; the paddle blade is of an oval form, 2 feet long by about 6 inches broad. The bailer is of the regular type, of one piece of wood with handle in the centre, and shaped to fit the canoe. The launch of one of these used to be the occasion of a feast. Kava was placed for the gods, after one of whom it was named and then supposed to be under his special protection.
>
> The tavane is only about 12 feet long and 8–10 inches deep; at the top it is usually about 6 inches broad, but bellied out considerably underneath. The outrigger is about 8 feet long and supported merely by two crooked sticks, lashed across the top of the canoe.
>
> The oie, or drum, is always stationary, and usually of very large size; it has generally a special roof. Its general shape [figures 6.2E and 6.2F] is the ordinary, but it is much more bellied and cut out deeper at the ends than is customary in Fiji. (Gardiner 1898:457–59)

In a section of his notes labeled "canoes," MacGregor recorded the names of canoe types and parts. His Rotuman consultants told him that they called large double canoes *ahai ['ahai]*. Some of them thought the name came from the English word "ahoy," used by English sailors, a derivation favored by C. M. Churchward, who wrote the definitive dictionary of the Rotuman language (Churchward 1940:348). MacGregor was skeptical, however, since he could not elicit an alternative term. The traditional term, he wrote, would not have died out so quickly. Gardiner also reported that the term *'ahai* was used for large double canoes, although

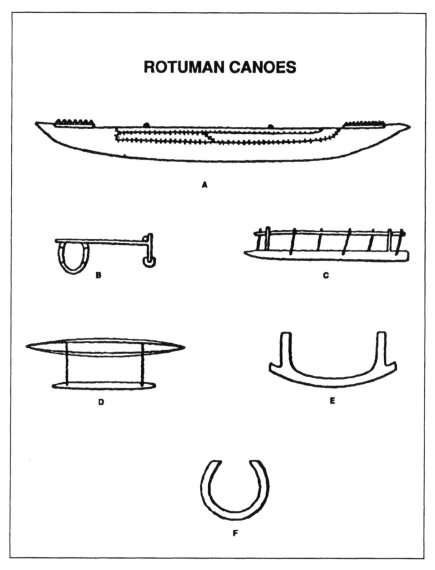

ROTUMAN CANOES

A

B

C

D

E

F

FIGURE 6.2. Rotuman canoe features: A—side view of the *tafaga*, showing planks let in at the side, also bow and stern; B—section of the *tafaga* through one of the supporting beams of the *sama*, or outrigger; C—side view of the *sama* to show method of fixing; D—top view of the *tavane* (the thin lines at the sides show the bulge of the canoe); E—longitudinal section through the *oie*, or drum; F— transverse section of the *oie*. (After Gardiner 1898:458)

he spelled it *ahoie;* like MacGregor, he doubted that it derived from English (Gardiner 1898:459). Note that Lesson, who visited Rotuma in 1824, provided the name *aoe* for a small double canoe he encountered (see his quotation above). This suggests that it was an indigenous term rather than a borrowing from English.

MacGregor wrote in his notebook that no one on the island remembered seeing a double canoe. Nevertheless, one of his Rotuman consultants told him that *'ahai* were made from five or six planks to a side, according to the size of the tree, and that they were about five to five and one-half feet tall. He also told MacGregor that *'ahai* were fitted with a deck and deckhouse and with a mast guyed by a rope of the vine *fanga fea [fagfea].*[6]

Churchward lists the Rotuman word *samtutuki* for the smaller double canoe (Churchward 1940:305), which MacGregor described as constructed of two hulls *(vaka)* joined by three crosspieces *(kiata).* The hulls were about eight feet high, according to MacGregor's consultants, and were completely covered over to keep out water. The covering had a trapdoor to permit access to provisions. Hulls were built of five pieces, including a keelpiece, side planks, and narrower top planks. The planks had flanges and were sewn together. Stitches tying the planks together were held fast by driving small wooden wedges under the knots. Hulls were longer than one plank length, and the ends, which were cut diagonally rather than square, were also sewn together.

Poles were set up in the hulls, and the deck *(pupui)* was held up on them about a fathom above the canoes' top planks. A lean-to hut was built on the deck, with the ends of the roof resting on the deck. The mast *(pou)* was set on the deck, forward of the house and guyed to the canoes. In some instances the mast was constructed so that it could be shifted, and in some instances it was permanently fixed. Sails *(läe)* were made of about twenty ordinary floor mats sewn together. They had two wings, or points, in the fashion of Fijian canoes. The steering oar *(hose)* was worked on the starboard hull. MacGregor's consultants told him that *samtutuki* carried about one hundred men, but it must be cautioned that they were reporting about the construction of a canoe type that had long since disappeared.

Like Gardiner, MacGregor also recorded that large, single-hull outrigger canoes were called *tafaaga [taf'aga]* and smaller ones *tavane [täväne].* Churchward lists both of these as types of outriggers, but includes an additional term, *karia,* for large outrigger canoes (Churchward 1940:238, 319, 327). MacGregor reported that *täväne* were made with the fore outrigger boom shorter than the aft one as an aid to steering. This gave the canoes an appearance of toeing in when viewed from above. "The stern is the wider part of the canoe because of the narrowness of the whole canoe for a man of any size to sit in and because it handles more easily," MacGregor wrote. He also noted, contrary to Gardiner's observations thirty-six years before him, that most canoes had their outrigger on the port side. This is confirmed by John Bennett, an American married to a Rotuman woman and an accomplished sailor. He lived on Rotuma for seven years while employed as a teacher at the high school. According to Bennett, outriggers today are commonly mounted on the port side, as most people are right-handed and find paddling on starboard more com-

fortable and unobstructed if the outrigger is mounted on the left. Turning with the
paddle is also easier (J. Bennett, personal communication).

An account of the steps involved in building *taf'aga* was provided MacGregor by
a craftsman from the village of Salvaka:

> The Rotumans build two sorts of large outrigger canoes, the tafaka oro [possibly
> taf'aga 'i'oro 'shark fishing canoe'] and the tafaka fonfonu [taf'aga fonfono 'canoe with
> built up sides'].[7] The first is a three piece canoe with a deep hull, the second a five
> piece canoe with a shallow keel piece and built up sides, two planks to a side. When
> the whole body of the canoe is considered these canoes are actually five and seven
> piece canoes, but the last two pieces are deck pieces and not in the walls of the canoes.
> . . . The difference in structure is determined by the material the carpenters have to
> work with. If a tree selected is not thick enough to give the proper depth to the hull, a
> five piece canoe is built.
>
> The machau [majau], or head carpenter, selects the tree from which the proposed
> canoe is to be built. Then a koua or feast is held, called foiang fua [faiag fua 'felling of
> a tree for the keelpiece'], at which is announced the intention of building a canoe, and
> whether it will be fuaora or not, that is "the way of constructing a tafakora."
>
> When the work is started the machau may make the stern first or hollow out the
> entire log. When the tree is hollowed out to form the fua or bottom piece of the hull,
> a second koua is held, called Saragfua [sarag fua 'completing the keelpiece']. The fua is
> then finished off and the beveled edge is made for joining the piece to be laid on top.
> In the five piece canoe this keel? [sic] is the vaka fonfonu [vak fonfono 'canoe with
> built up sides'], and the beveled edge is made to join the fonu. ?? [sic] In this case, the
> fua or keel piece is made much broader and shallower. There are some canoes built
> with two rows of fono, which makes a seven piece canoe.
>
> It has been stated that three piece canoes are in reality of five pieces. It can be seen
> here where the extra pieces come in. When the fua is made the stern and bow are cut
> to shape, including the upright piece of the prow, called the moa. Often this is impos-
> sible due to the size of the tree. Then deck pieces of purou are made to fit on top of
> the stern and bow of the level fua. These are necessary to carry out the height of the
> canoe established by building on the fono or wall pieces. In the standard three piece
> canoe, these should join at each end with the high bow and stern of the fua. The fono,
> probably originally one strip, is now made of three to each side.[8] The center fono
> which is laid on the completed fua first, is called the raurara. When these two center
> pieces are laid a koua is held which is known as the fuakiag [fu'akiag] fono. Then the
> end fono, two to each side which connect the raurara with the stern and bow, are laid
> on. These are the fonchichaki [fon jij'aki 'sideboards slipped into place']. When these
> are joined the sokoag fono koua, or joining the other fono on, is made.
>
> Next come the roa, if the canoe is to be a five piece one. These are the top planks
> or strips that are set over the fono to complete the walls. Then the bow and stern
> pieces are put on (these are called porou [purou] in one place and puka in another,
> puka being name given by Ismeli [another consultant] as well. The canoe is now fitted
> together and all the flanges are sewn down. The machau inspects all edges to see if
> there is a perfect fit.
>
> To insure that all the planks fit smoothly, the sides that are laid against each other
> are smeared with paint made of ura ['ura Indian mulberry] or pandanus mixed with

lime. The pandanus root is first pressed with water. This paint is smeared on the edge of the fua and then the fono is laid on. Any unevenness will show up by its lacking marking with paint.

Then the entire canoe is unleashed and the pieces taken off. Each piece is trimmed and smoothed to make it thinner and lighter. The inside portion is cut out more carefully. All holes for lashing are inspected, but they must not be touched again after corrections are made from the preliminary lashing of the canoe.

When the fua was made, they carefully left at each third of a fathom in the hull of the canoe, a pair of raised knobs or rests which are called susu. They are not in the exact center of the bottom of the canoe but about six inches apart. These form the rests for the rib supports or tokai of the canoe. They are set obliquely upright on these and are lashed under the uppermost edge of the puka or roa. The seats, manu, are set above pair [sic] of tokai. There should be three seats to each fathom of the canoe. The seats are cross boards lashed over the gunwale or roa. Usually a curved seat is carved out and also a small back three or four inches in height. The back of the seat is called the kiat rot. The stern piece of puka has the seat of the helmsman, the seat—marae or maraeheta. This puka is the last piece that is set in the hull of the canoe when she is put together. It has two arms or fork [sic], as has the bow piece, which come out and join the end of the roa. These are known as the U Rua ne Puka ['u rua ne puka], the hands of the puka. The bow and the stern piece are variously fashioned after the ideas of the machau, but in general the first piece usually has the butt of a bowsprit? [sic] or upright piece foremost. This is called the moa. Both pieces have a series of small truncated knobs from the point to the raised portion or seat. These are the moa ne puakta, and correspond to the decoration on Samoan bonito canoes and paopao. Very rarely I have seen cowrie shell attached to them.

A wooden bailer, tatahet [tata], is made for each canoe, in the shape of a grocer's sugar scoop, with the handle inverted or within the bowl.

The outrigger, sama, is attached with booms, as in the tavane, and when all is finished the final koua, avahiag tafaga [a'vahiag taf'aga 'finishing the canoe'] is given for the occasion.

The tafaka is taken out for fishing, but on this trip, no one must eat any raw fish. The catch is brought together, cooked and eaten in one place. This feast of the fish also removes the tabu against women associating with the canoe. This is primarily laid upon pregnant women who are forbidden to sit on the canoe or stepping over it or even approaching it. Other women are less seriously regarded.

If in the process of making the canoe a worker is cut and blood flows, a koua is held, hapagsue [hapagsu]. So also if a part is broken or cut so thin that the axe comes through, a koua is held to stop the bad luck.

The place where the canoe is built is tabu during the first trip out. No one is allowed to play there, and it would bring the worst sort of bad luck, armu [armou], if blood were shed on it. Armu is "bad luck, no fish, shedding of blood, or some bad happening." (MacGregor 1932)

The canoe associated with this description, inspected by MacGregor, was thirty-three feet long, 1.5 feet at the widest part, and twenty inches deep. MacGregor made a list of outrigger parts. Table 6.1 gives both MacGregor's terms and Churchward's corresponding dictionary entries.

TABLE 6.1.   Rotuman canoe lexicon.

Canoe Part	MacGregor	Churchward
keelpiece	fua	*fua*
sideboards	rorara, raurara, fono	*fono*
upper sideboards	roa	
upper end pieces	puka,* purou	*puka*
inside post supports	tuakai, tokai	*tokại*
seat in canoe	manu	*mạnu*
helmsman's seat	marae	
back of seat	kiat rot	
projections on ends	moa(he)	*moa*
figurehead		*ūläe*
bowpiece	perafoua	
sternpiece	tamakfonu	
bow	taumua	*puket e taumua*
stern	taumuri	*puket e taumuri*
hull	for ne vaka†	*katea*
mast	peri	*pou*
outrigger	sama	*sama*
outrigger boom	keata	*kiata*
outrigger brace	parsama	

* MacGregor notes that the *puka* "is the part that runs from the end of the roa on one side around the stern or bow to the end of the roa on the other side. It should be of one piece." He adds that this implies it is not necessarily the whole stern piece. (MacGregor 1932)

† lit. 'body of the canoe'

MacGregor also provided a list of wood types used in the construction of a canoe. The ratau *[ratu'a]* tree was used for the hull of a canoe; the outrigger and paddle *(hose)* were made from *penau* wood (*Thespesia populnea* L., Pacific rosewood tree); the outrigger boom from *hau* (hibiscus) wood; and the outrigger brace from either *hau* wood or bamboo. Paddles were 4.5 to 5 feet long, with a blade from two to two feet four inches; MacGregor described them as flat on one side and rounded on the other (MacGregor 1932). This may suggest more uniformity of construction than was the case. Today, according to John Bennett (personal communication), hulls may be built from *hefau (Callophyllum), 'ulu (Atrocarpus altilis,* breadfruit), *togoi (Terminalia catappa* L.), *'ura (Morinda citrifolia* L.), *ratu'a (Erythrina variegata* L.), or *sa'a* trees,[9] from which most paddles are now made. Bennett suggests that *sa'a* is used for paddles today because it is light and much easier to shape than paddles made of *penau*. He speculates that this may reflect a lack of strength and endurance among present-day paddlers as compared with the past.

For caulking *(pulu)* MacGregor recorded that breadfruit sap had been used, but a substance produced from the ripe seed of the *pipi* fruit *(Atuna racemose* Raf.) was a recent innovation that proved superior. The seed is pressed into a red watery fluid in the hand with a rock. It is worked into the seams where it becomes very hard and holds fast. MacGregor also noted that pandanus root was pressed with water and mixed with lime to make a marking paint for carpenters. His notes contain detailed drawings of lashings (MacGregor 1932).

Based on hull shape, outrigger attachment, and proximity, Hornell concluded that Rotuman canoes were an adaptation of a small canoe used on the northern Tuvalu island of Nanumea (Hornell 1936:281), but this conclusion is disputed by McQuarrie, who makes a strong case for their having a closer relationship to the canoes of Tonga and Samoa (McQuarrie 1980).

FISHING WITH CANOES

Gardiner and MacGregor also provide the most thorough accounts of Rotuman fishing techniques, including hook and line, fish traps of various types, and nets. Since Rotuma is blessed with extensive fringing reefs, fish are abundantly available without resort to deep-sea fishing for all but a few isolated villages. Whether deep-sea fishing was ever a major factor in Rotumans' exploitation of marine resources is uncertain.

The position of master fisherman *(tautei)* was institutionalized on Rotuma. Each district had a *tautei* who was in charge of fishing expeditions. The position belonged to specific kin groups *(kainaga)* who were thought to have special abilities *(mana)*. Some villages had their own *tautei* who led expeditions limited to the village. *Tautei* titles derive from fishing activities. For example, according to Elisapeti Inia, retired Rotuman schoolteacher and authority on Rotuman language and customs, the title Reuas derives from *räe ia'uas* 'to see a shoal of fish'; Tokoar from *tok 'o'oar ta* 'the canoe used as a receptacle during fish drives'; Tokroa from *tok roa* 'long pole' (used to direct communal fishing activities); and Urakmat from *ur'ak mat* 'to respect' plus 'wet', suggesting the importance of following taboos associated with fishing (Elisapeti Inia, personal communication).

Gardiner reported that Rotuman fishhooks were generally crude. He described them as follows:

> The fe, or shark-hook, was made from a shrub, the tiere, which, when it reached the height of about 3 feet, was twisted into an open knot, with a diameter of about 5 inches; it was then allowed to grow for about two years before being cut. The hook was then shaped, and a piece of hard wood spliced on as a barb projecting inwards. The bait was tied on over the barb; the fish working at this, as the wood was springy, gradually got its jaw between the barb and the stem of the hook. On being struck the barb caught in the gills, and the fish was hauled up sideways. A similar hook, but smaller, the oiniafa, was used for catching a large species of rock cod, the roog. Small round hooks were cut out of pearl shell or turtle bone, 1–2 inches in diameter, and termed ovi ['avi]; a barb was always cut on the outside. Those of pearl shell for certain

fish were not baited, nor towed behind the canoe. Proper spinning baits are termed pa [poa], and were of two kinds, the one large, of pearl shell fixed on bone 4 inches, or more, long, and the other small, 1–2 inches, of pearl shell alone. Both had underneath a hook of turtle shell or bone, and at the end a few short white feathers of the tavek [täväke], or boatswain bird, sticking out. Tjija [Jija], long fish with very narrow jaws [garfish], almost too small for any hook, are caught by a lump of spider's web at the end of a line on a long bamboo, when the tide is coming in. The teeth are numerous and long, and cannot disentangle themselves. (Gardiner 1898:425)

MacGregor provided additional information about spider web fishing:

> The spider web . . . is caught up from the corner of the house by twisting on the end of a stick. The web is made into a ball and colored with charcoal so that it will show up black. Charcoal of the leifau [hefau?] is used, called mahala. This ball is then tied on the end of the fish line.
>
> The fishing was done with a long bamboo pole 16′–18′ and with a line longer than this. The fish were only caught in a few places in Rotuma, one of them being off the reef, another off the islet Afngaha [Afgaha] off Noatau. The pole was held so that the ball of black web was suspended just over the water, and allowed to blow back and forth in the wind. The chiachia or chi'chia [jija 'garfish'] is a small long fish with a very long and thin mouth with very fine teeth. It would jump out of the water to bite at the web and be caught by its teeth in the mesh. (MacGregor 1932)

Gardiner described several techniques for catching fish on the reef, mostly involving traps and nets. In three instances he mentioned the use of canoes: while turtle fishing, during fish drives, and when catching flying fish. For turtle fishing, Rotumans used sennit nets, according to Gardiner. A net was put down in a reef passage just before the tide began to ebb. Canoes were stationed at each end of the net, and when a turtle was seen going into it, a man from each canoe dived after it, seized it by the front flippers, and turned it over so that it was compelled to come to the surface (Gardiner 1898:426).[10] MacGregor confirms this description, adding that the fishermen would frighten the turtles into the nets by drumming on the sides of their canoes. He also describes an alternative method of turtle fishing, involving taking canoes out at night on the high tide and searching for turtles with torches, then spearing them when they came to the light (MacGregor 1932). Today people dive for turtles using goggles or a diving mask and small spear made from a quarter-inch steel rod propelled by a flexible rubber tube (similar to surgical rubber), with a copper wire loop attached on one end and a tire-tube rubber loop, placed over the thumb, at the other. The spear is drawn like a bow and arrow (J. Bennett, personal communication).

Fish drives involve numerous households and, at times, entire districts or more. A large net is placed at a strategic location in a reef passage just before low tide, and fish are driven into it by lines of people beating the water. Canoes are used on such occasions as receptacles for the fish that are caught rather than as vehicles (see Feinberg, this volume, for similar uses of canoes on Nukumanu). Those picking the fish out of the net crush the skull between their teeth to dispatch them quickly and to prevent them from flipping out of the canoes in which they are stored. Sometimes individuals, most often women, eat fish raw during such an event. Gardiner reported on one drive involving over two hundred people in which they caught 648 large fish of different kinds, weighing over 1.5 tons (Gardiner 1898:427).

Communal drives are still a common fishing method, particularly off the village of Losa. Fish are driven out of the reef passage and, blinded by the setting sun, are caught in a net. This method is called *furamasa* 'to fish late in the afternoon' (Churchward 1940:208), or, more generically, *hagoat vao* 'net fishing'. The term *jau* 'to beat' (which in this instance refers to beating the water when driving fish to where they can be caught)[11] is commonly used for fish drives in which nets are not used. No lexical distinction is made between a communal drive involving an entire village or simply a few family members (J. Bennett, personal communication).

In the past, canoes were also used to catch "flying fish" using a special net *(seu)* about twelve feet long by six feet wide, fixed at the end of two bamboo poles. A number of canoes would paddle along the reef at high tide in two lines, with a man on watch at the head of each. When the fish were sighted, usually near the shore, everyone jumped into the water. While some of the men surrounded the fish with a net, others got ready to catch them when they jumped over it (Gardiner 1898:428). From his account it seems that Gardiner was referring to mullet *('anasi)* rather than true flying fish *(säsäve)*, since the former feed on the reef while the latter inhabit the deep sea outside the reef. Mullet often jump out of the water but do not have the anatomy to glide through the air.[12]

The *tautei* from the Noa'tau district provided MacGregor with detailed information concerning *seu* expeditions:

> The Seu is a fishing party of eleven canoes which are accompanied usually by a chief, for whom the fishing is done.[13] The fleet of canoes go out in two lines of five in file, and the eleventh canoe travels between the two lines opposite the last two in the files.
>
> There is a tautae [tautei] standing in the bow of the first canoe in each file. He wears an eyeshade (isau) [isao] made of coconut leaves, and a titi or vehnau which is a grass skirt made of hau. . . .
>
> When the fish have been sighted, the files separate to a greater distance to surround the school. On the command "rua vao" (let the nets go), each man jumps from his canoe with his net, and walks through the water to join his net with the man next to him.
>
> A complete net is thus formed on each side of the school, and these are joined together, at one end with the net of the center or eleventh canoe and at the other between the two canoes of the tautae.
>
> There are more than two men in a canoe. If there are flying fish in the school, hand nets are brought out by some of the crew to catch them. These nets are vauseu [vao seu]. The long nets are vau hapa [vao hapa].
>
> Each movement is carried out only at the tautae's orders.
>
> The seu is carried out inside the reef in shallow water so that the fish, when completely enclosed with the nets, are taken out by hand into the canoe. (MacGregor 1932)

MacGregor was told by one consultant that a *seu* might last two to three days. A number of taboos were associated with *seu*. For example, on the night before an expedition, the fishermen were supposed to sleep alone; if any one of them had sex, fish would jump over the net he was holding. No one could mention the names of the men who went fishing. The houses of the fishermen were shut during a *seu*, and no one was allowed to enter them while it was in progress. Making noise was taboo, and it was forbidden to make cooking fires. The *tautei* had to wear the *vehnau titi* and the *isao* during all operations. If any of these taboos were violated, it would bring bad luck. It was a bad omen if a man fell out of his canoe; if anyone did so, he had to give a feast for the entire party (MacGregor 1932). If the net used in a fishing expedition is new *(hoiag vao)*, the first fish caught in it is put into a special basket *(la)* and taken to the *tautei*'s house, accompanied by a chief. The doors of the house, kept closed until then, are opened, and an announcement of the catch *(ma hei'akia)* is chanted (Elisapeti Inia, personal communication).

MacGregor mentions two locations in which hook and line fishing were used for catching snapper in deep water by submerged reefs: off the islets of Haua and off the village of Losa. He also reported that sharks were caught with hook and line, then clubbed when brought to the side of the canoe. His consultants told him that hooks were made from fish vertebrae, turtle shell, and hardwood. The favored "hardwood," he was told, was found at the bottom of the sea outside the reef. (According to John Bennett, the substance referred to is black coral, commonly found off the island of Uea, which has no fringing reef.) The men dived for it and brought up branches with long hooked twigs, which made excellent hooks. Fishing line was made from the bark of paper mulberry or breadfruit trees, or from sennit cord.

The practice of closing up a house when a man goes deep-sea fishing is still common today. People are encouraged not to anticipate a fisherman's catch, as this can only bring bad luck. When one first takes out a new boat to fish, he is expected to acknowledge a good catch by providing fish to the chief and minister. Not observing this custom, Rotumans claim, will result in poor catches (J. Bennett, personal communication).

SHIPPING OUT: ROTUMAN SAILORS ON EUROPEAN VESSELS

It is clear from the reports of nearly all early commentators that Rotuman men were eager to leave Rotuma aboard European vessels and took every opportunity to do so (e.g., see Bennett 1831:480). Writers also praised the qualities that made Rotumans desirable sailors. The remarks of Joseph Osborn, aboard the whaling ship *Emerald* when it stopped at Rotuma in 1835, are typical:

> They love to visit foreign countries & great numbers of them ship on board the English whaleships. . . . On board a ship they are as good or better than any of the South Sea natives: diligent, civil & quiet, 3 very necessary qualities. They soon learn to talk English & there is but few of them but what can talk a few words. (Osborn 1834–1835)

John Eagleston, captain of the *Emerald,* echoed Osborn's sentiments. "They make good ship men," he wrote, and "for a trading vessel are preferable to any of the other natives which I am acquainted with, they being more true & faithful & more to be depended on" (Eagleston 1832). He noted that he had had a number of Rotumans aboard as crewmen in the past, as well as other islanders, but found Rotumans to be the best.

Some forty years later, Litton Forbes wrote:

> The men of Rotumah make good sailors, and after a few years' service in sea-going vessels are worth the same wages as white men. Scarcely a man on the island but has been more or less of a traveler. It is no rare thing to find men who have visited Harve, or New York, or Calcutta, men who can discuss the relative merits of a sailors' home in London or Liverpool, and dilate on the advantages of steam over sailing vessels. Thus the average native of Rotumah is more than usually capable and intelligent. (Forbes 1875:226)

Commenting in 1867 on the extent of emigration, Rev. William Fletcher, the first European Methodist missionary stationed on Rotuma, wrote that upward of seven hundred young men were known to have left the island in recent memory (Fletcher 1870). Anxiety over the unimpeded emigration of young men was one of the first issues raised by the chiefs of Rotuma in their negotiations with British authorities prior to cession. Thus, Arthur Gordon reported in 1879 that the chiefs desired regulations to check wholesale emigration. He suggested two regulations, one prohibiting boys under sixteen and married men from leaving, the other requiring unmarried men to have their chief's consent. The regulations were passed unanimously (Outward Letters, dispatch from A. Gordon to Colonial Secretary, 4 December 1879).

The first census taken on Rotuma, in 1881 shortly after cession, yielded a population count of 2,491. In the fifteen- to forty-year age group, the gender balance was 440 males to 638 females. The resident commissioner at the time, Charles Mitchell, attributed the surplus of females to the fact that so many young men had left the island (Outward Letters, dispatch from C. Mitchell to Colonial Secretary, 1 October 1881).[14]

W. L. Allardyce, who was on Rotuma about this time, commented on the shift in traveling destinations resulting from the demise of the whaling industry as well as the social price homestayers had to pay:

> Nearly all the men on the island have at one time or another been to sea, and while in the old whaling days Honolulu and Behring Straits formed the goal of their ideas, the sailors of the present day must needs [sic] visit New Zealand, Australia, China, and India, while others still more ambitious are not satisfied till they have rounded the Horn and passed the white cliffs of Dover. The few who have never been to sea at all have often to endure a considerable amount of banter at the expense of their inexperience. (Allardyce 1885–1886:133)[15]

Allardyce also noted that the majority of Rotuman men abroad were engaged in the Torres Straits pearl-diving industry, which was flourishing at the time. Writing in 1884, William Gordon reported that over one hundred Rotuman men were employed in the industry, mostly in the management of boats. The boatmen earned two to three pounds a month. Divers earned much more, up to forty pounds a month according to Gordon, but tended to squander it during binges in the city (Outward Letters, dispatch from Wm. Gordon to Colonial Secretary, 24 November 1884).

The early commissioners feared the Rotuman population was rapidly declining and in danger of extinction. They saw emigration as a significant part of the problem. Fortunately, however, Rotuma avoided the scourges of venereal disease,[16] a fact remarked upon by Commissioner Gordon with surprise, given the comings and goings of so many young men who had been sailors (Outward Letters, dispatch from Wm. Gordon to Colonial Secretary, 24 November 1884). Attempts to dampen emigration were aided by the British decision to govern Rotuma as part of the colony of Fiji and to close Rotuma as a port of entry. This significantly reduced the number of vessels calling at Rotuma and meant that men had to go to Fiji to sign aboard as seamen.

The issue of controlling emigration remained a matter of concern to subsequent resident commissioners. Following an inquiry into the matter, A. R. Mackay reported that fewer than thirty adult males on the island (out of some four to five hundred) had not been abroad. He reiterated what others had said before, that "it is a cutting reproach to cast at a man that he has not been away from the island; hence, partly, the anxiety of the young men to accomplish their long cherished dream" (Outward Letters, dispatch from A. R. Mackay to Colonial Secretary, 10 January 1887).

The concern for controlling emigration eventually led to the passage of Rotuma Regulation Number 3 in 1939, stating that "No native may leave Rotuma without the permission of the District Officer" (who replaced the resident commissioner as administrative officer in charge of Rotuma following a colonial governmental reorganization). It further specified that "No male adult responsible for the maintenance of his wife, children, or relatives may leave Rotuma without making adequate provision for the maintenance of said wife, children, or relatives to the satisfaction of the District Officer" (Rotuma Regulations 1939:457).[17]

Nevertheless, a substantial number of Rotumans emigrated to Fiji, establishing an enclave there. The outbreak of World War II accelerated Rotuman emigration to Fiji, and by 1946 approximately 17 percent of all Rotumans were residing there. Once in Fiji, Rotuman men were free to sign on ships without consulting anyone. The chiefs protested and demanded the right to choose who could go, but the governor of Fiji ruled that "the liberty of the individual must be respected and it is not for the Rotuman Chiefs to decide who shall and who shall not sign on ships" (Fiji Archives, Document F22/44).

Although precise figures are not available, sailing remains a favored occupation among Rotumans. In a survey of 414 households (85 percent) on Rotuma during 1989,[18] I identified sixty-nine men engaged in sailing at the time. This accounted for 20.7 percent of all men abroad on whom I have occupational data. Five of them were ship captains, two were pilots. Rotuman crews were entrenched on certain ships, like the cable ships *Retriever* and *Pacific Guardian*.

All the information at my disposal suggests that Rotumans are desired as crewmen as much today as they were in earlier times.[19] The reasons given are similar: that Rotumans are exceptionally conscientious, they learn fast, and are capable of taking responsibility.[20] I have elsewhere related these qualities, widely recognized by employers of Rotuman personnel, to socialization patterns and the social organization of the Rotuman community (Howard 1966, 1970).

SEAMANSHIP ON ROTUMA TODAY

With a few notable exceptions, Rotumans now residing on the island do not venture beyond the reef and have not developed seafaring skills. Almost all fishing is done on the reef, and canoes are used more as receptacles than as vehicles. The only type of canoe that has survived is the small outrigger, formerly called *täväne* but currently known only by the generic term for canoe, *vaka*. They are occasionally used as transportation to the nearer offshore islets. Both men and women fish on the reef, and women are as likely to take canoes for this purpose as men. It is common to find husbands and wives exploiting the reef together.

The most usual fishing techniques employed do not require canoes, however. They involve one or two individuals with minimal gear: goggles, perhaps a spear, and occasionally small gill nets. Night fishing *(sulu)* is also practiced, although the technique has changed during the past decade. Previously, benzine lanterns were used, and one would walk on the reef at low tide or spearfish from a canoe. Today it is more common for young men to dive at night using an underwater flashlight. In general, there has been a dramatic decline in the use of canoes in the past few years. Bennett reports that men with whom he previously fished in the deep sea no longer go out, and young men show little interest (J. Bennett, personal communication).

As the cash flow to Rotuma has increased, largely as a result of remittances (Rensel 1994), the islanders have exploited marine resources less, so that consumption of tinned fish now exceeds that of fresh fish. A few years ago a Fisheries Division report documented an islander's average annual per capita consumption of thirty tins of mackerel, a total wet weight equivalent to more than forty tons of fish for the population as a whole. The report's authors comment on the unimportance of fishing in daily life, in stark contrast to the strong fishing traditions of other Polynesian peoples (Fisheries Division n.d.:5).[21]

The 1989 household survey (see note 18) included an inventory of selected items, including canoes and boats. Seventy-six households (18.4 percent) reported owning a canoe, and seven households (1.6 percent) reported owning a punt or launch with an outboard motor. All canoes were owned by individual households, and nearly all had been built by a member of the household.[22]

One man, with the title Sautiak, owned a small fishing boat with an inboard engine. Sautiak identified five fishing areas that he exploits. Three were off the west end of the island, including Whale Bank Reef; one was to the east; and another was to the southeast of Noa'tau. The farthest destination, Captain Read Reef, is some forty-eight kilometers to the south-southeast of Rotuma.[23] It is approximately sixteen kilometers long and rises to within twelve fathoms of the surface. According to a report from the Fiji Ministry of Agriculture and Fisheries, this location "is likely to be very productive for both pelagic and bottom fish, and can be fished with a reasonable margin of safety during favourable weather in the SE trades, when prevailing winds would favour sail-assisted return of a disabled vessel to Rotuma" (Fisheries Division n.d.:18).

Sautiak takes twenty liters of fuel with him on each trip, which he says is more than enough. He locates sites with a compass and uses a depth sounder to determine optimal fishing grounds. When fishing close to Rotuma, he uses alignments of landmarks on the island and watches for seabirds feeding at the reef breaks. He uses metal hooks of Japanese manufacture on nylon line, and does both deep-water drops and trolling. He goes out once a week or so when his boat is in good repair. Most of his expeditions are extremely fruitful, and he distributes his catch to friends and family, although he usually sells a portion. Since demand far exceeds the supply, selling fresh fish is very easy. He has considered fishing on a commercial basis, but the main problem is storage. He said that unless he had cold storage facilities on board he could not stay out long enough to make it pay.

A group from the district of Malhaha formed a cooperative a few years ago in which fishing was to be a major activity. They bought two boats and a large walk-in freezer to store their catch. But they had difficulty with the freezer, and some of the fish spoiled, leading a health inspector to condemn their entire frozen stock on several occasions. As a result, they endured financial losses, and their backers, a group of Rotumans in Fiji, withdrew financial support. After a while the freezer broke down completely. One of the boats was repossessed by the bank and sold to a group from Hapmak; the other developed a leak and was still in dry dock on our last visit to the island. The Hapmak group uses the boat for commercial fishing on a sporadic basis, going out when there is a special need for fish and when sailing conditions are optimal. Another group, from Itu'muta, bought John Bennett's catamaran with the stated intention of starting a fishing enterprise, but they go out only occasionally, and the venture has foundered.

Despite a consistent demand for fish and recognition of commercial possibilities, little has been done to capitalize on the potential. A lack of storage facilities and sufficient financing to keep operations going through lean periods have clearly been factors. But the fact that many Rotumans in Fiji are engaged in commercial deep-sea fishing suggests that an aversion to the rigors of the deep is not at issue.[24] While it is probably true that economic payoffs on Rotuma are insufficient to offset investment costs in time and money,[25] a more important factor may be a failure in leadership. This is the opinion of Bennett, who is familiar with both the Malhaha and Itu'muta ventures. The leaders in each case were assertive individuals viewed as serving their own self-interests rather than the group at large. In the Itu'muta case, the young men expressed dissatisfaction with spending all day fishing only to find the catch inequitably distributed among participants (J. Bennett, personal communication). Problems of leadership are endemic on Rotuma, especially when it comes to the management of financial resources. It may well be, therefore, that the kind of leadership required to sustain a fishing enterprise is absent on Rotuma and that Rotumans engage in seabound ventures so much more readily abroad (and aboard European vessels) because they find the leadership much more palatable.

SAILING AS A FOCUS OF CULTURAL EXPERIENCE

The importance of sailing as a focus of cultural experience for Rotumans is evident in many ways. It is a source of solidarity between men who have sailed together and is the subject of reminiscences when men congregate. Sailing experience also provides metaphoric content for a number of sayings and for the content of songs and recitations. In some instances it constitutes the core of personal identity, as in the case of a woman who changed her name to *Al 'e Sasi* 'Died at Sea' after her son was lost while serving aboard a ship. Travel abroad, in general, is metaphorically a sailing experience, and at its core remains a canoe journey. Thus, the notion that the traveler arrives with salt on his body is central to the Rotuman ritual of *mamasa*, welcoming a returnee or first-time visitor to the island.

The Mamasa 'Welcoming Ceremony'

The term *mamasa* means 'to be dry' or 'to become dry', and it is used in reference to a ceremony performed when people return from a sea voyage or, in earlier times, from a dangerous deep-sea fishing expedition (Churchward 1940:258). Presumably when people arrived by canoe, or by steamer prior to the building of a wharf at Oinafa in the 1970s, they landed wet and had to be dried and provided with clothes; hence, the reference to drying out. The *mamasa* is one of several life crisis events that involve the central symbols of Rotuman ceremonial performances: sacrificial pigs, kava, sweet-smelling oil, garlands, and fine white pandanus mats *(apei)*.

The recipient of a *mamasa* ceremony *(forau)* is seated in the place of honor on a pile of mats *(päega)* topped with an *apei*, which symbolizes his or her elevation to a godlike status for the duration of the event. *Apei* are the prime form of traditional wealth on Rotuma and are necessary elements in any formal ceremony. Each *apei* is consecrated by a *koua* 'sacrificial slaughter and cooking of a pig in an earth oven'; it symbolizes life and blessings from the gods.

While seated on the *päega*, the *forau* is presented with a *tefui* 'garland', tied around his or her neck by a woman designated to play the welcoming role. The woman then performs the *mamia*, which in ordinary circumstances means 'to wash a person or fishing net in fresh water after having been in the sea' (Churchward 1940:259), but in this instance is symbolized by anointing the honoree with sweet-smelling oil, which must be pure Rotuman oil. This highly symbolic act signifies cleansing the body of salt from the sea (Nilsen 1977:80). In earlier times, the woman would take off the *forau's* shirt and put a new one on him or her, then present him or her with a new lavalava (Marseu 1986:5).[26]

This act is followed by a kava ceremony and formal presentation of food. The *forau* is given the head of the largest pig (reserved for the person of highest status during feasts), which is placed in front of him or her on a ceremonial table *('umefe)*. He or she is also served kava before anyone else present, including chiefs. If the ceremony is an elaborate one, for a person of high status or someone whose achievements abroad brought honor to the community, dances and songs composed for the occasion may be performed, glorifying the person's adventures or accomplishments.

The *mamasa* ceremony has at least two clear functions. One is to reintegrate sojourners back into Rotuman life by communicating their importance to the community and elevating their status, if only for the duration of the event. Attention is called to their absence and return, to their bravery in leaving the island, and to their accomplishments. They are made to feel special. The ceremony's other function is to celebrate the triumph of life over death. Like all Rotuman ceremonies, the symbolism of the *mamasa* emphasizes the regeneration of life forces: the sacrificial pig is a gift to the gods, who are supposed to respond by giving life to the land and its people; kava symbolizes bodily fluids that give life; and fragrant oils and flowers (in the form of a garland) suggest the sweet smells of life as opposed to the stench of death.[27] Journeying beyond the reef for long periods was regarded as dangerous in the past; the *mamasa* was a way to offer thanks for a safe return. Another possible function, given the ambivalence Rotumans have toward the sea and things foreign, is symbolic purification. By washing away saltwater residues with fresh water, they perhaps ritually cleanse sojourners of contamination not only by the sea but by foreign influences of all kinds.

Sayings

Rotuman sayings referring to sailing experiences can be grouped into four categories: (1) those calling attention to the special status of travelers; (2) those used metaphorically to call attention to hardships and fatigue; (3) those referring to chaos; and (4) those calling attention to undesirable behavior. The following examples are illustrative:[28]

1. The special status of travelers. *'Ou la mat la'mou* 'Your legs (or feet) are still wet'. This phrase is said to newcomers, suggesting that they have not yet fully integrated into community life. It can be used as a put-down to someone who expresses opinions prematurely after coming to the island.

2. Hardship and fatigue. *Na ta lu* 'Give a rope'. This phrase is used for people who work slowly, as if fatigued. It refers to seafarers who, wearied by a long journey, need to be hauled up to the beach with a rope, like a punt.

3. Chaos. *'Itake vak lo* 'Like a capsized canoe'. This phrase is used when there is a sudden crisis, and everyone starts talking at once, but no one knows what to do, and nothing gets done. It also applies when one cannot hear because of the noise.

4. Undesirable Behavior. *Vak ta lelei ka sam ta raksa'a* 'The canoe is good but the outrigger is bad'. Metaphorically, the man is good, but his wife is not. This phrase is generally used in reference to a chief and his wife, since the term *vaka* is a common metaphor for a chief.

Songs

Songs are composed in several formats that refer to travel abroad, including chants that accompany action dances, and compositions in a modern pan-Pacific format accompanied by guitar, ukelele, and other instruments. An example of such a song is presented by Mosese Kaurasi (1977:145–46):

Rotuman Version
Tefui hata vasa 'e tier
Ma noa la se maoen 'ae 'e fue
Api ma roa 'ae 'e matit fak use
Tari te Rotuma noh fak rotue

English Translation
The garlands of pandanus fruit and gardenia.
Be careful not to get lost out there.
You've lingered long in the cold of the rain.
Your relatives are awaiting you in Rotuma.

Recitations

Ritual presentations of kava occupy a central place in nearly all Rotuman ceremonies. A key part of the ritual is the recitation of a *fakpeje*, a text generally associated with the legendary coming of kava to Rotuma. Recitations are given by male elders *(mafua)*, usually in a language so esoteric that most people cannot follow their meanings. Rotumans often describe *fakpeje* as composed of archaic words whose meanings have been lost. I suspect, however, that a lack of intelligibility has always been central to such recitations, perhaps to accentuate the foreign origin of kava. The prevailing myth concerning kava's origin has it coming from "Tonga," which in its generic sense is a place over or under the sea inhabited by potent beings or spirits.

That Rotumans associate experiences overseas and aboard ships with the foreignness (and potency) attributed to kava can be seen in a *fakpeje* recorded by Hocart on Rotuma in 1913. In this instance, intelligibility is obscured by the seemingly random juxtaposition of English phrases with Rotuman words interspersed:

A below,
way about
riepouj
how many nu le for here
ten mile and a quarter
two far off
all pull up to which
you can't go up there
it's too heavy
good kuretemene hard
Adele
lee o four yar
forty gunsale
forty mainsail
pull off the guff topsail
French ship
jib
stay sail jib
fore poren
where your head
saw pau es
you takes up

UNPREDICTABILITY AND AMBIVALENT EMOTIONS

Collectively, Rotuman attitudes toward the sea are ambivalent. It has been a source of wondrous adventures for some, of seasickness for many, and of grief over losing kinsmen for others. For all Rotumans, boats represent connections to the outside world. For those on the island, boats are bridges to relatives abroad, transporters of vital supplies, and the means by which money is earned through the shipping of copra. The days on which boats arrive and leave are major occasions.

That the sea beyond the reef is dangerous comes home repeatedly. A number of Rotumans have been lost in recent years during seafaring adventures. Some have gone fishing and never returned. News of crew members aboard vessels that have sunk arrives periodically. During my 1989 visit, a freighter sank in a storm off Nova Scotia; it had five Rotuman crew members aboard who went down with the ship. Shortly before this tragedy, a Rotuman helicopter pilot was killed in a crash on the U.S. mainland,[29] lending even more emphasis to the dangers of sailing, since the sea and sky are associated in Rotuman cultural idiom (airplanes are called 'ahai fere 'flying ships').

Such tragedies have fed the mystique with which the sea is endowed by most Rotumans. They conceive of the sea, and what happens in and on it, as dangerous and unpredictable on the one hand, enriching and vitalizing on the other. Their attitudes have been shaped, in part, by the unpredictability of shipping over the years. Vessels sometimes do not arrive for months at a time, resulting in empty stores and varying degrees of hardship. At other times several ships may arrive within days of each other. Despite numerous efforts on the part of well-placed officials, shipping to Rotuma has remained erratic since the initial arrival of Europen vessels. It has been the source of much black humor on the island. For example, when I heard on Fiji Radio that a boat was scheduled to sail for Rotuma in a week and mentioned it to my Rotuman friend, he laughed and told me always to multiply the time interval by two or three.

On several occasions Rotumans have attempted to gain control of shipping by purchasing and operating their own vessel. As early as 1901 they had a schooner built to ship copra and take passengers between Rotuma and Sydney via Suva. The fifty-ton vessel cost over 2,000 British pounds and operated for eighteen months before sinking on a reef at Rotuma (Eason 1951:89–90). Most recently, in 1992, a Rotuman group purchased an interisland vessel, the *Wairua*, at a cost of Fiji $250,000. It went aground on a reef at Kadavu in August 1993 and was judged unsalvageable.

CONCLUSION

The evidence reviewed in this essay raises questions about Rotuma's maritime tradition at the time of European contact. Although there is no doubt that Rotumans occasionally voyaged to islands in their general vicinity, and perhaps beyond, their canoes were described by European observers as of poor quality, and their navigational knowledge was characterized as limited. Taken at face value, these observations suggest that Rotuma lacked the highly developed maritime traditions that characterized some of its mid-Pacific neighbors. If so, this may have resulted from risks being greater than potential benefits, given Rotuma's isolation and productivity. Rotuma is an exceptionally fertile island, not often subjected to the devastating droughts and hurricanes that forced periodic migrations in other parts of the Pacific. There may have been little motivation to develop long-distance sailing skills.

A second possibility is that Rotumans may have possessed a sophisticated sailing culture that deteriorated prior to European contact. The only hope of verifying such a prior tradition would be through archaeological investigations yet to be done. A third possibility is that Rotuman seafaring skills were in fact highly developed, but opportunities to sail aboard European vessels led to an extraordinarily rapid erosion of traditional maritime technology and knowledge. Perhaps, it might be argued, the most skillful sailors took advantage of the opportunities European ships offered, and they distinguished themselves because they already had the personal characteristics that made them good sailors, regardless of the craft involved. That sailing, and canoes in particular, have remained central symbols in Rotuman culture lends weight to such an argument. Regardless of the scenario one favors, it seems clear that the character traits developed on this remote island were consistent with those required for seafaring, especially where responsibility to one's shipmates was central.

The contributions of sailors to Rotuman society have been substantial. Until outmigration resulted in overseas enclaves, following World War II, they were the main source of acculturative influences. Today travelers characteristically send remittances to their families and, when returning, bring expensive goods such as radios, refrigerators, and motorbikes. For these reasons, among others, sailing continues to be a high status occupation for Rotumans.

NOTES

1. For detailed information concerning the geology of Rotuma, see Woodhall 1987.

2. W. E. Russell, who served as resident commissioner on Rotuma in the 1920s, published an account taken from the notes of F. Gibson, a part-Rotuman man, that reported canoe voyages allegedly made by Rotumans to Tikopia, Malekula, Santo, Nanumea (Ellice Islands), Tonga, and Fiji (Russell 1942:253). A man by the name of Pani and two other unnamed men from Malhaha and Losa, respectively, were said by Gibson's informants to be the last canoe voyagers to go abroad and return. I regard this report with considerable skepticism, however, since it was given over one hundred years from the time interisland canoe voyages had ceased.

3. Allen served as a Methodist missionary on Rotuma for several years during the 1880s.

4. Hocart, during his visit to Rotuma in 1913, elicited the names of several constellations, some of which were associated with sailing directions, but it is unclear whether this information represented indigenous knowledge (Hocart 1913:4944–46). MacGregor's notes also contain a number of entries concerning astronomy, but only one entry refers to the navigational use of stars. He records the name *Takirua* as two stars between which the course is laid from Wallis to Rotuma (MacGregor 1932).

5. The spelling of Rotuman words was standardized following Churchward's publication of his *Rotuman Grammar and Dictionary* in 1940. I use Churchward's orthography in my own writing, and following other authors' usage I include Churchward's spelling in brackets if it is different. For an explanation of the orthography, see Churchward 1940:13.

6. MacGregor also records in his notes from this consultant, a man named Niua, "These canoes carried from 60–100 people and traveled to Fiji, Futuna and Sufaia? [sic] in the Ellice. Ngofe was a famous captain of the last Oinafa ahoi *['ahai]*. Planks still in Oinafa" (MacGregor 1932). Again, given the time lapse from the period in which such voyages might have been made, one must be cautious in interpreting this report as factual knowledge.

7. *Ororo* refers to a "contrivance made of large numbers of half coconut-shells threaded on a wooden hoop, and drawn up and down in the water, thereby making a noise which attracts sharks to the proximity of the baited hooks that are out for them" (Churchward 1940:275). It is also used in reference to fishing for sharks with the help of *ororo*.

8. MacGregor's consultant mentioned this to him when asked why there were only two strips on one border of his canoe. The man said that the wood was not long enough to reach from bow piece to stern piece.

9. Identification of *penau, togoi, 'ura,* and *ratu'a* trees are from Whistler (1989). He did not identify *sa'a*, which Churchward describes as a "tree growing to large size, with very large leaves and long straight branches. The bark, at first, is greyish-green and very smooth. Bears bunches of small whitish flowers. Timber, white, much used in house-building and canoe-making" (Churchward 1940:307).

10. Hocart, in a brief article published in 1914, reported that, as the result of a curse, turtle nets were no longer being made in at least one district.

11. According to Churchward, the phrase *jao 'atua* 'beating ghosts' is sometimes used (1940:231).

12. I am indebted to John Bennett for pointing this out to me.

13. Another consultant told MacGregor that the last *seu* involved twenty-one *taf'aga* canoes.

14. Two years earlier, Arthur Gordon inquired into labor recruiting on Rotuma and obtained figures for five districts (Itu'ti'u, Itu'muta, Juju, Pepjei, and Malhaha). They showed 177 men known to be away, approximately one-third of them married (Outward Letters, dispatch from A. Gordon to Colonial Secretary, 4 December 1879).

A significant portion of the men who were away had been recruited as laborers to work in the Hawaiian Islands and Samoa, and had difficulty returning. In a series of dispatches during 1883, William Gordon, the resident commissioner, requested assistance in having the 50–60 men in the Hawaiian Islands, and an unspecified number from Samoa, repatriated. He commented that the men in Samoa had been paid in goods instead of money and were thus unable to pay for passage home.

15. Gardiner (1898:407) also commented on the disgrace endured by Rotuman men who had not been to foreign lands. He speculated (p. 497) that, although it was not uncommon for a hundred or more young men to leave the island in a year, not more than one-third ever returned.

16. The population may have been protected as a result of the prevalence of virulent yaws, which has a complementary distribution with syphilis (see Howard 1979).

17. The practice of informing chiefs when departing the island is still carried out to some extent, although it has noticeably declined over the past fifteen years. Chiefs enforce the regulation to varying degrees. Protocol requires an individual to inform his village chief *(fa 'es ho'aga),* who in turn informs the district chief, who then informs the district officer (J. Bennett, personal communication). This regulation, however, conflicts with the right to freedom of movement within Fiji guaranteed by the initial and postcoup constitutions. A recent case, in which the district officer attempted to confine a woman to the island on the grounds that her children might not be properly cared for, highlighted this contradiction and resulted in a threatened lawsuit.

18. The survey was conducted by schoolteachers hired as research assistants, supervised by myself and my wife, Jan Rensel, who was pursuing doctoral research on the island at the time. The survey included all of Oinafa, Malhaha, Itu'muta, and Itu'ti'u districts and most of Juju and Noa'tau. Pepjei was omitted as a result of interviewer difficulties.

19. In late 1990 a recruitment program was launched in Fiji for up to sixty Rotumans to become the core crew for a newly commissioned cable ship having English officers (J. Bennett, personal communication).

20. These are the same reasons given by supervisors at the Vatukoula gold mines for favoring Rotuman workers (see Howard 1966:266).

21. The Fisheries Division report concludes that the sea around Rotuma offers considerable opportunity for commercially viable fishing enterprises, but they identify three major problems: (1) the lack of suitable vessels to exploit the productive areas; (2) inadequate facilities for fishing vessels, including lack of an all-weather anchorage; absence of maintenance facilities; occasional fuel shortages; and the lack of ice, gear, storage, and marketing facilities for fishermen; and (3) the isolation of the island (Fisheries Division n.d.:18–20).

22. Household size averaged 5.8 persons in 1989. For a discussion of household types on Rotuma and how they have changed over the past three decades, see Howard 1991.

23. The reef is named after its discoverer, Captain Read, aboard the hydrographic vessel *M. V. Tangaroa,* which carried out a survey for phosphate deposits in the region in 1976.

24. According to information provided by Vilsoni Hereniko, obtained from his sister Vamarasi, his brother Mua, and Isireli Motofaga, a boat owner in Lautoka, at least five Rotumans in Fiji own fishing vessels and are engaged in commercial fishing. Their boats were purchased with the help of bank loans. Two of the boat owners captain their own vessels and sail with a hired crew ranging from two to four, depending upon availability. The other owners remain on land while a hired crew goes out to sea. One of the boats is quite large, and the crew sometimes remains at sea for up to one month. The other boats are smaller and usually stay out for about two weeks at a time, depending upon the weather. The large boat's catch can bring in between Fiji $3,000–5,000 per trip, while the smaller ones usually bring in catches worth between Fiji $2,000–3,000 per trip. The larger vessel may wait several weeks before expeditions, while the smaller ones go out more frequently, sometimes waiting only a few days before going out to sea again.

25. According to Hereniko's brother, Mua, the absence of reefs beyond the fringing reef around Rotuma limits access to such commercially profitable fish as tuna or walu, which eat smaller fish that feed off reefs. Mua believes that this at least partly accounts for the absence of commercial fishing on Rotuma. Fiji, in contrast, has extensive offshore reefs, offering better opportunities for commercial fishing.

26. This practice is occasionally followed today but is not now regarded as essential to the ceremony.

27. These symbolic associations are my inferences and were not explicitly provided by informants. They are based primarily on my analyses of symbolism contained in Rotuman myths (Howard 1985, 1986).

28. The sayings included here have been obtained from an unpublished collection by Elisapeti Inia. Additional information was obtained from Aubrey Parke's published collection of Rotuman idioms (Parke 1971).

29. The young man was flying mercy missions for a company located in Spokane, Washington.

REFERENCES

Allardyce, W. L.
1885–1886 Rotooma and the Rotoomans. Royal Geographical Society of Queensland, Proceedings. 1st sets:130–44.
Allen, William
1895 Rotuma. Report of Australasian Association for Advancement of Science, pp. 556–79.
Anonymous
1938 Isle of Rotuma: curious place in Central Polynesian history. Pacific Islands Monthly, December 15, 1938. Sydney, Australia.
Bennett, George
1831 A recent visit to several of the Polynesian islands. United Service Journal 33:198–202, 473–82.
Cheever, George N.
1834–1835 Log of the Ship Emerald. Pacific Manuscript Bureau, frame 31.
Churchward, C. Maxwell
1939 Tales of a Lonely Island. Oceania Monographs No. 4. Sydney: Australian National Research Council.
1940 Rotuman Grammar and Dictionary. Sydney: Australasian Medical Publishing Co., Ltd.

Dillon, Peter
1829   *Narrative . . . of a Voyage in the South Seas.* London: Hurst Chance.
Eagleston, John Henry
1832   *Log of the Ship Emerald,* Vol. 3. Salem, Mass.: Peabody Museum.
Eason, William J. E.
1951   *A Short History of Rotuma.* Suva, Fiji: Government Printing Department.
Fiji Archives
1947   Rotuman crews on overseas vessels. Archive F22/44.
Firth, Raymond
1961   *History and Traditions of Tikopia.* Wellington: The Polynesian Society.
Fisheries Division, Ministry of Agriculture and Fisheries
n.d.   *The Fishery Resources of Rotuma.* Suva, Fiji.
Fletcher, Wm.
1870   *The Wesleyan Missionary Notices,* No. 13, Vol. III. Sidney: Australasian Wesleyan
        Methodist Conference.
Forbes, Litton
1875   *Two Years in Fiji.* London: Longmans, Green, and Co.
Gardiner, J. Stanley
1898   Natives of Rotuma. *Journal of the Royal Anthropological Institute* 27:396–435,
        457–524.
Hocart, A. M.
1913   Field notes on Rotuma. Wellington, New Zealand: Turnbull Library.
1914   The disappearance of a useful art in Rotuma. *Man* 14:162–63.
Hornell, James
1936   *The Canoes of Polynesia, Fiji and Micronesia.* Special Publications No. 27. Hon-
        olulu: Bernice P. Bishop Museum.
Howard, Alan
1966   Plasticity, achievement and adaptation in developing economies. *Human Organi-
        zation* 25:265–72.
1970   *Learning to Be Rotuman.* New York: Columbia Teachers College Press.
1979   The power to heal in colonial Rotuma. *Journal of the Polynesian Society* 88:243–75.
1985   History, myth and Polynesian chieftainship: the case of Rotuman kings. In *Trans-
        formations of Polynesian Culture,* edited by A. Hooper and J. Huntsman, pp.
        39–77. Auckland: Polynesian Society.
1986   Cannibal chiefs and the charter for rebellion in Rotuman myth. *Pacific Studies*
        10:1–27.
1991   Reflections on change in Rotuma, 1959–1989. In *Rotuma: Hanua Pumue: Precious
        Land,* edited by Anselmo Fatiaki et al, pp. 227–54. Suva, Fiji: Institute of Pacific
        Studies, University of the South Pacific.
Jarman, Robert
1838   *Journal of a Voyage to the South Seas, in the Japan, Employed in the Sperm Whale
        Fishery, under the Command of Capt. John May.* London: Longman and Co. and
        Charles Tilt.
Kaurasi, Mosese
1977   Rotuman chants, sports and pastimes. In *Rotuma: Split Island,* edited by Chris Plant,
        pp. 143–52. Suva, Fiji: Institute of Pacific Studies, University of the South Pacific.
Lesson, René
1838–1839   *Voyage Autour du Monde . . . sur . . . 'La Coquille'.* Paris: Pourrat Frères.

Lucatt, Edward
  1851   *Rovings in the Pacific, 1837–49... by a Merchant Long Resident in Tahiti.* London:
          Longman, Brown, Green, and Longman.
MacGregor, Gordon
  1932   Rotuma field notes. Honolulu: Bishop Museum Archives. SC McGregor.
McQuarrie, Peter
  1980   Canoes of Rotuma. *Archaeology and Physical Anthropology in Oceania* 15:51–55.
Marseu, Fesaitu
  1986   The Rotuman mamasa ceremony. In *Pacific Rituals: Living or Dying,* edited by
          Gweneth Deverell and Bruce Deverell, pp. 3–22. Suva, Fiji: Institute of Pacific
          Studies, University of the South Pacific.
Nilsen, Aileen
  1977   The Mamasa ceremony. In *Rotuma: Split Island,* edited by Chris Plant, pp. 79–87.
          Suva, Fiji: Institute of Pacific Studies, University of the South Pacific.
Osborn, Joseph W.
  1834–1835 *Log of the ship Emerald.* Pacific Manuscript Bureau, Reel 223, Frame 359.
Outward Letters.
  n.d.   Rotuma District Office. Suva: Fiji Central Archives.
Parke, Aubrey
  1971   *Rotuman Idioms.* Auckland: Te Reo Monographs, Linguistic Society of New
          Zealand.
Rensel, Jan
  1994   For Love or Money: Interhousehold Exchange and the Economy of Rotuma.
          Ph.D. Dissertation, Anthropology Department, University of Hawai'i.
Rotuma Regulations
  1939   *Legislative Council Papers.* Suva, Fiji: Government Press.
Russell, William
  1942   Rotuma. *Journal of the Polynesian Society* 51:229–55.
Thompson, Basil
  1915   *Voyage of H.M.S. 'Pandora'.* London: Francis Edwards.
Whistler, Art
  1989   Ethnobotany of Rotuma. Manuscript.
Wilson, James
  1799   *A Missionary Voyage to the Southern Pacific Ocean.* London: Chapman.
Wood, C. F.
  1875   *A Yachting Cruise in the South Seas.* London: Henry King.
Woodhall, Derek
  1987   *Geology of Rotuma.* Suva, Fiji: Mineral Resources Department, Ministry of Lands,
          Energy and Mineral Resources.

FROM OUTRIGGER TO JET:
FOUR CENTURIES OF SIKAIANA
VOYAGING

William W. Donner

•   Sikaiana relations with foreigners have always been full of excitement and danger, both in the past, when voyagers traveled hundreds of miles in outrigger canoes, and in the present, when the Sikaiana people regularly travel in cargo ships. Over the past four hundred years, the Sikaiana experience with voyaging and outsiders has developed into a "voyaging ethic" that shapes the behavior and meanings found in Sikaiana's present-day contacts with other cultures and in their modernizing social life. Voyaging is not only a set of nautical skills and techniques; it is also a system of symbols and meanings that organizes experience and behavior (see also Carucci; Howard; Feinberg, all this volume). Although this system of symbols and meanings was formed in the past, when Sikaiana was an isolated atoll and a few brave men voyaged in outrigger canoes, it continues in the present, as the Sikaiana have become incorporated into a regional social system and have come to use modern technology.

Sikaiana is located at 8°22' S, 162°45' E, about 170 kilometers east of Malaita Island in the Solomon Islands. The atoll is about thirteen kilometers long, eight kilometers wide, and includes four small islets. Of necessity, life on an atoll is oriented to the sea. Fish is a main staple in the diet, and the roar of the surf is heard from any location on the islets. Sikaiana is geographically isolated, the nearest high island being Malaita. Isolation is magnified by a small population size: fewer than two hundred people inhabited Sikaiana during the nineteenth century. Throughout the twentieth century, about 200–250 people have resided on the atoll.

For the isolated Sikaiana people, outsiders are a source of excitement and novelty but are also the cause of exploitation and plunder. In pre-European times, some foreigners settled on Sikaiana and became the ancestors of the present-day population; other foreigners were marauders who threatened and killed the atoll's inhabitants. In the nineteenth century, whalers and traders brought trade goods (steel tools, tobacco, and calico) that became necessities in Sikaiana's economic life. In the twentieth century, contacts with outsiders intensified, providing Sikaiana with new technology and opportunities, and at the same time radically altering their institutions and practices. Western institutions were established on the atoll, and most of the population spent at least some time away from home in other parts of the Solomon Islands. At present, the Sikaiana are involved in national and international institutions: Christianity, formal education, courts, and a cash economy. The population has tripled in size since the beginning of the century. Although the number of residents on the atoll has remained stable since 1900, those residing overseas have steadily increased. By the 1980s, the number of Sikaiana migrants living in the area around Honiara, the capital of the Solomon Islands, was greater than the number residing on the atoll.

The Sikaiana no longer undertake long-distance voyaging in small boats. The last occasion when anyone did so was in the early part of this century when a resident trader, low in supplies, set off for Malaita in his own dinghy with some Sikaiana crew members. The Sikaiana no longer even construct outrigger canoes. Instead, they make single-hulled dugout canoes *(manaui)*, which are suitable for fishing in the lagoon or close to shore outside of the reef, but not for long-distance voyaging.

Nevertheless, now, as in the past, the sea and voyaging are essential elements in Sikaiana life. More than ever before, the Sikaiana are voyagers. Although they no longer travel in outrigger canoes, they board cargo ships to find work in other parts of the Solomon Islands, to further their education, or to visit other Sikaiana emigrants. Migrants living away from the atoll travel to Sikaiana during their holidays.

In the present essay, I will describe the centrality of voyaging in Sikaiana life, both in the past and at present. I begin with an overview of Sikaiana voyaging, from the legends of pre-European long-distance voyaging to the present time of Sikaiana travel on steamships and airplanes. Then I examine the symbols and metaphors of voyaging in contemporary speech and social life. I conclude with an examination of how both opportunity and risk are recurrent themes in Sikaiana views of voyaging and in their interactions with foreigners. Although their modes of transportation and their destinations have changed over the past four hundred years, the Sikaiana remain a cautiously adventuresome people who, curious and vulnerable, face the world beyond their reef.

THE HISTORY OF SIKAIANA VOYAGING

Before contact with Europeans, both legends and historical sources suggest that some Sikaiana men were master navigators. Sikaiana legends recount that the atoll's population was founded by Tehui Atahu, a man from an unidentified place called Luahatu. Although some younger Sikaiana propose various locations for Luahatu, these locations are based upon modern knowledge of geography, and older people are consistent in their uncertainty about its exact location. Tehui Atahu took on crew members from various islands, including those of the Santa Cruz group. He arrived at Sikaiana, but the land was submerged under a few feet of water. After marking a claim, he traveled on to Ontong Java (five hundred kilometers to the northwest), where he befriended a chief, Tehui Luaniua, with whom he returned to

Sikaiana. Tehui Atahu and his followers are the original ancestors of the present-day population of the atoll. According to legend, later immigrants arrived from Nukumanu Atoll, north of Ontong Java (see Feinberg this volume), and from somewhere in the east, either Kiribati (Gilbert Islands) or Tuvalu (Ellice Islands). An immigrant named Levao is said to have come from "Samoa."[1]

Sikaiana legends also recount an invasion from "Tona," which they now identify with Tonga, although *tona* is also a common Polynesian directional term. After feigning friendship, the people from Tona slaughtered most of Sikaiana's men. These invaders sailed off with a Sikaiana hostage for Taumako, four hundred kilometers to the southeast, where they were slain after the hostage warned the Taumakans about the slaughter on Sikaiana.

The Sikaiana have a song genre, *tuuhoe* (literally 'stand-paddle'), that describes the long-distance voyages *(holau)* of two ancestors, Semalu and Kaetekita. Semalu is reported to have been the hostage taken to Taumako; according to genealogies, Kaetekita was a contemporary of his. The *tuuhoe* are repetitive, simple songs that briefly recount the activities of these men and the places they visited, including Honohono (perhaps Santa Cruz), Hiti (at present the Sikaiana associate this with Fiji), and Pileni (in the Santa Cruz group). At the turn of the century, the resident commissioner of the Solomon Islands, Charles Woodford (1906:167), collected a story of how Kaetekita had journeyed to Malaita, Isabel, Taumako, and Tikopia, in addition to other islands. By the early 1900s, when Woodford collected this story, some Sikaiana people had traveled widely with European traders, and many place names may have been incorporated into this legend as a result of such travels. Pre-European contacts with Samoa, Tonga, and Fiji are unlikely in my opinion. Contacts with Tuvalu, Ontong Java, and the Polynesian-speaking peoples of the Santa Cruz group clearly occurred, although it is impossible to determine the extent or frequency of these contacts (see Davenport 1964). It seems likely that there were at least occasional contacts with other Polynesian outliers, including Nukumanu, Takuu, and perhaps Tikopia.[2] Presumably, Sikaiana voyagers used their knowledge of stars and wave configurations to navigate. By the time I arrived in 1980, however, no one knew these techniques, and some people expressed the opinion that voyagers, such as Semalu and Kaetekita, were led by powerful spirits *(aitu)*.[3]

The fact that there was knowledge of, and contact with, many other islands is supported by historical documents. In 1606 the Spanish explorer de Quiros met a man named Luka on Taumako. Luka was not a native of Taumako; rather, he came from an island about a four days' journey away. De Quiros referred to this island as "Chikayana," and most scholars identify it as Sikaiana (Woodford 1916:39; Jack-Hinton 1969:149). Given oral traditions of contact between Sikaiana and Taumako, this inference is plausible.

Luka knew about many of the islands in the area. He claimed that a double canoe with about 110 people came from "Guaytopo" to Sikaiana. Jack-Hinton (1969:149–50) infers that Guaytopo is Vaitupu in the Ellice Islands (Tuvalu), although he does not rule out other possibilities. Luka also described the island of Tikopia, where he took de Quiros, and then beyond Tikopia, an island called

"Manicolo," which Jack-Hinton suggests could refer to Fiji and Tonga, although other scholars suggest Vanikoro. Luka set what at that time must have been the Sikaiana record for distance in voyaging when he accompanied de Quiros to Peru (see Jack-Hinton 1969:148–53).[4]

In traditional times, voyaging also took place as the result of insult or shame. After being embarrassed, a person might climb into a canoe and leave his or her fate to the currents. This practice was a form of suicide in that these voyagers did not seem to have had any particular destinations in mind, although survival was a remote possibility (see Firth 1967). I am aware of one case of this type of voyaging in the nineteenth century, but none since.[5]

Sikaiana was first sighted by Europeans in 1791. In the nineteenth century, because of the friendliness of its inhabitants, Sikaiana became a popular place for traders and whalers. By the middle of the nineteenth century, European visitors reported that some Sikaiana people could speak "broken" English (Schertzer 1861:602; Webster 1863:51–52; Anonymous 1848:575). During this period of time, it seems likely that most Sikaiana who wanted to leave their homeland did so, not by setting sail in an outrigger canoe but by climbing aboard visiting whaling and trading ships (see also Bennett 1987:39). In 1828 a whaling ship brought back a Sikaiana castaway from Ontong Java (cited in Bennett 1987:27). In the mid-nineteenth century, John Webster wrote that there were eleven bachelors on the atoll, three of whom left on his ship, the *Wanderer*. He adds, "all [were] young men, who seemed glad to join us" (Webster 1863:60). In 1863 the log of the *Ontario* reports leaving two consumptive crew members on Sikaiana and taking on some Sikaiana women and two men (in PMB 886: ship's log, 18 December 1863). By the turn of the century, a visitor reported that some Sikaiana people had left the atoll on visiting ships and returned, while others had left and never returned (Nerdum 1902). German ethnologist Ernst Sarfert reported the arrival by steamship of some Sikaiana on Ontong Java early in this century (Sarfert and Damm 1929–1931). The Sikaiana still recount stories about ancestors who worked on European ships in the nineteenth century.

In the mid-nineteenth century, a group of about thirty refugees from internal wars in Kiribati were found adrift in the ocean by a trader and were taken to Sikaiana. These Kiribati were most likely refugees from the attack of Tem Binatake and Tem Baitake on Kuria in 1863 (see Maude 1970:210; Woodford 1906:168). Sikaiana people claim that most of the Kiribati men died following a battle after they plotted to kill the Sikaiana men. The surviving women married Sikaiana men. There are still some Kiribati influences in Sikaiana culture, including techniques for collecting and fermenting coconut sap, and many genealogies include Kiribati women from this time.

The British incorporated Sikaiana into its Solomon Islands Protectorate between 1897 and 1899, although the administrators' visits were sporadic until the 1930s. By the early twentieth century, there were several trade stores that were supplied by foreign traders. Copra and coconut oil were used to trade for steel tools, cloth, and tobacco, which had become important in the local economy.

In the early part of the century, fearing the outbreak of disease, the British de-
clared Sikaiana a closed district for labor recruitment. But they hired many Sikaiana
to work as crew members on the Protectorate's ships, in particular the *Rinadi*, probably on the assumption that Polynesians would make good seafarers. Sikaiana men
working on the *Rinadi* requested that the Anglican Melanesian Mission send missionaries to their home atoll after a resident white trader tricked them into burning
down their traditional ritual houses.

In 1929, in response to this request, some Anglican missionaries came to Sikaiana. There followed a rapid—and, within ten years, virtually complete—conversion of the atoll's population. The missionaries provided Sikaiana with regular
transportation by sending the mission's ship, the *Southern Cross*, to Sikaiana once
every year. The ship maintained contacts with the missionaries overseeing Sikaiana's
conversion and transported Sikaiana students to the mission's schools, especially at
Maravovo on Guadalcanal and at Pawa on Ugi Island. By the early 1930s, a government vessel also visited Sikaiana once every year to oversee administrative matters, but the Melanesian Mission was the primary source of contact with the outside
world for most of the atoll's population. By this time many of Sikaiana's mature
men had left the atoll, mostly to work on government ships, and many of the older
boys were attending mission schools elsewhere in the Solomon Islands. In the
1930s the Melanesian Mission schools also began accepting Sikaiana girls.

Prior to the outbreak of World War II, in anticipation of the Japanese invasion,
most Sikaiana were repatriated to their atoll. Although there were some visits from
combatants, especially on Allied seaplanes, the government and mission visits
ceased (see Donner 1989). Some Sikaiana claim that by the end of the war they
were so low on trade cloth used for clothing that they considered making an outrigger canoe voyage to Malaita to find some. But the voyage was never undertaken.

Following the war, Sikaiana was again a closed district for labor recruitment. It remained so until labor shortages, resulting from the Maasina or Marching Rule movement, forced the government to allow recruitment there. But the Protectorate's government continued to recruit Sikaiana men for the crew of their ship, *Kurimarau*. In
the late 1940s and early 1950s, many Sikaiana men spent time working on this ship,
returning to Sikaiana when the boat made its yearly visit there. Sometimes these men
signed on for another year; other times they were replaced by different men.

By the end of the 1950s, fewer Sikaiana were working on ships, perhaps because
the government was beginning to require specialized training and certification for
crew members. The Sikaiana, moreover, were no longer restricted from working
abroad. They were emigrating, taking jobs, and raising families away from the atoll.
The majority of these families lived in Honiara.

The government increased its shipping service to Sikaiana in the 1950s and
1960s. In the 1980s one boat was scheduled to go there every month, although this
was variable depending upon repairs and competing demands for its service to other
parts of the Solomon Islands. The boat left Honiara, stopped at Auki, the capital of
Malaita Province, and then continued to Sikaiana, sometimes stopping at Dai Island, off the north coast of Malaita. The trip from Honiara to Sikaiana takes about

thirty-six hours. Usually, the boat arrives at Sikaiana at about 9:00 A.M. and departs at 4:00 P.M. the same day.

As the Sikaiana people became frequent voyagers on steamships, their indigenous seafaring technology changed and was simplified. From the late 1960s until the present, the Sikaiana constructed only two outrigger canoes. Instead, they construct single-hulled dugout canoes *(manaui)*, which are adequate for travel inside the lagoon and, when at sea, close to the reef. I was told that the *manaui* is not indigenous to Sikaiana; rather, it is modeled on canoes seen on trading ships earlier in this century.

Sikaiana people frequently move back and forth between Honiara and Sikaiana. They leave Sikaiana for training programs, education, work, or to visit relatives. They return on their holidays or for longer periods between employment to enjoy Sikaiana's lifestyle, which many find to be relaxed in comparison with the demands of earning wages in Honiara. Most Sikaiana people now reside in one of two locations, Sikaiana or Honiara, but they still form one community of interest and association. Sea travel between Honiara and Sikaiana is integral in the present-day life of their community.

The departure of the ship from Honiara and its arrival on Sikaiana are important events. When the boat departs from Honiara, many people go to the dock to talk with other Sikaiana, to bid farewell to departing friends and relatives, and to send messages or supplies for those on the atoll. On Sikaiana, people listen to the national radio service on their portable radios for news of the ship's arrival. Until destroyed by a cyclone in 1986, the atoll's cooperative store was supplied by this ship. Many of the items sold in the store, including rice, tea, sugar, tobacco, and kerosene, are considered necessities in the local economy. The store's stock was financed by selling its members' copra to a supplier in Honiara. After the cyclone, the government's ship brought needed relief supplies.

The day of the ship's arrival on Sikaiana is very busy. People unload arriving relatives and supplies; they load copra and departing relatives. Government officials sometimes take the boat to Sikaiana and hold community meetings or court cases. The boat cannot dock inside the reef because there are no passages that are deep enough, and the ocean floor outside the reef falls so steeply that ships cannot anchor. The boat circles in the ocean as canoes travel two or three kilometers across the reef to reach it. The arrival of the ship is also an emotional time. Relatives, lovers, and friends arrive and depart. There are usually good-bye parties on the nights before the expected arrival, and good-bye songs are an important genre in Sikaiana song composition (see Donner 1987).

No history of Sikaiana voyaging would be complete without describing the tragic event in July 1958 when one of the government's vessels, the *Melanesia*, disappeared, and everyone was lost. The *Melanesia* was taking Sikaiana people and government administrators to the atoll when it disappeared. A government investigation could find no evidence of abnormal weather, unbalanced load, or faulty navigational equipment. The report also discounted the various rumors that the boat had been sunk by a submarine, a drifting mine left from World War II, or the explosion of dynamite hidden on board (which some Solomon Islanders use for fishing). The report did note that several months earlier a section of the hull, 24' by 4'6", was so badly corroded that it had to be replaced, although the ship was only two years old. The report concluded, based on the few remains, that the boat went down suddenly; but the cause could not be determined (BSIP 13:II:3, 4, 5, 6, 7, 8).

The event was tragic for Sikaiana. The government report lists eighteen Sikaiana people lost, although there may have been more. Every family felt the loss of relatives. In the 1980s many Sikaiana still did not believe that the ship had sunk. They suspect that the boat was hijacked by some foreign power, most often said to be the Soviet Union, where they believe its passengers continue to reside. During my stay there were rumors that someone had actually heard about these relatives from a crew member of a ship from the Soviet Union that supposedly docked in Honiara. One well-educated Sikaiana man speculated that either the United States or the Soviet Union hijacked the ship to use the passengers in experiments for their space programs, which, he pointed out, were just beginning at that time.[6]

Certainly the Sikaiana reaction to the loss of the *Melanesia* involves elements of denial: many still cannot believe that their relatives are dead. But in my opinion their denial can also be understood as part of their cultural understandings about voyaging and the outside world. They do not fear drowning as much as they fear the potential for harm that comes from isolation. The *Melanesia,* in the view of many Sikaiana, did not sink, but, isolated on the seas, it was hijacked by a strong and malevolent foreign power. This sense of vulnerability to the devious motivations of powerful outsiders is a frequent theme in Sikaiana attitudes toward voyaging and interaction with the outside world.

THE SEA AND SEAFARING: METAPHORS OF SOCIAL LIFE

There are two locations for life on the atoll: the sea and the land. The distinction between these areas is marked by two words that are among the most frequently spoken: *uta* 'landward' and *tai* 'seaward'. Like the nautical terms *bow, stern, starboard,* and *port, uta* and *tai* are relative. The Sikaiana person standing at the shore will motion toward the interior of the islet and describe it as 'landward' and then will look toward the direction of the ocean and describe it as 'seaward'. The reef itself is a giant oval that surrounds the lagoon and is surrounded by the Pacific Ocean. The reef is always 'landward' from both the lagoon and ocean side. 'Seaward' can be opposite directions, depending upon where one is standing. Outside the reef, it is always away from the atoll, toward the open ocean; inside the reef, it is always in the opposite direction, toward the center of the lagoon (see Feinberg 1988b). The Sikaiana residing in Honiara have adapted these terms to their lives there. The business district of Honiara, with its stores and market, is 'seaward', while the suburbs and residential areas away from the business district are 'landward'. A Sikaiana person from the suburbs of Honiara will describe going to town as going 'seaward', and returning home as going 'landward', even though the entire trip in both directions is along the coast.

Terms and metaphors for seafaring pervade the daily speech of Sikaiana people and have been adapted to modern circumstances. The term for 'boat', *vaka*, is used to designate all sailing vessels, from yachts to aircraft carriers. The term is also extended to other types of vessel, including airplanes (*vaka lele i anna*, literally 'vessel that flies above') and submarines (*vaka uku i lalo*, literally 'vessel that dives below'). Sailing terms apply to some, although far from all, aspects of travel by automobile. Turning both an automobile and a canoe is described by the word *pale* 'turn'. But *huli*, which can also mean to 'turn' direction in a car, means 'turn over' when describing a canoe. Steering either a canoe or car is designated by the verb *lulu*. The term for a car's steering wheel, *lulu hoe*, is formed by combining *lulu* 'steer' with *hoe* 'canoe paddle'. The automobile itself, however, is called *motokaa*, a borrowing from English.

Older people sometimes use the term *vaka* 'vessel' or 'boat' to refer to a group of people who are living together or cooperating, but younger people do not use this idiom. In the Sikaiana card game *kaihulihuli*, however, there are round-robin games between different teams. These teams are always called *vaka*. Teams in other sports competitions are not referred to by this term; usually they are called *timi*, derived from the English word 'team'. Before the atoll's conversion to Christianity in the 1930s, there were some men who claimed to be possessed by the spirits of their deceased ancestors. These spirit mediums were described as the spirits' *vaka*.

Idioms concerning sailing are still used in everyday speech. A person who has fallen onto some misfortune, usually as a result of his own ineptitude or bad luck, can say, "*toku vaka ku pili*" 'my boat has run aground'. Another idiom describes someone who gives bad advice, "*taatou ka ppili i a koe*" 'we are going to run aground on account of you'. In both usages, the term for running ashore in a boat, *pili*, and the resulting damage to the vessel are used as a metaphor for general misfortune.

The verb describing the activities of the go-between in courtship, *hakasaosao*, is related to the term for taking a canoe across the reef, *hakasao*. On Sikaiana the passages are shallow, and the surf hits directly upon the reef. It takes considerable skill to move a canoe into the ocean without swamping or battering it against the reef. In their romantic affairs, young men and women should not be seen together in public. Initial courtship is usually conducted in secrecy, and it takes some skill to arrange a meeting. *Hakasaosao* was used to depict the activities of a go-between who arranged secret adulterous liaisons in traditional society. At present, it is used to describe someone who helps lovers arrange their secret meetings.

The sea and seafaring are common metaphors in Sikaiana song composition. Traditional songs composed before the middle of this century refer to boats and seafaring in a variety of contexts. In one song, a young man compares his secret love affair to a dangerous sailing voyage—he and his lover lack the necessary skills and materials to complete their voyage. A pair of songs, one composed as an insult and the other its reply, describe a man without any children as a person waiting for a boat that does not arrive. In another song, a young man laments his inability to find a wife, describing himself as an outrigger canoe without the parts that are essential for navigation. One song pokes fun at an overly fastidious man by comparing him with the captain of the government's ship, the *Rinadi,* always trying to keep his ship clean.

Songs in traditional style are rarely composed at present, but composition for guitar accompaniment has become very popular among Sikaiana's younger people. The ocean, voyaging, and boats are frequent images in these songs. Departure songs, composed for separating friends or lovers, often depict the imminent arrival of a government ship. Other guitar songs use images from seafaring. Rough seas, high winds, and drifting are frequent metaphors for adversity or loneliness. One young man composed a guitar song referring to *Hine Taulani,* a traditional spirit associated with long-distance voyaging in outrigger canoes. Another song, composed to tease the young men, uses the metaphor of a traveling canoe to describe a young maiden's enticing, but for the young men unattainable, beauty (see Donner 1987).

Seafaring and work associated with the sea are often viewed as masculine activities in Oceanic cultures, as noted in most of the essays in this volume. Often this association is part of a symbolic distinction between the sea as a male domain and the interior of the island as a female one. In general, this distinction holds for Sikaiana, but there must be some qualifications. Women go to the sea to collect shellfish and sometimes to fish. Men go to the interior bush to clear gardens, plant some crops, and collect coconuts. Some men acquire reputations for being good workers on land but not being adept in salt water; other men are notorious for their lack of interest in working on land but are known for their ability at sea. Sikaiana expect men to be able to do both kinds of work, although more prestige is associated with being capable at sea.

Men are more involved than women with the world beyond the reef. Men manage relations with foreign visitors, control the atoll's administrative institutions, and are more likely to emigrate to other parts of the Solomon Islands. But Sikaiana women also have a long history of involvement with outsiders. In the nineteenth century, whalers and traders took a few women away from Sikaiana. Missionaries took men to their schools before they took women, although, even before World War II, many young women left the atoll to attend mission schools. In the 1930s a group of Sikaiana women persuaded the leaders of the Melanesian Mission to establish a sisterhood, and these women became its first members. At present, many women live in Honiara and work for wages, and they travel almost as much as men.

BEYOND THE REEF: CULTURE CONTACT AS RISKY OPPORTUNITY

Throughout Sikaiana history, the sea and sea voyaging have offered both opportunity and danger. Sikaiana's isolation makes its people both suspicious of, and fascinated with, outsiders and their cultural traditions. Sikaiana legends depict the vulnerability of the atoll's inhabitants. Its founder hero, Tehui Atahu, staked his original claim when the atoll was still submerged. He returned to find the atoll above water and inhabited by people, the *Hetuna,* whom he proceeded to deceive and slaughter. The atoll's vulnerability to invasion is reflected in the legends concerning marauders from Tona, the plot by Kiribati (Gilbertese) immigrants to murder their Sikaiana hosts, and the hijacking of the *Melanesia.* One person told me that, in former times, men rather than women worked on a back-strap loom. The men found, however, that their legs were too cramped to fight in emergencies, and women took over the work. Even today, Sikaiana people are somewhat mistrustful of outside visitors to their atoll, wondering about their motivations and, at the same time, curious to meet them.

In traditional times, new arrivals to Sikaiana were called the *tonu* of the chief. The chief had the right to decide whether the immigrants should live or die. If allowed to live, as seems often to have been the case, the chief decided where they would reside, usually assigning some family line to look after them. In some cases, immigrants and their descendants had special ritual roles, notably as *pule*, who served as ritual guardians enforcing prohibitions on harvesting special fruits. Perhaps chiefs trusted these migrants because they were dependent upon the chiefs' patronage. From genealogies and family histories, it is also clear that many immigrants were warmly received, perhaps because their host families learned new rituals, technology, songs, and dances.

The Sikaiana's feeling of isolation is enhanced by their sense that the atoll offers limited resources. Oral traditions depict a period known as *te tulana o te sekeseke* 'the period of famine', a time before coconuts were planted, when Sikaiana's inhabitants constantly suffered from food shortage. Even today, although proud of their atoll, people often say that Sikaiana's resources are limited.

Novelty is valued in present-day Sikaiana life. New fashions, new clothes, new songs and dances, and even new fishing techniques are enthusiastically, if only temporarily, adopted. In their traditional life, long-distance voyaging was probably undertaken in part as the result of curiosity and excitement for contact with outsiders.

This sense of curiosity and excitement pervaded Sikaiana relations with Europeans. In the nineteenth century, traders and whalers found the Sikaiana to be very friendly, probably because the Sikaiana people appreciated both the novelty and material goods such contacts brought them. A writer (possibly Andrew Cheyne) in the *Nautical Magazine* of 1848 wrote:

> I would advise all ships bound to China and Manila from South Wales to sight this group for the purpose of their chronometers. No danger need be apprehended from the hostility of its inhabitants, as they are very hospitable, and few in number, there being only 38 able bodied men on the group. . . . I have had much intercourse with these natives and can recommend them as being trustworthy. (Anonymous 1848:575)

Another mid-nineteenth-century visitor wrote:

> If the inhabitants of the Solomon group were the most savage race of men we encountered throughout our cruise, these amiable Sikayanese left on us the impression of being the most moral and peacefully disposed race of aborigines that we became acquainted with, and even to this day the few fleeting but highly suggestive hours we spent with these primitive people are among the most singular, yet delightful, on which memory rests, when recalling the incidents of our circumnavigation. (Schertzer 1861:622–23)

In a paper read to the Royal Geographical Society, which was published in 1916, Charles Woodford cited Andrew Cheyne's quite favorable impression of the Sikaiana people and added his own agreement:

> He [Cheyne] describes the natives as "without exception the best disposed he has met with among the islands." This character I have great pleasure in being able to confirm. (1916:41)

This favorable European impression continued into the twentieth century and certainly enhanced Sikaiana interactions with Europeans (see Lambert 1941:109–10; WPHC 1925:938; *Time* 1943[41]:38, 40).

In the nineteenth and twentieth centuries, Sikaiana people were interested in leaving the atoll, in part to make money and acquire trade goods, and in part to have contacts with the outside world. As early as 1902, one visitor wrote about the Sikaiana people:

> They wanted to learn reading and writing. My friend was asked if he would stop on the island as a teacher. They offered him a house and a certain number of coconut palms. (Nerdum 1902:24)

This interest in education seems to have been partly a result of a desire for access to Western material goods. It was also partly the result of a desire to know more about the outside world. In 1936 the bishop in charge of Anglican missionary activities in the Solomon Islands described

> A growing restlessness on the part of the [Sikaiana] people who want more and more to be in touch with the wider life of the group. (BSIP 1:III:F 49/6, letter from Walter Baddley dated 31 August 1936)

In a comparative study of migration patterns on Polynesian outliers, Bayliss-Smith (1975) found that Sikaiana was the atoll that had both the earliest contact with outsiders and the most extensive emigration. (His figures actually underestimate emigration.) Ontong Java, by contrast, had a reputation for hostility toward outsiders in the nineteenth century, and today the people of Ontong Java are considered to be conservative by the Sikaiana people. Firth (1963:chapter 1) describes Tikopian curiosity about the outside world in 1928 and 1929 in a manner that is very similar to Sikaiana. But, perhaps because of lack of opportunity, present-day Tikopians and Anutans remain more traditional and conservative than most Sikaiana, both in their migration patterns and in their reluctance to adopt Western practices.

There is long and continuing debate about the reasons for Oceanic seafaring (Buck 1938; Sharp 1956; Lewis 1972). Feinberg (1988a:chapter 8) has suggested that Anutan seafaring is in large part the result of a sense of adventure and excitement. In a review of Feinberg's book, Alkire (1990) challenges Feinberg's analysis and argues that interisland voyaging most often has economic value. In the Sikaiana case, it is difficult to find strictly utilitarian value in pre-European long-distance voyaging. The trips were hazardous, and the canoes were small. Nor does voyaging seem a practical way to resolve environmental crises, as it may have been in the Caroline Islands (see Alkire 1965). A sudden cyclone probably would destroy most canoes and supplies. After the shock of a cyclone, it seems unlikely that many Sikaiana families would have wanted to risk the hazards of long-distance voyages, especially in light of uncertain receptions at destinations where their unprepared hosts had population burdens of their own.

It is doubtful that, in the time before European contacts, maintaining ties with other islands and accepting some strangers with hospitality provided the Sikaiana people with trade and material resources. Instead, it provided them the wealth of ideas that are carried in the mind and do not take up valuable space in the canoe. New songs, new dances, new rituals, and new fashions were the result of this contact. These contacts also may have provided knowledge about new technology and methods of food production.[7]

The direct material and utilitarian advantages of interactions with outsiders became great only after European contact, because manufactured technology, especially steel tools, offered immense advantages over the shell technology used by the Sikaiana. Today, because of their increased population, the Sikaiana must emigrate to survive. Nevertheless, even at present, when imported technology is essential for their economy and emigration is a necessity, the excitement of interaction with others remains very important in their relations with the outside world (see Carucci; Howard; Feinberg, all this volume).

CONCLUSION: THE VOYAGING ETHIC AND THE SPIRIT OF SIKAIANA MODERNIZATION

The Sikaiana have rapidly incorporated many Western institutions into their lives, and they have eagerly pursued opportunities to emigrate from the atoll. Nevertheless, they have maintained a sense of themselves as a separate community. This community is maintained through ties of kinship, fosterage, exchange, ceremonial events, and common interests and commitments. This process parallels the history of Sikaiana voyaging and, more generally, their relationships as the residents of a small and isolated atoll with outsiders. They look beyond themselves at the same time that they preserve their distinctiveness.

Over the past four centuries, the modes of transportation have changed and, although voyaging is no longer undertaken in outrigger canoes, the percentage of the population that travels has increased. During Luka's time in the sixteenth and seventeenth centuries, voyaging, probably quite rare, was the activity of a few adventurous men. In the nineteenth century, contacts with traders and whalers provided opportunities for men to voyage on European vessels. During the twentieth century, voyaging in cargo ships became a regular part of Sikaiana life, both for the men who worked on government ships and for those who migrated to other parts of the Solomon Islands. As manufactured goods became important in the local economy and as the Sikaiana became partial to many consumer goods, life overseas offered opportunities to earn the money needed to purchase these goods. In the early twentieth century, men worked abroad to earn cash, usually with the intention of returning to the atoll. After World War II, many Sikaiana families became permanent migrants, and their children were raised abroad. These people maintain ties with other Sikaiana and visit the atoll, although their lives are centered elsewhere, and many have bought land in other parts of the Solomon Islands. Moreover, the population increase has made it impossible for the atoll to support all the people who have claims to its resources. Living abroad has been transformed from a temporary adventure to a permanent way of life.

Throughout Sikaiana's history, the sea has provided the food resources necessary for survival on the atoll. The sea, however, is more than a resource. It is also an avenue for contact with outsiders. This relationship with the sea and voyaging saturates Sikaiana social life, not only in former times when they voyaged in outrigger canoes but also today when they travel in boats and jets. The Sikaiana have been consistently interested in meeting foreigners and, over the past fifty years, in adopting and participating in Western institutions. But in doing so, whether migrants in Honiara or participants in the Western institutions established on the atoll, they have preserved themselves as a separate community. By choice they are no longer isolated; more than most other local communities in the Solomon Islands, they have adopted Western institutions and made them into their own. Still, they maintain themselves as distinct and separate; whether working in Honiara or residing on the atoll, they remain, at least through the latter part of the twentieth century, a group of people with special commitments to one another.

The cautious desire for foreign contacts and adventure while maintaining ties with one another are constant themes in Sikaiana social life, from the legendary times of Kaetekita and Semalu to the present. They are fascinated with the world beyond, but they are also somewhat enclosed, in the past by their vulnerable isolation and at present by their communal institutions.

NOTES

1. Jacob Love (personal communication) informs me that Levao is a plausible name for a Samoan.

2. The only direction in which sea travel is relatively safe is toward the west, where the land mass of Malaita is hard to miss. But the Sikaiana say they generally avoided this direction out of fear of Malaitans, who had reputations for hostility and violence. Instead, they maintained contacts with the much smaller and more distant atolls inhabited by Polynesian-speaking peoples—in particular, Ontong Java and the islands of the Santa Cruz group (notably Nukapu, Taumako, and Pileni). Reaching these islands would have taken considerable navigational skill, and missing the destination would probably have resulted in death in the open expanses of the Pacific Ocean.

3. I have found one minor indication of traditional interisland sailing techniques. In a song that metaphorically compared an adulterous relationship with a long-distance voyage, one verse described a *tai polau.* During my first stay from 1980 to 1983, none of the older

men could tell me this term's meaning. In 1987 a younger man who had traveled to other Polynesian islands while working on freighters suggested to me that the term referred to wooden boards used as navigational charts.

4. There was no legend about Luka known by Sikaiana people at the time of my stay, although a few had read accounts of him in history books. It cannot be assumed with absolute certainty that the inhabitants of Sikaiana at Luka's time were ancestral to the present-day inhabitants, but his story does fit nicely with other Sikaiana legends about contacts with Taumako. Semalu and Kaetekita lived about ten to twelve generations ago.

5. According to my informant, this suicide voyage was undertaken by a humiliated woman.

6. Similarly, Anutans believe that two canoes whose crew were lost in the 1940s made landfall in either 'Uvea or Samoa, where they still reside (Feinberg 1988a:26–27, 158–59, and personal communication).

7. The Sikaiana have a legend, about which I am skeptical, that says coconuts were brought there by an immigrant. In any case, this contact was accidental, not the benefit of maintaining a seafaring tradition.

REFERENCES

Alkire, William
  1965   *Lamotrek Atoll and Interisland Socioeconomic Ties.* Illinois Studies in Anthropology No. 5. Urbana and London: University of Illinois Press.
  1990   Review of *Polynesian Seafaring and Navigation: Ocean Travel in Anutan Culture and Society,* by Richard Feinberg. *American Ethnologist* 17:588–89.
Anonymous
  1848   *Nautical Magazine,* Vol. 17.
Bayliss-Smith, Tim
  1975   The Central Polynesian Outlier populations since European contact. In *Pacific Atoll Populations,* edited by Vern Carroll, pp. 286–343. ASAO Monograph No. 3. Honolulu: University of Hawai'i Press.
Bennett, Judith A.
  1987   *Wealth of the Solomons: A History of a Pacific Archipelago, 1800–1978.* Pacific Islands Monograph Series No. 3. Honolulu: University of Hawai'i Press.
BSIP
  n.d.   British Solomon Islands Protectorate, Government Correspondence. National Archives, Honiara, Solomon Islands.
Buck, Peter (Te Hiroa Rangi)
  1938   *Vikings of the Pacific.* Christchurch, N.Z.: Whitcombe and Tombs.
Davenport, William
  1964   Notes on Santa Cruz voyaging. *Journal of the Polynesian Society* 73:134–42.
Donner, William
  1987   Don't shoot the guitar player: tradition, assimilation and change in Sikaiana song composition. *Journal of the Polynesian Society* 96:201–21.
  1989   'Far-away' and 'close-up': World War II and Sikaiana perceptions of their place in the world. In *The Pacific Theater: Islander Representations of World War II,* edited by Geoffrey White and Lamont Lindstrom. Honolulu: University of Hawai'i Press.
Feinberg, Richard
  1988a *Polynesian Seafaring and Navigation: Ocean Travel in Anutan Culture and Society.*

Kent, Ohio: Kent State University Press.

1988b   Socio-spatial symbolism and the logic of rank on two Polynesian outliers. *Ethnology* 73:291–310.

Firth, Raymond
1963   *We the Tikopia: A Sociological Study of Kinship in Primitive Polynesia.* (1936) Abridged by author. Boston: Beacon Press.
1967   Suicide and risk taking. In *Tikopia Ritual and Belief.* (1961), pp. 116–40. Boston: Beacon Press.

Jack-Hinton, Colin
1969   *The Search for the Islands of Solomon, 1567–1838.* Oxford: Clarendon Press.

Lambert, S. M.
1941   *A Yankee Doctor in Paradise.* Boston: Little, Brown and Company.

Lewis, David
1972   *We the Navigators: The Ancient Art of Landfinding in the Pacific.* Honolulu: University of Hawai'i Press.

Maude, H. E.
1970   Baiteke and Binoka of Abemama, arbiters of change in the Gilbert Islands. In *Pacific Island Portraits,* edited by W. Davidson and Deryck Scarr. Canberra: Australian National University Press.

Nerdum, J. G. B.
1902   Indtryk og oplevelser under 7 aars ophold paa Salomonderme. *Norwegian Geographical Society Yearbook* 1901–1902:22–55. (English translation courtesy of Roger Green, Department of Anthropology, University of Auckland.)

PMB
n.d.   Pacific Manuscripts Bureau. Microfilm rolls. Hamilton Library, University of Hawai'i.

Sarfert, Ernst, and Hans Damm
1929–1931   *Luangiua und Nukumanu, Ergebunsse der Sudsee Expedition 1908–1910,* Vol. 12. Abt 2 Ethnographie B. Mikronesien.

Schertzer, Karl
1861   *Narrative of the Circumvention . . . by the Austrian Frigate Novara.* London: Saunders Otley and Company.

Sharp, Andrew
1956   *Ancient Voyagers in the Pacific.* Polynesian Society Memoir No. 32. Wellington: The Polynesian Society.

Time
1943   Seductive Sikaiana. *Time* 41(24):38, 40.

Webster, John
1863   *The Last Cruise of Wanderer.* Sydney: F. Cunningham.

Woodford, Charles
1906   Some account of Sikaiana or Stewart's Island in the British Solomon Islands Protectorate. *Man* 6:164–69.
1916   On some little-known Polynesian settlements in the neighbourhood of the Solomon Islands. *Geographical Journal* 48:26–54.

WPHC
1925   Western Pacific High Command. Correspondence. Microfilm. University of Auckland.

CONTINUITY AND CHANGE IN NUKUMANU MARITIME TECHNOLOGY AND PRACTICE

Richard Feinberg

• Nukumanu, also known as the Tasman Islands, is an atoll populated by Polyne-sian-speaking people on the eastern border of Papua New Guinea's North Solomons Province. It is small and geographically isolated, and largely for that rea-son, much of the community's traditional culture has been retained. Indeed, Nuku-manu is one of a mere handful of Polynesian communities that have rejected Chris-tian missions in favor of older religious practice and belief, even through the time of my field study in the 1980s. Although a century of European contact has led to changes in the atoll's social and economic life, those changes have been integrated into a distinctively traditional cosmology (Feinberg 1985, 1986, 1990).

These observations are as true of the community's relations to the sea as they are of spheres of life discussed in detail elsewhere. Nukumanu use their maritime envi-ronment in much the same way as their forebears, often utilizing traditional craft, equipment, and techniques. Yet, the sea is also used in new ways and for new pur-poses. The old craft are being modified in response to the new purposes for which they are employed, and techniques are similarly undergoing alteration. In this essay, I explore issues of continuity and change in Nukumanu maritime technology and practice.

NUKUMANU USE OF THE SEA

As an atoll, Nukumanu consists of a narrow strip of land surrounding a large in-ner lagoon and surrounded by the ocean. No one on the atoll is ever more than a few meters from the sea. The sight and sound of waves and water are constant facts of life. Children play in the sea, and adults derive much of their livelihood from the lagoon and ocean. As in earlier times, islanders' major source of protein consists of fish and shellfish. The most efficient means of travel to outer islets for purposes of gardening and collecting coconuts as well as for procuring fish and shellfish involves crossing the lagoon by canoe. And interisland voyaging, particularly to Ontong Java Atoll, Nukumanu's nearest neighbor just over forty kilometers to the south, has for generations been a major focus of social and symbolic interest.

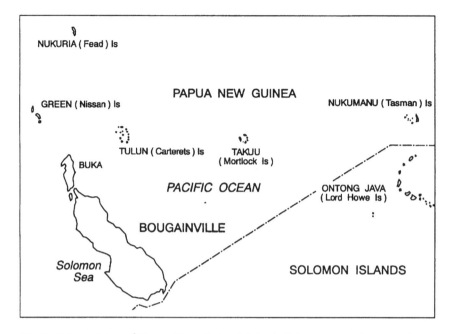

FIGURE 8.1.   Map of Papua New Guinea's North Solomons Province and international border with the Solomon Islands, including Ontong Java Atoll in the Solomon Islands.

While old uses of the sea have been maintained, several new ones have been added in the recent past. European contact has led to dependence on imported wheat flour and rice as staple foods. Metal tools, monofilament fishing line, kerosene lanterns, and other commodities of European manufacture are now regarded as necessities, and dependence on imported goods requires cash with which to purchase them. Nukumanu's major sources of cash in 1984 were bêche-de-mer, trochus, and copra, the first two being marine products.

Nukumanu sailors travel regularly to Ontong Java. During my field study in 1984, an average of one to two journeys a week took place between the two communities. Otherwise, interisland canoe voyaging has been almost wholly discontinued. With the exception of sailors who are blown off course between Ontong Java and Nukumanu, interisland contact is by European ship. As such vessels are both safer and more comfortable than voyaging canoes, and as interisland visitors no longer live in fear of being killed by hostile or suspicious hosts, modern shipping has expanded the Nukumanu's geographical and social universe. Moreover, shipping has provided wage employment for many Nukumanu (cf. Donner; Howard this volume). Many men now work as crew aboard government or commercial ships. At the time of my visit, one young man had taken a job as navigator aboard a national defense force patrol boat. Another managed a commercial shipping company.

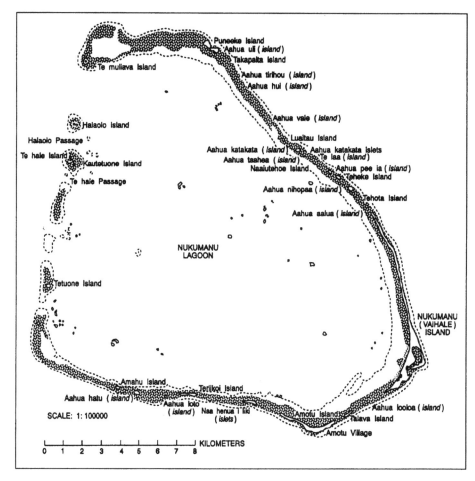

FIGURE 8.2. Nukumanu Atoll (based on North Solomons provincial government map).

VESSELS

Nukumanu employ several types of craft. These include European-style ships and launches, fiberglass canoes, and wooden outrigger canoes. In earlier times, long-distance voyaging canoes constituted an additional variety.

European-style ships and launches are not constructed on Nukumanu, nor are any owned or under the control of an atoll dweller. Over the past century, however, islanders have grown accustomed to such craft. In the years since contact, European shipping has become the major means of interisland travel. Until recent civil strife on Bougainville, Nukumanu maintained contact with the outside world via ships that were either owned by the North Solomons provincial government or chartered by the government from a commercial shipping company. At the time of my study,

authorities tried to arrange for visits to the atoll by official vessels at three-week intervals. An assortment of mechanical failures, bad weather, and emergencies elsewhere in the province, however, resulted in the schedule being honored primarily in
the breach.

Nukumanu often journey to other parts of Papua New Guinea seeking wage
employment, hospital care, schooling, a break from the routine of atoll life, and to
visit relatives. Sale of copra, bêche-de-mer, and trochus and importing food and European goods also require interisland contacts. Occasional visits by private sailing
yachts bring news about the outside world and a chance to trade for supplies.

Nukumanu has a fairly wide passage into its large lagoon, and neither government ships nor sailing yachts have difficulty traversing the channel. Most of the
islets, however, have extensive reef flats, in some cases extending almost a kilometer
into the lagoon. Therefore, any vessel with much draft must anchor a good way
from shore. To transport passengers and cargo to and from the beach, most ships
have a launch, and yachts are usually equipped with dinghies. Still, movement of
personnel and cargo most often is accomplished by canoe. Canoes are the vessels
commonly used on the atoll for most other purposes as well—for fishing, transportation among the atoll's many islets, and, to a limited degree, interisland travel.

CANOES

Western observers have commented on the canoes of Nukumanu and the essen-
tially similar ones of Ontong Java for over a century. One of the earliest accounts
was published in 1897 by Richard Parkinson, the German planter, on the basis of
repeated visits in his capacity as a supervisor for the Forsayth copra company.
Parkinson's description is as follows:

> The Nukumanu and Ontong Javanese must depend on driftwood for building their
> canoes, since they do not have trees large enough for this purpose. By the number of
> vessels in the area, one would judge that the sea provides sufficient materials. Almost
> every canoe shows signs of long and hard use, with many patches on its planks. The
> pieces of driftwood are not always big enough for a boat; thus, several pieces must be
> joined, so that you may find light and dark woods used together without regard for
> pattern or distribution. . . . The canoes vary in size from small ones which hold only
> two people to 16 meters long, accommodating twenty people. However, they all have
> the same shape: a long trough with straight keel and rectilinear edge, the ends bent
> slightly back of the keel. Some have short decks fore and aft, which serve as a seat for
> the helmsman. Stability is provided by an outrigger. Many canoes also carry a triangu-
> lar sail, and it is amazing how fast these clumsy and often fragile boats can go even in
> stormy weather outside the lagoon. If the boat capsizes no great harm is done, as the
> people easily right it and swing themselves on board. If women or children are taken
> aboard, they are protected from sun and/or rain by a shed made of pandanus leaves.
> (Parkinson 1986 [1897]:20–21)

Parkinson's observations figure prominently in the accounts presented by Sarfert
and Damm (1929) and Haddon and Hornell (1975 [1936–1938]). Except for ex-

aggerated claims regarding the atolls' dependence upon driftwood (see below), a misplaced characterization of Nukumanu canoes as "clumsy and fragile," and evident abandonment of the pandanus-leaf sheds, Parkinson's description could serve as well for 1984 as for a century earlier.

Today, Nukumanu vessels include outriggerless fiberglass craft of European manufacture and locally produced wooden outrigger canoes. The former are known as *na faipa* (from 'fiberglass') and are a recent introduction. At the time of my investigation, there were just two on the atoll. They are expensive to acquire and operate, as they must be purchased overseas and are invariably powered by outboard motor. On the other hand, they are durable and require little maintenance. Outrigger canoes, by contrast, are abundant. They cost little or no cash to produce, and they may be propelled by paddle, pole, or sail as well as outboard engine, making them far cheaper to operate. However, they do require a substantial investment of time and effort to build and maintain.

Haddon and Hornell (1975 [1936–1938]:II:70), following Sarfert and Damm, list five classes of outrigger canoe:

Pepekau: the old interisland voyaging canoes.

Haitakui: large sailing canoes, up to eighteen meters in length but of less refined construction than *pepekau*.

Vaka loloa: literally 'long canoe', of similar dimensions to the *haitakui* but not equipped with sails, and used primarily for fishing.

Vakalo: an evident misrendering of *vaka alo*, literally, 'paddling canoe'. These were large vessels sometimes equipped with mat shelters in the center.

Papau: a probable misrendering of *paopao*. These were small canoes, not more than five meters in length. The larger canoes of this type, according to Sarfert and Damm, were termed *papau lahi* 'large *papau*'; smaller ones were *papau soliliki* 'small *papau*'.

Either Nukumanu words for canoe types have changed a good deal over the past century, or a number of these terms were misconstrued by Sarfert and his predecessors. On the other hand, Parkinson's observation (1986 [1897]:20) that Nukumanu outrigger canoes vary more in size than fundamental design is as true today as it was in the 1890s. Size, however, is important. The smallest canoes (*paavaka* or *paopao*) are utilized exclusively for fishing and collecting mollusks near the village islet. They hold only one or perhaps two passengers at a time, and they only are propelled by pole and paddle.

Larger canoes present a very different picture. In contrast with small ones, which may be little more than two meters in length and boast but two or three outrigger booms, *Solair*, one of the atoll's largest vessels, measures 12.5 meters at the gunwales. The canoe is equipped with seven outrigger booms. The outrigger float is 9.5 meters in length. At the ends, the canoe's height is 1.1 meters; even amidships, it is 85 centimeters from keel to gunwales. From the outrigger float to the opposite gunwale is 2.4 meters amidships and 2.2 meters at the ends; and the bow deck extends a full two meters. As of 1984, Nukumanu had three other vessels in this size range. Five more were a half meter shorter.

Nukumanu also carefully note the width of their canoes. *Solair* was cited as the widest vessel on the atoll; *Arovotahi*, which I thought looked equally wide, was described as having the highest gunwales. From the amount of cargo that it holds, however, I was told that one can see it is "not nearly as wide" as *Solair*.

Large vessels such as these, as well as many in the middle range, may be rigged with bow and stern decks and either sails or outboard motors. Sailing canoes *(puke)* may take several sailors at a time and are used for travel to distant islets for purposes of collecting copra, taro, bêche-de-mer, and trochus as well as fish. If a canoe is sufficiently large and seaworthy, it may also be employed for the forty-kilometer voyage over open ocean to Ontong Java (see figure 8.1). Such trips typically include eight to ten voyagers per canoe.

In addition to *faipa* and outrigger canoes, Nukumanu recognize outriggerless canoes, which they term *mola*. They do not make such canoes themselves, nor are there any on the atoll. However, they are familiar with *mola* as a canoe design preferred by many Melanesians, whom Nukumanu know from their travels around the Solomon Islands and Papua New Guinea (see Hviding this volume). One informant commented that there is a large *mola* in Pelau, Ontong Java, built by a Melanesian who was resident there for some years. It is seaworthy and is sometimes rigged for sail or outboard motor. Outrigger hulls, because of their narrow contours, will not stay upright should the outrigger become detached. By contrast, *mola* are constructed in such a way as to remain stable without the additional support of an outrigger.

In former times, the Nukumanu vessels par excellence were *vaka hai laa*, great interisland voyaging canoes in which informants claim their predecessors journeyed to isles hundreds of miles distant. Sarfert and Damm (1929:196–98) cite the term *pepekau*, a name not used by my informants. Their descriptions make it clear, however, that *vaka hai laa* and *pepekau* designate a single canoe type.

According to Sarfert and Damm (1929:198), the great voyaging canoes were going out of use on Nukumanu and Ontong Java by the late eighteenth century. Early descriptions, however, indicate that they were made from "sound wood" (not driftwood) and resembled in contours the model sailing canoes currently produced on Takuu, a neighboring atoll. They were captained by accomplished navigators called *tinohiti*, who were fortified with magical, as well as technological and astronomical, knowledge.

Accounts given me in 1984 supported this description. One of my primary informants on matters having to do with the ocean and navigation told me that the *vaka hai laa* were huge vessels, almost more like small ships than canoes. The gunwales, he said, would be up to his neck (over 1.5 meters high), and the bow and stern would be a good three meters in the air when standing on land. The craft were more than thirteen meters long, with a full deck and outrigger platform as well as a hold below. Another man claimed *vaka hai laa* carried small canoes on their decks so that sailors could repair the outrigger or hull of the main vessel while at sea.

Vaka hai laa were also known as *vaka tapu* 'sacred canoes'. By contrast, smaller nonsacred canoes were called *paopao*. *Vaka tapu* were *tapu* 'sacred' or 'restricted' in the sense that only certain people could travel in or use them, and they were associated with certain rituals. In particular, for shark fishing, a special food oven would be kindled prior to the expedition. The ceremony would go on for six days and involve extensive use of *tilo*, white leaves from the very top of a coconut palm, which are prominent in many Nukumanu rituals (see Feinberg 1990).

Takuu models of what they claim are their old voyaging canoes, termed *vaka fai laa*, confirm the descriptions of my Nukumanu informants. In addition, the models show a deep-V hull with a great deal of "rocker," in contrast with the round bottoms and straight keel of contemporary vessels on both atolls.

Surprisingly, Nukumanu informants asserted that in the old days, the Takuu did not make or have *vaka hai laa* and did little traveling. Until European times, they said, Nukumanu people had no contact with Takuu or Nukuria, Polynesian outlier atolls to the west and north, nor did they even know of their existence. Other commentators claimed that Nukumanu occasionally voyaged to their western neighbors but that the Nukuria and Takuu did not have voyaging canoes and, therefore, did not reciprocate such visits. Most informants held that virtually all Nukumanu voyaging was to the east, to islands as far-flung as Sikaiana, Tikopia, Anuta, and even (rather implausibly) to New Zealand, Tahiti, and Hawai'i.

My informants' claims about the sparsity of contact with Takuu received some confirmation from Roy Moffatt, an Australian who had worked for the Papua New Guinea government for many years as a ship's captain. Moffatt reported to me that the currents between Nukumanu and Takuu are powerful and treacherous. On one trip, he said, the current "horseshoed around" so that it actually reversed its direction of flow—from south to north—at about the halfway point. The weather was overcast, so he could not get a bearing for many hours at a time. He set the bow of his diesel-powered ship off considerably in an attempt to compensate for the current. Still, when he was able to get a bearing, he found that he was well off course to the north. He calculated the current at that point at 1.8 knots. In a wind-powered canoe, without instruments, the current would pose an even greater hazard than it did for Moffatt. In addition to distance and current, Nukumanu and Takuu are so low as to be visible, even from the deck of a ship, only at distances of ten to fifteen kilometers. Islands to the south and east present a very different picture: they are mostly large volcanic outcroppings, visible from dozens of kilometers away.

Not surprisingly, people from Takuu have quite a different view of their seafaring history. They claim that in olden days they were first-class navigators, while Nukumanu neither had great vessels nor traveled farther than Ontong Java on a regular basis. Sarfert and Damm (1929:197) present a sketch of a model Takuu *vaka fai laa* that looks indistinguishable from those made there currently, while a sketch on the same page of a Nukumanu–Ontong Java–type canoe looks much like those in use today on those two atolls. At the very least, these data indicate that voyaging canoes went out of use much earlier on Nukumanu than Takuu. Sarfert and Damm's review of the historical literature supports this conclusion.

In their inventory of interisland contacts, Sarfert and Damm (1929:183) list just one voyage to Takuu and one to Nukuria from Nukumanu. As for voyages to Nukumanu (pp. 185–86), they cite one from Ontong Java, three from Nukuria, one from Tikopia, one from Tonga, one from Samoa, three from "Tokolau," one from Apemama, one from Moina (?), one from Moleai (?), and one from Anuta. The writers list all of these voyages as "accidental." In addition to these, Nukumanu indicated knowledge of Sikaiana, Nissan, Niutao, Nanumea, Rotuma, New Caledonia, Nukulaelae, Tarawa, Motuiti (?), Manahiki, Rarotonga, Tonga, and a number of other locations (pp. 178–81). It is not clear, however, how the Nukumanu came to know these place names.

Vaka hai laa have not been made for a long time, in part because they were associated with the old *hale aitu* 'spirit houses'.[1] In the days of the traditional religion, the *aliki* 'priest' or 'sacred chief' would captain great canoes and conduct ceremonies in the *hale aitu* to guarantee good weather and a safe journey.[2] Early during the plantation period, a Roman Catholic mission was temporarily established and effectively undermined such practices. Moreover, since contemporary interisland canoe travel is restricted to Pelau and Luangiua (Ontong Java's two communities), great canoes and special rituals no longer are deemed necessary.

Nukumanu boasts a large number of canoes per capita. With a resident population of about four hundred people, I counted a total of eighty canoes, or one for every five persons. By contrast, on Anuta, a Polynesian outlier in the eastern Solomon Islands, in 1972, I counted twenty-two canoes for a resident population of 156 people—a total of fewer than one canoe for every seven persons on the island (see Feinberg 1981, 1988a; for comparable data on Ontong Java, see Bayliss-Smith 1974, 1975). This difference can most likely be attributed to the fact that Anuta is a volcanic island with a fringing reef and no lagoon. Therefore, vessels are used only on the open sea, and for that reason, most canoes are large craft, carrying from three to eight persons. In comparison, many Nukumanu craft are small, narrow, unstable, and designed for use on the lagoon by one or two paddlers.

Perhaps because of the relatively nonstressful conditions under which Nukumanu canoes normally operate, atoll vessels often appear to be somewhat carelessly slapped together. Lack of care in Nukumanu canoe construction, however, is easy to exaggerate, as the difficulty of obtaining quality wood impairs the aesthetics of even the best vessels. Several commentators (e.g., Parkinson 1986 [1897]) have reported erroneously that trees suitable for making canoes do not grow on the Polynesian outlier atolls and that craftsmen are entirely dependent upon driftwood. Such reports are partially correct for the postcontact period: on Takuu, the Forsayth copra company had all large trees cut down to make room for coconut palms (J. Howard, personal communication). On Nukumanu, however, several types of local tree, in addition to driftwood, are used for the construction of canoes, and unauthorized felling of such trees forms the basis of at least occasional court cases. Yet, even on Nukumanu, the wood used for canoes tends to be knotty, insect-eaten, and often partially rotten. In contrast with many atolls, Nukumanu do not appear to make canoes from breadfruit logs.[3]

Canoe Design

Gladwin (1970), in his discussion of Puluwat canoe design, notes four major components: hull, outrigger, sail and rigging, and lee platform. Nukumanu vessels do not have lee platforms. The other three components are the same.

Hull. The hulls of most Nukumanu canoes are low, narrow, and unstable. Especially in the smaller canoes, it may be necessary to place one's feet one in front of the other rather than side by side because of the hull's narrow contours. And more than once I almost swamped a small vessel by unconsciously shifting my weight or moving to sit on one of the gunwales rather than the thwart.

According to Friederici (1912; see also Sarfert and Damm 1929:200), small paddling canoes, at least through the beginning of this century, were built with outriggers permanently attached to the port side, giving the vessels a fixed bow and stern in the usual Polynesian manner. Today, all Nukumanu outrigger canoes are double-ended, following the common Micronesian pattern. Bow (*matavaka i mua* 'front end') and stern (*matavaka i muli* 'back end') are identical and interchangeable. To change tack, the mast and sail are moved to the opposite end of the canoe and their rake reversed. The old bow becomes the new stern, the old stern the new bow, and the canoe sets off in a reciprocal direction. The outrigger is always kept to windward to avoid the possibility of its submerging in a heavy breeze. Both bow and stern are squared off. On larger canoes, this may facilitate the mounting of an outboard engine. However, all canoes are similarly shaped, making me believe that this design is traditional and not a recent accommodation to Western technology.

Hulls are not symmetrical; rather, the nonoutrigger side *(vahi katea)* bulges slightly more than the outrigger side. This is intended to provide additional stability and to help keep the canoe from capsizing in a stiff wind.

Nukumanu canoes are normally operated as completely open boats. However, removable stern, and particularly bow, covers are sometimes added, especially for sailing on windy days or for interisland travel on the open sea, whether the voyage is propelled by sail or motor. The bow cover on a large canoe is about two meters long. The last fifty to seventy-five centimeters of the bow cover is a removable piece. The piece contains a number of ridges projecting upward many centimeters. In addition to providing a kind of socket to brace the end of the yard (see below under "Sail and Rigging"), these ridges help prevent water from pouring over the bow and into the vessel. In a modest chop, even with the bow cover in place, constant bailing is necessary. The Nukumanu bow cover and the system for attaching it to the canoe are illustrated in figures 8.3 and 8.4.

Nukumanu canoe builders do most of their work in one of two areas at either end of Amotu, the main village. Workers carry the log from which the lower hull is to be cut to one of these areas in order to be hollowed out and shaped with an adze. The major tools for such projects are known as *takuu* 'adze' or 'axe'. A chopping axe is *te takuu tuutuu* 'severing adze'; a *takuu taataa* 'hewing adze' has a blade hafted onto a bent shaft with a long handle and short neck; and a *homi* has a blade

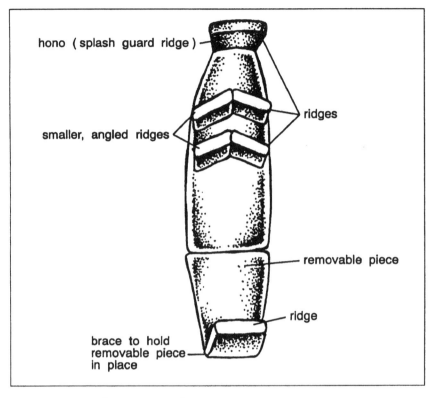

FIGURE 8.3.   Nukumanu canoe bow cover, top view.

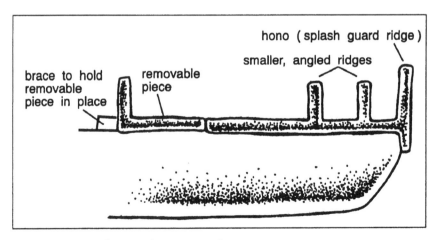

FIGURE 8.4.   Nukumanu bow cover, side view.

hafted to a shaft with a neck almost as long as the handle. *Homi* are primarily for shaping the inside of the narrow hull; *takuu taataa* are for shaping the outside. These types of adze are depicted in figure 8.5.

The lower hull is called by the same term as the canoe, *te vaka*. It is rounded, in contrast with the Carolinian and Anutan deep-V designs, and the freeboard is augmented by the addition of a single plank *(hono)*. The plank is lashed *(hakatau*

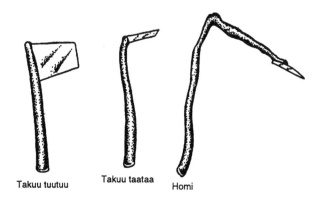

Takuu tuutuu   Takuu taataa   Homi

FIGURE 8.5.   Tools used in canoe construction.

FIGURE 8.6.   Carpenter working on the inside of a canoe hull with a *homi*.

'fastened') to the lower hull with nylon monofilament fishing line and secured with nails *(katana)*.

Outrigger.   As in other Polynesian languages, *ama* is the Nukumanu word for both 'outrigger' and the 'outrigger float'. The outrigger float is hewn from any reasonably light wood. It is approximately three-quarters the length of the hull, more or less circular in cross-section, and the ends are tapered to points.

The float is attached to the 'outrigger booms' *(kiato)* by a system of pegs. Pegs toward the bow and stern are *hakatuu*. Their job is primarily to hold up the "outrigger platform." The *hakatuu* are lashed onto—not inserted into—the outrigger float. *Ttuki* are pegs that hold up the *kiato* amidships. There are two or three *ttuki* per *kiato*, made from relatively hefty sticks. In addition to being lashed, they are driven into the float.

Directly above the float, a sturdy pole called *te aviha* is lashed parallel to the hull and perpendicular to the 'outrigger booms'. Additional rigidity is produced by yet another pole called *te halo*, lashed across the *kiato*, parallel (and close) to the hull.

A number of short poles called *kiato motu* 'shortened *kiato*' or 'severed *kiato*' are lashed between the full-length 'outrigger booms' *(kiato mauni* 'true *kiato*'). The shorter poles are not integral to the vessels' structure; their purpose is to make a better "platform" for storing gear. The term "platform" may be somewhat misleading as this is not a solid structure; rather, it is a network of poles on which objects such as masts or paddles may be set. Sometimes smaller objects also are laid on this structure, and were it not for the *kiato motu*, they might well fall through the spaces, especially in rough weather. The Nukumanu outrigger's design is shown in figure 8.7.

Sail and Rigging.   In common with most Pacific Islanders, Nukumanu traditionally equipped their sailing canoes with triangular sails of plaited pandanus matting. In recent decades, this material has been replaced with cotton cloth of European manufacture or, in a few cases, plastic sheeting. Modern cloth and plastic sails are termed *puke*, in contrast with the old pandanus sails, known by the common Polynesian term *laa*. Despite the change in materials, the traditional triangular shape has been retained in order to maintain maneuverability—particularly the ability to beat into a head wind. In this respect, Nukumanu corresponds with many Polynesian and Micronesian communities (e.g., see Gladwin 1970) but differs from Anuta, where square sails have been adopted (Feinberg 1988a).

The Anutan rationale for adopting a square sail is that it makes possible a larger sail without increasing the height of the mast, thereby increasing speed without sacrificing stability. I mentioned this rationale to Ahuti, one of my more outspoken Nukumanu informants, one day as we were crossing the lagoon. He responded scornfully that with a triangular sail you can put up a large one and go as fast as you want. If the wind is too strong, you put up a smaller sail. Indeed, as he spoke, I noticed that he had along a second sail in case the weather should change while we were at sea.

This conversation took place on a windy day. Our speed was seven or eight

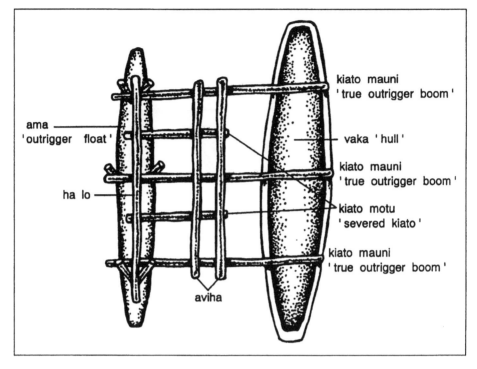

FIGURE 8.7.   Structure of Nukumanu outrigger.

knots, and Ahuti's son was bailing constantly as water poured across the gunwales. We were heeling about as far as we could without being in danger of capsizing—because of the force of the wind in the sail, not the height of the mast, which actually is not great, being tilted well forward (see below). As we sped through the chop, heeling precariously, with waves towering above the gunwales, I had to admit that the canoe had all the sail it could handle.

Nukumanu use two rigging systems, the more common of which is depicted in figure 8.8. In this system, the bottom of the mast *(te hukilani)* is forked and set on the middle *kiato* 'outrigger boom' on the outrigger side *(te vahi ama)*. The sail is attached directly to a yard and boom. The yard *(tila)* is lashed to the mast about one-third of the way from the top and to the boom *(tou olo)* near the bottom; the bottom is wedged against the inside of the bow or foredeck. The mast is tilted forward at perhaps a 60-degree angle, or 30 degrees from perpendicular

The mast is held up by four stays *(na le)*. The forestay goes around the forward *kiato* and is doubled back to the middle *kiato*, where it is tied on the outrigger side, near the gunwale. The outrigger and outboard stays are tied to the middle *kiato*, the former on the windward (i.e., outrigger) and the latter on the leeward (nonoutrigger) side *(vahi katea)*, just beyond the gunwales. The outrigger stay is *te tau ama;* the

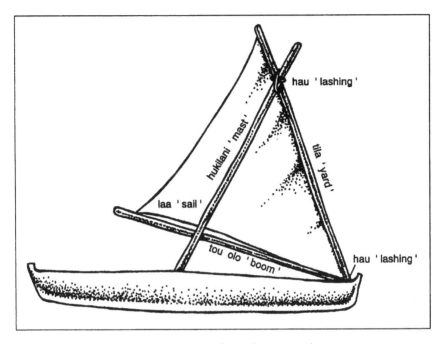

FIGURE 8.8. Common rigging system for Nukumanu sailing canoe.

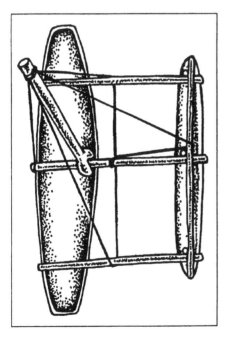

FIGURE 8.9. Nukumanu sailing canoe rigging for mast, top view.

FIGURE 8.10.   Nukumanu sailing canoe rigging for mast, side view.

FIGURE 8.11.   One system of rigging and mast for sail.

forward, rear, and outboard stays are *na le*. The fore and aft stays are also called *na tuku* 'keepers'. Figures 8.9 and 8.10 illustrate the system of stays holding the mast to the canoe. The sheet is attached to the boom about three-quarters of the way to the end, and the sail is raised *(hakatuu)* with a halyard *(mea laa tootoo)*. This, I was told, is the old system once used on the interisland voyaging canoes.

The second rigging system uses only one stay attached to the mast. It is located amidships, on the outrigger side. The base of the mast is set inside the stern of the canoe rather than up on the middle *kiato*. The force of the wind against the sail is necessary to keep the mast and yard in place. There is no halyard; the yard is lashed to the mast and boom before they are set in place. To raise or lower the sail, the whole assembly must be put up or down. This system, illustrated in figure 8.12, is said to be a recent innovation and is generally considered to be as serviceable as the older one. It has the advantage of being quicker and easier to put up and take down, although it may be less sturdy than the older system.

If the weather is extremely calm *(marino)*, a second sail is sometimes raised. In that case, the mainsail is located amidships, not at the bow. The second sail is on the stern *kiato*.

Canoe Maintenance

To keep the canoes in working order is as vital to survival out at sea as is construction. Still, time spent on maintenance cannot be devoted to other productive

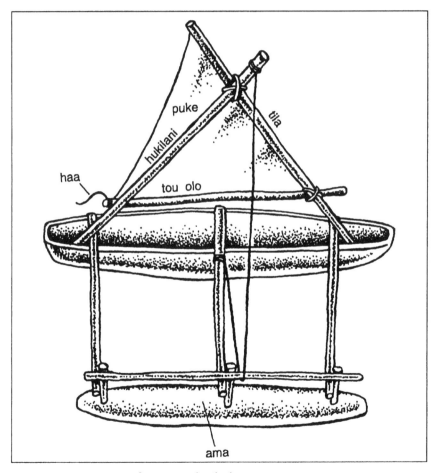

FIGURE 8.12.   Rigging for mast and sail, alternate system.

pursuits; and the attention Nukumanu give it is not great compared with many other Oceanic peoples.

As elsewhere, enamel paint has been a boon to Nukumanu sailors and craftsmen. In addition to reducing the drag of the hull as it travels through the water, paint protects the wood from the effects of dampness, salt, and sun. It is in chronic short supply, so many vessels are badly in need of a new coat. New craft may wait many months for their first application, and then only the exterior is painted. Still, paint is eventually applied to the outsides of most canoes and to all large ones.

Nukumanu usually pull their canoes out of the water and well up onto the beach when they are not in use (cf. Montague this volume). In contrast with many other island peoples, however, they do not construct canoe sheds. They cover their canoes with coconut fronds—a process known as *uhiuhi*—to provide protection from the sun and rain; but the *uhiuhi* process is not particularly involved or effective (cf. Feinberg 1988a:81–86). The fronds laid atop the hull help somewhat to protect the wood from sunlight, but rain gets inside. After a rain, the canoe is uncovered, the water bailed out, and the canoe left in the sun to dry.

The Nukumanu pattern of canoe storage and use exposes vessels to the forces of decay, and canoes must be repaired periodically. Because of the shortage of wood, canoes are rarely discarded when they begin to rot. Instead, the rotting part is cut out and replaced with a new piece that is lashed, nailed into place, or both. When a canoe is so badly damaged that it can no longer be repaired, whatever solid parts remain are saved and used to repair other vessels.

SOCIAL RELATIONS

Symbolism and the Sea

As in many Pacific Island cultures, Nukumanu men were traditionally associated with the sea and women with the inland area and gardens. With few exceptions, men have always been responsible for fishing and canoe building. Women have been exclusively responsible for the taro swamps, for plaiting mats and thatch, and, by and large, for cooking. When women go to sea, it is to travel from one island to another, as when they go to work their gardens on Nukumanu islet[4] or to visit kin on Ontong Java. Furthermore, they go as passengers while men paddle, pole, control the sail, or operate the outboard motor. By contrast, while men also terminate their voyages on land, the focus of the voyage for them is the time spent on the water.[5]

Even in relation to commodity production, men's realm is the sea. The two most important income-producing activities, bêche-de-mer and trochus collection, are maritime activities and predominantly masculine endeavors. Men spend most of their waking hours on the sea, preparing to go to sea, or talking and singing about ocean voyages. A faux pas on the ocean evokes ridicule and shame; and among the surest ways to provoke a fight is to impugn another's seamanship abilities.

Along with the sea, a second focus has been added to the masculine worldview: *kaleve* 'toddy'-drinking. Toddy is the sap of the coconut palm. It may be used in cooking, but more often it is fermented to form a moderately potent alcoholic beverage. The practice of fermenting toddy is said to have been introduced to Nukumanu in the early 1950s by Maatau, a man from Pelau, Ontong Java, who had learned the art himself on Sikaiana in the Solomons. *Kaleve*-drinking quickly became popular among Nukumanu men, and today its production and consumption have been incorporated into the daily routine.

Drinking is a masculine activity on Nukumanu. Women indulge only at special celebrations like Christmas and New Year, when normal rules are suspended. Moreover, alcohol consumption usually occurs in places marked as singularly masculine. The most prominent of these areas are *soa* 'friend' houses: small, elevated, rectangular platforms covered by low roofs and no walls. When not otherwise in use, the *soa* may be utilized by boys and teenaged youths for respite from the sun and as a place to play cards or draughts; but their primary purpose is as a common drinking area for adult males. Women may gather around the *soa* but never get up on the platforms. There are three *soa*: one at each end of the central corridor between the two main rows of dwelling houses and one on the lagoon beach toward the eastern end of the village.

The other major drinking areas are the places where men build canoes. These areas are along the lagoon beach to the east and west of the main village, and they are areas of focal symbolic significance. Canoe construction *(taataa vaka)* is an exclusively male activity, associated with other male activities such as voyaging and fishing and with the preeminently male domain of the sea. It takes place on the beach—the point of articulation between land and sea. The most popular canoe-

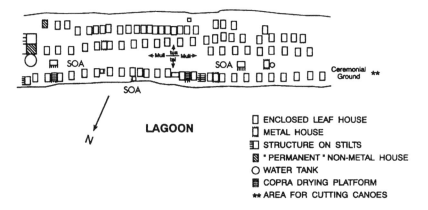

FIGURE 8.13.   Map of Amotu Village.

cutting area is said to be watched over by an evil spirit *(tipua haaeo)* (see Feinberg 1990 for a discussion of Nukumanu spirits) and considered dangerous for women or children to enter.

Canoe Construction

During my four months on Nukumanu, I did not observe complete construction of a new canoe. Sarfert and Damm, however, offer a description of the process from the early part of this century. A loose translation of their account is as follows:

> The construction of boats is a matter that the men undertake on the outer islets. . . . The raw material is furnished from the forest. Good driftwood blown in by the northwest wind is also used.
>
> All male relatives of the future canoe owners are called upon to cut the trees. Then they pull the tree trunk—or drift log—to the work place. The men are expected to work without compensation. As the trees are being moved and trunks prepared, songs are sung. Songs for dragging trees are called . . . holo lakau. . . . Songs for preparing the trunk are . . . holo vaka. . . . These work songs are supposed to cheer the workers who also strike up songs when pulling a heavy canoe into the water or onto the land.
>
> The preparation of the trunks takes place under the supervision of an 'expert', known . . . as . . . tanata iloa na vao. This 'expert' brings the family members of the customer together to participate in the canoe work. Before sunrise, payment is made at the house of the 'expert' and is in the form of . . . loincloths. In return, the 'expert' ties around each of the men red-colored pandanus leaves and a young coconut leaf knot, and he pleads for his father and various spirits (such as Kimunoho, Kimulani, Kimupapa, Kimuhora, Hearepakupaku, Hearemela'oa, and others) to preserve the canoe workers from sickness, make the construction proceed quickly, and allow the wood not to splinter or shatter. After sunrise, the 'expert' goes with his workers to the tree trunk. He takes leaves and a whole young coconut whose liquid contents he splatters for the actual canoe spell. . . . Similar ceremonies are repeated as well on the following work days. Daily, around noon, the canoe 'expert' announces the workers' quitting time. . . . The 'expert' again splatters water from a coconut bottle over the canoe and then goes to his house with his coconuts and leaves. Every morning he begins the work with this ceremony.
>
> On the last day, boys bring the outrigger rods and booms, and with their installation the work is done. After that, the 'expert' ties a coconut leaf knot on the front of the outrigger, in the boat's interior, and on the stern. The first is supposed to represent his father, the latter his mother. If the parents of the 'expert' are still living, the knots mean his paternal grandfather and his maternal grandfather. At the tying of the knots, he makes a long speech requesting watchfulness for the canoe, the bringing of many fish for the owner, and protection for the owner from illnesses.
>
> Next, the orderer takes over the canoe and pays the 'expert'. . . . The canoe is pushed into the sea and turned around with the bow in the beach sand. Then, the new owner . . . lays down the payment. . . , loosens the ties of the 'parents' of the 'expert', and replaces them with his own in the form of red-colored pandanus leaves. While this is going on, he asks them for protection and assurance of success in catching fish. Now the 'expert' goes to the canoe and gets his own 'parents'—which he

later throws into the sea—and the payment. With this, the delivery ceremony is complete, and the 'expert' goes to his house where the family of the new canoe owners bring food. At this time, the 'expert' ties around the owner a red-colored pandanus knot and lays fine white sand on his head, shoulders, and stomach. . . . He then blows away the sand under invocation to the spirits . . . to protect the owner from illness and to defend his canoe. Again, he ties around the canoe owner a coconut leaf knot and smears him as before with sand before he covers the seated owner with coconut oil. He then repeats the ceremony with the remaining canoe workers. (Sarfert and Damm 1929:203–6)

Canoe construction now involves less ritual than at the time of Sarfert's study. Still, ceremony is a vital part of Nukumanu life. All able-bodied males participate in boat building from time to time. For older men who find it difficult to spend long hours diving, paddling, and fishing in the hot sun, construction and maintenance of canoes may be the primary productive activity. Even younger men, however, cut small canoes and assist their elders in construction of midsized and large ones.

Canoe building also provides a focus for social gathering. Toward late afternoon, men return from their day on the sea and gravitate to the construction sites, joining those already at work there. Sometimes they lend assistance; often they just come to sit, chat, and drink the ubiquitous *kaleve*. Such gatherings are informal in nature; if a man should walk near another who is working on a canoe, unless already on a pressing mission, he will probably strike up a conversation. Should a group already be extant, he is likely to join. Even men who are not on good terms with one another often socialize at such casual gatherings and appear for all the world to enjoy each other's company until normal inhibitions are erased by ethanol.

Canoe Ownership

Today, a canoe is "owned" by the man who builds it and other men in the builder's household. Most Nukumanu households consist of nuclear families, sometimes augmented by close kin in any number of relationships. Decisions as to when a canoe is to be taken out, by whom, for what purpose, where it will be taken, and how it will be powered are made by the builder or the head of the builder's household. In addition, a father and son, or occasionally a brother, who are not living under the same roof but who have remained on good terms share canoes and accessories. Usually when one of the 'owners' wishes to use a canoe, he speaks to the co-'owners' to make sure that he is not interfering with their plans and to get their approval. This, however, is not always done, particularly if the co-'owner' is not readily available and one needs to use the vessel right away. These rules also apply to other forms of property, especially such maritime accessories as outboard motors, sails, paddles, poles, and fishing nets.

Ritual Activities

Nukumanu is one of the few remaining Polynesian communities in which aspects of traditional religion continue to be openly practiced. The areas in which appeal to pagan spirits remains most pronounced involve curing and the sea. This is not surprising, as these are activities in which both life and limb of individuals and overall community well-being are at stake; very likely these were major foci of religion in precontact times as well.[6]

Sarfert and Damm (1929:206) report that early in this century, when a canoe was readied for a lengthy voyage, a piece of wood called *te hetipuna* was attached to one of the outrigger booms. Hetipuna was the name of a male deity who guided and protected the canoe at sea. One side of the *hetipuna* was left "white"; the other was dyed red. Upon landing at the intended destination, a 'priest' would tie pandanus leaves onto the *hetipuna* and sing a song to a local deity in one of the community's *hale aitu* 'temples'. On Ontong Java, the deity thus addressed was Keluahine. The following day, the 'priest' would destroy the leaf knots, crush the stem, and discard the bundle. Another Nukumanu deity with a function similar to that of Hetipuna is Loatu.

According to Sarfert and Damm (1929:206), the captain (whom they term *te tinohiti*) was responsible for ritual procedures to control the wind, rain, water spouts, lightning, thunder, large fish, and dangerous currents. Access to such knowledge was hereditary or available through purchase. In order to perform his ritual duties, the *tinohiti* tied coconut leaves around his elbow joints and called upon protective spirits for assistance. In addition, when problems arose at sea, two men stationed in the bow of the canoe would toss young coconut leaves overboard to placate angry spirits, particularly the ghosts of men who had been killed by sharks. Simultaneously, a green, unhusked coconut was cracked and the liquid expelled with a kind of "swirling" motion. In addition, Sarfert has reported that while out at sea one must "urinate so that it will not be noticed on the water" and that one may neither eat nor spit into the ocean when out of sight of land (Sarfert and Damm 1929:207).

I cannot confirm Sarfert's account directly on the basis of my informants' comments or my own experience, and any practices associated with the ancient 'temples' have been long abandoned. Still, many ritual procedures associated with canoes and voyaging have been retained.

When a new canoe has been constructed, it is dedicated to one or more pagan spirits. A guardian spirit to whom a canoe is dedicated is known as *mahaunani*. In the old days, every canoe had one, and many still do. Each major descent group (*hale* 'house') has specific spirits looking after its canoes. Some of the more prominent include Nahuiavaka, Nahuiahau, Nahuitinilau, Nupani, and Matuahano. The latter is responsible for the well-being of canoes in two separate 'houses'. In addition, before major fishing expeditions on the ocean—particularly deep-sea fishing for *lavena*—and sometimes before interisland voyages, spells are recited and rituals performed. Canoes of adversaries may be cursed to bring them bad luck in fishing or an unsuccessful voyage.

Such prayers and spells are still remembered, and many are written down in family notebooks, along with genealogies and other vital secret information. I was permitted to copy one such notebook, containing a total of forty-nine prayers. Of these, twenty-nine are *kavai*, prayers having to do with canoes, fishing, and the sea.

The following verse is a rough translation of one sample—a prayer to improve the luck of an unsuccessful fisherman. I will not produce the text and offer only an approximate translation in order to protect the secrecy of my informants' formulas.

> You Tehiu, Teutua's child.
> You Kaititi and Kaveau, look after me.
> I have forgotten the guardian spirit Telakau.
> Lighten the side Mapauanuku.
> Lift it up in the sea.
> I am finished—a parumea below.
> Paru uri below.
> A vaeloti below.

Tehiu is the name of a stone with power to affect the behavior of fish. Kaititi and Kaveau are names of two spirits. Telakau 'The Timber' is presumably the name of a 'guardian spirit' *(mahaunani)*, and Mapauanuku is the name of the *tipua* 'spirit' that looks after fish. *Parumea, paru uri,* and *vaeloti* are types of fish.

Some prayers are intended to attract fish of specific types. Others cause them to bite the hook. I have on record one prayer performed by a man to keep others from approaching his wife while he is at sea. There are *kavai* for lashing planks *(hono)* and outrigger *(ama)* to the hull to ensure that they will be secure. Yet another is performed before the craftsman drills a hole for lashing parts together. One is spoken by sailors marooned on an outer islet to cause the wind to shift so they can return home. In these prayers, spirits are addressed by name. In many cases, these are recently deceased kin; in others, they are spirits never taken to have been human and not associated with any particular descent group. Prominent among the latter type are several variants of Hina or Sina, a widely known Polynesian heroine of supernatural capabilities. Sinatai is goddess of the lagoon; Sinauta, goddess of the land; and Sinaurutahua, goddess of the ocean.

SEAMANSHIP

I divide this section into two parts: handling and navigation. The first refers to operation of canoes; the second to techniques for finding one's way at sea to an unseen destination.

Handling

Nukumanu propel their canoes by a variety of techniques. These include walking, poling, paddling, sail, and outboard motor. In considering propulsion of a boat, one rarely thinks of walking. Yet, much of the time that Nukumanu spend with their vessels is devoted to pushing or pulling them through shallow water. The reef flat extends a kilometer or so into the lagoon, and during low tide, much of the reef is exposed. Therefore, canoes must be pushed or carried a good way before they can be floated with their crews aboard.

Even when one plans an expedition to the ocean, canoes are almost always launched on the lagoon. This means that one must find a passage between islets to get to the open sea. During high tide, it is possible to float canoes through many of these passages, but only the main channel at the north end of the atoll is reliable at low tide. Therefore, sailors often have to push their vessels through a passage, and sometimes they must walk as much as several hundred meters.

Lastly, searching the reef flat for bêche-de-mer and trochus frequently is done in waist-deep water. The collector walks along, bent over at the waist, peering down through plastic diving goggles. As he walks, he grasps the bow painter, pulling the canoe behind him. The boat, in this case, serves more as a basket for collected bêche-de-mer and shellfish than a means of human transportation.

Even during high tide, most of the reef flat is only a meter or two deep. Consequently, it is feasible to pole *(toko)* as long as one stays close to shore. This involves one man standing on the gunwales near the stern, using a pole three to four meters in length to push off on the bottom. In shallow water, poling is more efficient than paddling.

Once one ventures into deeper water, a pole is no longer serviceable. In this case, for relatively short trips—especially if the canoe is a smaller one or if the wind should be unfavorable—Nukumanu seamen employ paddles. Nukumanu paddles are small and light, with narrow blades, at least in comparison with those of many Polynesians. The blade is pointed at the tip and may be one-half meter long. The shaft is about another meter long, with a smoothed, somewhat rounded end but no special enlargement for a grip. The most distinctive feature of the Nukumanu paddle is that the blade is curved, more or less like a modern kayak paddle, so that it has a distinct power face and back face. Informants told me that this is the traditional style. Paddles with flat blades, which are also common on the atoll, are of a style said to be borrowed from Takuu. Paddles are employed as well for steering with a sail and for close maneuvering in deep water for such purposes as dropping anchor. To propel a canoe with standard forward "bow strokes" is *alo;* to scull is *hue.*

For longer trips, Nukumanu use either a sail or an outboard engine. With an engine, one may travel straight toward the destination and is not dependent on the wind. Motors, however, are expensive to purchase and operate. Gasoline and oil are scarce, so one often must wait for several months to replenish the supply. And engines tend to break down.

Voyagers usually take sails and paddles on extended trips, even when they plan to use their motors. Not only does the sail act as insurance against engine failure on a distant islet or the open sea, but it costs nothing to operate, is more of a challenge to the expert mariner, and, if the wind is favorable, can be as fast as a small outboard.

On a calm day, a small canoe may be rigged with a mast and sail without any added covering. On a windy day, only large canoes are likely to be taken out, and these are fitted with removable bow and stern covers *(pui)* to keep the craft from shipping too much water as they cut through the large waves at speeds of several knots. The decking fits into a notch carved in the hull, and each deck piece is made to fit a specific canoe.

Still, under the best of circumstances, canoes take on water and must constantly be bailed. Bailers are made of wood, with roundish bottoms to fit the hulls' interiors. A handle is carved into the same piece of wood and projects forward from the bailer's rear wall. The person bailing holds the handle of his implement; with one motion he swings it forward through the water at the bottom of his boat and dumps it over the gunwale. Especially in small canoes, a seaman must be careful not to let too much water accumulate since, if the canoe is riding low, it may be swamped instantaneously by a single wave.

Unlike some Pacific mariners (e.g., see Gladwin 1958, 1970), Nukumanu do not steer using the sail alone. Rather, steering is accomplished with a paddle employed as a rudder. Nor do Nukumanu make special steering paddles. An ordinary paddling paddle is tucked under the helmsman's armpit and braced against the gunwale in such a way that it takes just one hand to control it. This leaves the other hand free to work the sheet when, as is often the case, a canoe is occupied by a solo voyager.

For lengthy voyages, such as the trip to Ontong Java, one of the larger canoes is always used. These may be anywhere from ten to fifteen meters and may take a half dozen or more passengers. They normally are fitted with outboard motors, although one, or sometimes even two, sails are taken along. The exception is fiber-

FIGURE 8.14.   Canoe under sail, view from leeward.

glass canoes, which Nukumanu generally do not rig with sails. They are preferred for long trips because they are faster and more durable than wooden outriggers, but in case of engine failure, the sailors are helpless.[7]

Assuming all goes well, the trip from Nukumanu to Pelau, the more northerly of Ontong Java's two communities, is estimated to be about six hours with an outboard motor. By sail, if tacking is necessary, the trek may take up an entire day. Once the travelers arrive at their destination, they usually stay for several days to visit friends and relatives or simply to recuperate from their long day at sea. Partially for this reason and partially as a hedge in case of loss at sea, Nukumanu try to provision themselves thoroughly for lengthy trips. One trip that I observed about to set off for Ontong Java in Nukumanu's second largest canoe is depicted in figure 8.15.

Navigation

Methods used by Nukumanu for navigational purposes constitute a variant on those reported in other parts of the Pacific. The navigator finds his way over the high seas by following the stars at night, the sun during the day, swell patterns when the sky is overcast, and birds for homing in as the destination approaches.

Directions. Nukumanu presently do not have a complex wind or star compass comparable to those of the Carolinians, precontact Tongans, or even present-day Anutans. Nor does their directional system show the kind of extreme relativism that

FIGURE 8.15.   *Teatutava,* loaded with supplies and crew, departing for Pelau, Ontong Java.

I found among Anutans. Rather, it is similar to that found in the West. It has four cardinal directions: *te anake* 'east', *te kupu* 'south', *te laki* 'west', and *te tokolau* 'north'. As in the Western system, points between these cardinal directions are indicated with compound terms. For example, 'northeast' is *te anake-tokolau*, 'southwest' is *te laki-kupu*, and so forth.

Each cardinal point is said to be guarded by a whale *(taholaa)*. These four whales are known formally as *Na Ika i te Ava* 'The Fish in the Passage'. The one in the east is named Tetau, that in the south is Pupunu, that guarding the west is Haukaniu, and the one in the north is Hinateoro. These names are commonly known on the atoll; particular descent groups have alternate sets of names by which they are invoked. The whales punish wrongdoers by wrecking their canoes through such maneuvers as surfacing underneath and capsizing them. My informants denied that they are *tipua* 'spirits', but they seem to be in some sense supernatural.

Stars.   Stars and constellations are the most important navigational "tools" for Nukumanu, as they are for other island mariners. Genuine long-distance voyages are only undertaken at the present time when a canoe is blown off course and the sailors cannot make their way back home. For intentional visits to islands more distant than Ontong Java, Nukumanu rely entirely on European ships, and largely for that reason, much detailed astronomical information has been forgotten. Still, informants could cite a number of important constellations and had some idea of the relationship between their movements and the bearings of a number of islands. Several of the better-known constellations are similar to those found on other islands. These include Manu 'Bird' (Sirius), Te Kapakau Looloa 'The Long Wing' (Canopus), Te Kapakau Nounou 'The Short Wing' (Monocerus), Mataliki 'Small Eyes' or 'Small Face' (Pleiades), and Talo 'Taro' (Scorpius' head and claws). Atolu 'Three' is Orion's Belt, Te Melemele is Orion's sword, and Teaounu is a group of three stars including Orion's shoulders plus one unidentified star nearby and slightly off center. Te Mano 'The Shark' was described as coming immediately after Talo and is probably Scorpius' tail. The Southern Cross, an important navigational constellation throughout the South Pacific, generally is called Te Kros, although one of my older consultants cited as an indigenous name Te Himu 'Trigger Fish'. Centaurus, two bright stars near the Southern Cross, are Sahalapolu, a name for which I have no English gloss. Other constellations recognized on Nukumanu include Samono 'Dolphin' (Big Dipper), Kaavei 'Octopus Tentacle', Kaipea 'Crab', and Te Ula 'The Crayfish'. Of these, Samono is well known; the others are less so. They were never pointed out to me in the sky, and I cannot make a positive identification (but cf. table 8.2). My data on Nukumanu constellations are summarized in table 8.1 and illustrated in figure 8.16.

Sarfert and Damm (1929:187–95) list thirty-three astronomical bodies (see table 8.2). Aside from differences in spelling, some inconsistency in use of articles, and inclusion of the sun and moon, this list is similar to mine. However, it is more extensive. In addition, Sarfert and Damm cite mythological and religious associations

TABLE 8.1.   Names of Nukumanu constellations with tentative English glosses and Western identifications, as of 1984.

(Te) Aounu	(?)	Orion's Shoulders plus one star off center
(Te) Himu	'Trigger Fish'	Southern Cross
Kaipea	'Crab'	unidentified
(Te) Kaniva	(?)	Milky Way
Kaavei	'Octopus Tentacle'	unidentified
Mataliki	'Small Face' or 'Small Eyes'	Pleiades
(Te) Mano	'Shark'	Scorpius' Tail
(A) Manu	'Bird'	Sirius
(Te) Melemele	(?)	Orion's Sword
Sahalapolu	(?)	Centaurus
Talo	'Taro'	Scorpius' Head and Claws
(A) Tolu	'Three'	Orion's belt
(Te) Ula	'Crayfish'	unidentified

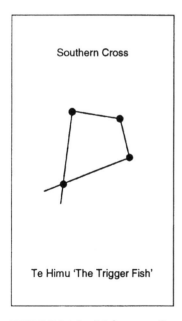

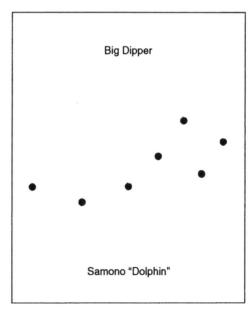

FIGURE 8.16.   Nukumanu Constellations.

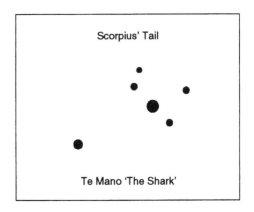

Scorpuis' Tail

Te Mano 'The Shark'

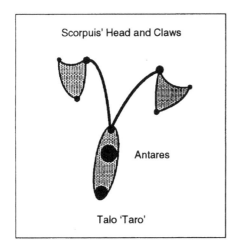

Scorpuis' Head and Claws

Antares

Talo 'Taro'

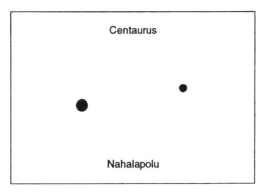

Centaurus

Nahalapolu

FIGURE 8.16.   Cont'd.

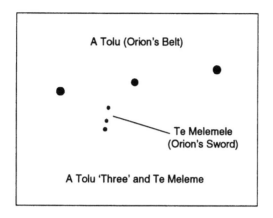

A Tolu (Orion's Belt)

Te Melemele
(Orion's Sword)

A Tolu 'Three' and Te Meleme

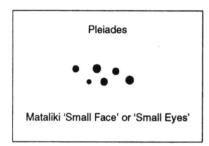

Pleiades

Mataliki 'Small Face' or 'Small Eyes'

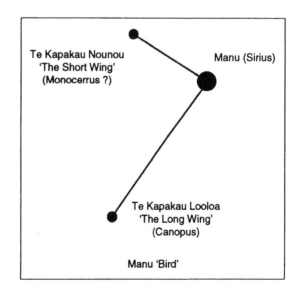

Te Kapakau Nounou
'The Short Wing'
(Monocerrus ?)

Manu (Sirius)

Te Kapakau Looloa
'The Long Wing'
(Canopus)

Manu 'Bird'

FIGURE 8.16.   Cont'd.

TABLE 8.2.　Nukumanu names and Western identifications of astronomical bodies as reported by Sarfert and Damm, based on data collected in 1908–1910.

Nasimu	Southern Cross
Namahu	Magellanic Clouds(?)
Nahalapolu	Part of Centaurus(?)
Ura and Malepu	Two stars in the Milky Way, below Canis Major
Aipea	A small star or nebula between Capella and Castor
Mano	Seven stars including the back and tail of Scorpius
Mailapa	Altair
Toki	Vega
Kumete	Delphinus
Tauha	Includes stars from Andromeda and Pegasus
Kavei	Part of Cassiopeia
Matariki	Pleiades
Kounu	Four stars in middle of Centaurus
Tolu	Three stars of Orion's Belt
Manu	Includes Sirius and a number of surrounding stars, including Procyon, Regulus, Canopus, and several others
Hamana Tolo	Includes parts of Aquarius and Pegasus
Pupula Hano	Three small stars
Una	Part of Taurus
Hela	Sun
Malema	Moon
Hanalulu	Four head stars of Draco
Matila	Grus
Mataku Matamea	Corvus
Pora	Spica or Venus(?)
Melemele	Orion's Sword
Laki Popoto	Part of Taurus
Pula	?
Ko	A dark spot in the Milky Way, a little south of Mailapa
Polata	Five stars near Mailapa
Kaniva	Milky Way
Kotaro	?　(see Talo, table 8.1)
Tapakea	?
Karoupu	?

with a number of the asterisms they describe. Evidently, within the last three generations, a good deal of information has been lost.

Star Paths.   I could not get even the best navigators to recite specific star paths. Indeed, I was told there never were widely accepted conventions but that each sailor figured out his own guide stars. This is likely an exaggeration. Nukumanu are aware that stars rise and set in a definite sequence and that this may be useful for navigational purposes. One informant went so far as to identify as the "primary sequence" Kaavei, Mataliki, Teaounu, Atolu, Te Melemele, Amanu, Kaipea, and Te Ula. Nukumanu, however, maintain much secret knowledge, and an accomplished navigator, even in the old days, might well have been reluctant to share information with anyone other than close relatives. Furthermore, although elaborate star paths involving a succession of rising and setting stars were not cited, a number of informants noted individual stars or constellations that they regarded as the primary guides to particular destinations.

Swells.   When out of sight of land during the day, or at night in overcast weather, the Nukumanu helmsman maintains a steady course by following swells *(heau)*. As is true of other Pacific navigators, Nukumanu keep track of the swell primarily by feeling their vessels' movement rather than by sight. Competent sailors should be able to maintain a steady course with reference to the dominant swell. My informants, however, made no reference to secondary swells (utilized by Carolinian navigators), reflected waves (used for purposes of land finding by Tikopians and Anutans), or interference patterns (utilized by Marshall Islanders).[8]

For purposes of homing in on an unseen island, Nukumanu rely primarily on birds rather than reflected waves. Birds are more plentiful, both in number and variety, on Nukumanu than on the islands further east. The most important species for navigational purposes are those that sleep on land, fly straight out to sea in the morning to feed, and return straight back at dusk. As in other parts of the Pacific, boobies *(te nonoo* and especially *te kanopu* 'large brown booby') and noddies *(lakia)* are considered particularly useful in this respect. The frigate bird *(te kataha)* was also mentioned as useful for land finding.[9]

In addition to such mundane methods of land finding, some informants cited natural phenomena with spiritual significance as being helpful. In the old days, I was told, sailors might follow lightning *(te uila)*, a rainbow *(te umata)*, or a meteor *(te tanaloa)*, and it would guide them to an island. Today, each descent group *(hale* 'house') has what might be called a totemic relationship with a particular species of bird, fish, or other marine animal. This animal, if treated with respect, is thought to help group members when they have problems on the ocean. I was told by members of one group with the great white shark *(ulukao)* as its totem that, if they should be shipwrecked, a shark would swim by, allow them to climb onto its back, and carry them to shore. One tale has a heroine named Asina riding across the lagoon on the back of a turtle. And my friend Hatutahi told me that when he was lost at sea in 1962, his totemic bird *te lupe* 'the pigeon' led him to an island (see below for an account of this voyage).

Missed Landfall.   Most of Nukumanu's intentional interisland voyaging in recent memory has been to Ontong Java Atoll in the Solomon Islands, a little more than forty kilometers to the south. Ontong Java is one of the world's largest atolls, with a lagoon over fifty kilometers in diameter. Therefore, the likelihood of getting lost on the outward trip is slim. For the voyage home, however, the destination is less than twenty kilometers in diameter, with little possibility of an expanded target (cf. Lewis 1972:part 4), making successful landfall in bad weather problematic. A number of canoes have been lost on the voyage between the two atolls in recent decades, and most of those have been on the northward segment of the journey.

At first blush, missed landfall at either atoll would seem to be a fatal error. The nearest alternative destination is well over 150 kilometers distant. However, if one ventures in the realm of three to five hundred kilometers, there are several large islands: New Ireland to the northwest, Bougainville to the west, Choiseul to the southwest, Santa Isabel directly south, and Malaita approximately south-southeast. Furthermore, people skilled in survival techniques can sustain themselves for many weeks at sea, and if one is prepared to spend a week or two upon the ocean, there is an excellent chance of making landfall somewhere.

In precontact times, a Polynesian crew landing at one of the Melanesian islands in the western Solomons may have fared little better than one that remained at sea. Since the days of European contact and "pacification," however, these large islands have provided a genuine haven for lost sailors. Therefore, a voyage is likely to be provisioned well in excess of what is necessary for one day on the ocean, and a crew that veers off course presumes that, with adequate conservation of supplies, successful landfall will be made. The following account of one such experience is compiled from my notes of several conversations and from a taped narrative.

In 1962, four canoes got lost on a voyage between Nukumanu and Pelau. Two of these—named Lorean and Molosuhi—eventually made landfall at Bougainville; the other two landed at Gizo in the western Solomon Islands. Lorean and Molosuhi carried seven men apiece; the former was led by Hatutahi and Tuunehu; the latter by Kipano, Nukumanu's 'paramount chief' *(tuku)*.

They left Nukumanu for Ontong Java and spent three days in Pelau, the closer of that atoll's two communities. They then went on to Luaniua for sporting competition *(hulo)* and stayed for an entire week. On their return, they spent four more days at Pelau, then put back out to sea for the last segment of their voyage.

When they were close to Nukumanu, the wind shifted and prevented any further progress. They took down the sail and paddled through the rainy, windy night; but when day broke, they couldn't see the island. They reraised the sail and looked around in vain for the island. After some time and an acrimonious debate, they gave up the search as hopeless and decided to make for Bougainville.

During the day, they followed the sun; at night, they followed the stars. In Hatu-tahi's canoe, he and Tuunehu took major responsibility for working the sail and steer-ing paddle. The sail was kept up day and night, and at least one of them stayed awake at all times. Others in the vessel slept at night but were awake by day. They were for-tunate to have clear weather through their journey. And the *heau* 'swell' was always there to help guide them.

They set their destination as Kieta, at that time the main administrative center on Bougainville. Hatutahi said they did not know exactly where Kieta was, but they had a clear enough idea to know which stars to follow and how to use the sun. The main navigational constellation was Te Mano 'The Shark' (Scorpius' tail), which rises in the southeast and sets in the southwest. Hatutahi's "totemic" bird, the pigeon *(te lupe)*, helped by flying out and guiding the voyagers to shore.[10]

They were on the ocean for seven nights before arriving at a plantation in Buin, near the southern tip of Bougainville. A man from Nukuria, another Polynesian atoll, was working on the plantation. With his help, they explained to the manager what had happened. The manager then contacted authorities by radio. They were flown up to Kieta and repatriated by ship. At length, the canoes were also returned by ship.

While at sea, the sailors trolled constantly and ate raw fish. The staple, however, was coconut. In the morning and again about mid-afternoon, they ate and drank—two men sharing one nut. At night they fasted. Because of their careful rationing, they still had a plentiful supply of nuts when they arrived. Their lives were never in imme-diate danger, and Hatutahi claimed that they had enough nuts for at least a month or two, if necessary. If they were to perish, it would have been for lack of 'water', and they had (with appropriate conservation) a good supply.

Loss of a canoe at sea is fairly common: about one voyage (one to five canoes) every four or five years. Yet, no one seems particularly worried. No one in recent memory has died at sea, despite an average of approximately two canoes a week making the trip to Pelau—and for the most part under sail until the early 1980s. This is quite a respectable safety record. Still, over the generations, loss at sea has been a significant cause of death, particularly among the atoll's male population.

CONCLUSION

The Nukumanu appear to have lost much of their old maritime technology and skill over the past century. Some of what was lost has been replaced by Western borrowings; some has simply dropped out of existence. Still, they have retained more of their traditional seafaring practices than most contemporary Pacific Is-landers.

Prominent among the objects dropped from Nukumanu's repertoire of maritime technology are the old voyaging canoes *(vaka hai laa)* and possibly some types of smaller inshore paddling canoe as well (cf. Friederici 1912; Sarfert and Damm 1929:200). Along with this, the Nukumanu have now given up intentional long-distance canoe voyaging, in which they claim they once excelled. With the cessation of long-distance voyaging, knowledge of celestial bodies and star paths appears to have eroded; it is likely that the Nukumanu system of direction-designation has grown less complex; and skill in reading wave configurations probably has atrophied.

Vessels are no longer lashed with sennit cord, nor are sails plaited from pandanus leaf. Sails themselves are superseded to a large degree by outboard motors, while wooden boats are giving way to fiberglass (cf. Hviding; Donner, both this volume). For lengthy trips, canoes have been replaced by European ships (cf. Donner this volume). And ritual activities associated with canoe construction, voyaging, and fishing have become attenuated.

Despite these changes, wooden single-outrigger canoes far exceed all other types of vessel on the atoll; and—outboard motors notwithstanding—canoes are usually propelled by paddle, pole, or sail. While islanders no longer use canoes for voyaging to distant lands, the trip to Ontong Java has become routine. This voyage takes one out of sight of land for several hours and requires an ability to navigate by swells, wind, sun, and stars as well as skill at handling canoes upon the open sea. Lastly, the association of Nukumanu men, canoes, and maritime activity remains as strong as ever. As elsewhere (e.g., see Carucci; Hviding; Donner, all this volume), Nukumanu cultural identity is represented in terms of the sea, canoes, and voyaging; and gender relations are expressed symbolically in terms of the relationship of land and sea.

Both continuity and change in Nukumanu maritime technology and practice must be understood in terms of the articulation between ecological constraints, the atoll's history of cultural contact, and the values and symbolic systems that have shaped islanders' experiential worlds. This articulation may be illustrated by Nukumanu use of double-ended canoes with interchangeable bow and stern and the practice of sailing with outrigger to windward. Such a system is widely distributed among the Polynesian outlier atolls (Lewis 1972:261–62; but cf. Feinberg 1988a:88–89) and perhaps reflects some borrowing from the surrounding populations.[11] Furthermore, as I have argued elsewhere (Feinberg 1988b), Nukumanu sociospatial symbolism may have made the atoll's dominant canoe design particularly attractive.

Ecological constraints affecting Nukumanu's style of seamanship include the atoll's sandy, salty soil and the sparsity of rainfall. These conditions make it difficult to raise crops and livestock. As both commodity production and subsistence practices must rely on marine resources, the sea could hardly fail to be a major factor in life on the atoll. The kinds of wood available for fashioning canoes and the importance of driftwood are also attributable to the atoll environment. The presence of a resource-rich lagoon precludes the necessity of highly stable vessels with a great deal of freeboard for most purposes. And the large reef flat makes poling an efficient means of propulsion.

The extent to which the Nukumanu have retained their navigational and sailing skills is largely a function of their intermediate position on the continuum of isolation. On large, high, fertile islands, residents had little motive to embark on difficult and risky journeys. Similarly, islands like Rotuma, which are readily accessible by ship or plane, gave up long-distance canoe journeys relatively early. At the other end of the continuum, such extremely isolated islands as Sikaiana, Nukuria, or Takuu lacked practicable destinations for any would-be voyagers. In general, communities that have retained their old seafaring practice are small enough that people feel a need for interisland contact, sufficiently isolated that ships and planes do not completely meet those needs, and close enough to one or more potential target islands to provide fair prospects of a safe, successful voyage. Nukumanu meets all these criteria as well as any island discussed in this volume, and it has been among the most successful at maintaining old seafaring traditions.

NOTES

Acknowledgments   This essay is based on research conducted on Nukumanu Atoll in Papua New Guinea's North Solomons Province in 1984. The study was sponsored by the Kent State University Research Council. I am indebted to participants in three stimulating sessions at meetings of the Association for Social Anthropology in Oceania for thoughtful critiques of earlier versions of my manuscript. In particular, I would like to thank Phil De-Vita, Bill Donner, Ward Goodenough, and Harry Powell for their helpful suggestions. I am grateful to Susan Win for assistance in the translation of the relevant sections of Sarfert and Damm (1929) and to the people of Nukumanu for their hospitality and support during the period of my research.

1. Sarfert and Damm (1929:198) attribute the demise of Nukumanu voyaging canoes to the absence of suitable trees on the atoll.

2. Sarfert and Damm (1929:198) give *tinohiti* as the Nukumanu term for the supernaturally fortified captains of old voyaging canoes.

3. Cf. Puluwat (see Gladwin 1970); Kapingamarangi (Emory 1965).

4. Nukumanu is the name for the atoll's largest islet as well as the entire atoll. In precontact times, the village, known as Vaihale, was located on this islet; today the old village name is sometimes applied to the islet as well. The *vakkehu* (*Cyrtosperma* "taro") swamps are also found here and have been for generations.

5. It is possible to overstate the male-female dichotomy. Women swim and dive; infrequently, they hunt for clams and trochus; and on rare occasions, a few women even fish. This, however, is exceptional and evokes derogatory comments from both sexes. Likewise, women very rarely pilot canoes. They are comfortable in small craft and frequently observe men handling their boats; so if called upon in an emergency, most Nukumanu women undoubtedly could do the job. But they have little opportunity to hone their skills through practice.

6. For a description of Nukumanu curing practices, see Feinberg (1990). For evidence of traditional concern with these spheres of cultural life on the closely related atoll of Ontong Java, see Hogbin (1930, 1931, 1932, 1961).

7. I heard some difference of opinion on this point. One informant in particular asserted that these vessels can be rigged with sails and taken on long trips. Others denied that this was done.

8. See Gladwin (1970:145–46); Feinberg (1988a:114–15); and Lewis (1972:194–201), respectively.

9. This assertion contradicts those of Anutans, who insist that frigate birds fly too high and have flight patterns too erratic to be useful for navigational purposes (see Feinberg 1988a:116).

10. For further information on Nukumanu "totemism," see Feinberg (1990).

11. Of the outlier atolls, Nukuria, Takuu, Nukumanu, Ontong Java, and Sikaiana are situated in northern Melanesia and accessible by canoe from Micronesian islands of the Carolines and Kiribati. Nukuoro and Kapingamarangi lie between the southern Carolines and northern Papua New Guinea. Thus, the double-ended canoe, common both in Micronesia and Melanesia, could easily have reached the Polynesian outliers through a process of diffusion. The suggestion of central Carolinian influence is also consistent with the relative egalitarianism of the outlier atolls in comparison with much of Polynesia, the practice of loom weaving cited by a number of observers, and the physiognomy of outlier populations noted by Shapiro (1933).

REFERENCES

Bayliss-Smith, Tim P.
1974   Constraints on population growth: the case of the Polynesian outlier atolls in the pre-contact period. *Human Ecology* 2:259–95.
1975   Ontong Java: depopulation and repopulation. In *Pacific Atoll Populations*, edited by Vern Carroll, pp. 417–84. ASAO Monograph No. 3. Honolulu: University of Hawai'i Press.

Emory, Kenneth P.
1965   *Kapingamarangi: Social and Religious Life of a Polynesian Atoll.* Bulletin No. 228. Honolulu: Bernice P. Bishop Museum Press.

Feinberg, Richard
1981   *Anuta: Social Structure of a Polynesian Island.* Lā'ie and Copenhagen: Institute for Polynesian Studies in cooperation with the National Museum of Denmark.
1985   Custom and development on Nukumanu. *Bikmaus* 6:89–100.
1986   Market economy and changing sex-roles on a Polynesian atoll. *Ethnology* 25:271–82.
1988a   *Polynesian Seafaring and Navigation: Ocean Travel in Anutan Culture and Society.* Kent, Ohio: Kent State University Press.
1988b   Socio-spatial symbolism and the logic of rank on two Polynesian outliers. *Ethnology* 27:291–310.
1990   Spiritual and natural etiologies on a Polynesian outlier in Papua New Guinea. *Social Science and Medicine* 30:311–23.

Friederici, Georg
1912   *Beitrage zur Volker- und Sprachenkunde von Deutsch-Neuguinea,* No. 5, pp. 1–324. Deutschen Schutzgebieten, Mitt. Erganzungsheft.

Gladwin, Thomas
1958   Canoe travel in the Truk area: technology and psychological correlates. *American Anthropologist* 60:893–99.
1970   *East Is a Big Bird: Navigation and Logic on Puluwat Atoll.* Cambridge: Harvard University Press.

Haddon, A. C., and James Hornell
1975   *Canoes of Oceania.* 3 vols. (1936–1938) Honolulu: Bernice P. Bishop Museum Press.

Hogbin, H. Ian
1930   Spirits and the healing of the sick on Ontong Java. *Oceania* 1:146–66.
1931   Tribal ceremonies at Ontong Java. *Journal of the Royal Anthropological Institute* 61:27–55.
1932   Sorcery in Ontong Java. *American Anthropologist* 34:441–48.

1961   *Law and Order in Polynesia.* (1934) Hamden, Conn.: Shoe String Press.

Lewis, David

1972   *We, the Navigators.* Honolulu: University of Hawai'i Press.

Parkinson, Richard H. R.

1986   Ethnography of Ontong Java and Tasman Islands with remarks re: the Marqueen and Abgarris Islands. (1897) Translated by Rose Hartmann. Introduced and edited by Richard Feinberg. *Pacific Studies* 9:1–31.

Sarfert, Ernst, and Hans Damm

1929   *Luangiua und Nukumanu.* 2 vols. Hamburg: Friedrichsen, De Gruyter.

Shapiro, Harry L.

1933   Are the Ontong Javanese Polynesian? *Oceania* 3:367–76.

NAVIGATION PRACTICES OF THE BUGIS OF SOUTH SULAWESI, INDONESIA

Gene Ammarell

Narékko takkala mallebbani sompe'é
ulebbirenni tellengngé nanréwe'é.

'The sail once raised,
Better to sink than to go back.'

•   This chant[1] is from the Bugis of South Sulawesi, one of the major seafaring peoples of eastern Indonesia. Numbering over two million, the Bugis of central South Sulawesi are the most populous of the six major ethnic groups from eastern Indonesia who engage in interisland shipping and trade. The other groups are the Makasar of southern South Sulawesi, the Mandar of northwestern South Sulawesi, the Buton of Southeast Sulawesi, the Madura of an island bearing the same name as well as the nearby East Java coast, and the Sama "sea gypsies," whose homeland is in the southern Philippines. Of these major ethnic groups, the Bugis and Makasar are the best known, dominating trade both in timber and in general cargo along the Surabaya-Banjarmasin-Makasar triangle (see figure 9.1).[2] Fabled as seafarers and traders, these Austronesian-speaking people have guided their vessels over open sea and along the often treacherous coastlines of Southeast Asia and northern Australia for at least three centuries. Powered by the wind and, only recently, by auxiliary engines, Bugis ships remain a highly visible and important feature of the Indonesian economy, carrying valuable agricultural products and timber from port to port in a country made up of over thirteen thousand islands. In this essay, I explore the practice and technology of Bugis seafarers, highlighting both points of continuity and differentiation from seafaring in Oceania.

INDONESIAN TRADING SHIPS

Accounting for approximately 40 percent of Indonesia's interisland shipping, a fleet of about ten thousand vessels of various designs annually transports approximately seven million tons of dry cargo (Hughes 1986:103–13). The bulk of this trade is carried out on three types of large sailing ship: the large and exotic schooners, called *pinisi,* and the somewhat smaller *lambo* and *baggo* (see figure 9.2). All three are evolving hybrids of Indonesian construction, often reflecting widespread Austronesian patterns combined with European design. As in the Pacific Islands, hulls are built not with blueprint or written plan but according to formulas and procedures that the shipwright commits to memory during his long apprenticeship. Thick, roughly squared beams of hard timber are carved by hand and joined edge-to-edge with dowels to form a shell. Only after this shell is laid up are the ribs and floors inserted and joined to the shell, again with dowels. These building techniques and designs have been well documented (e.g., Horridge 1979a, 1979b, 1985).

Pinisi, sailed exclusively by the Bugis and Makasarese, represent the largest, and perhaps most famous, Indonesian ship design. Until recently, the hull of a *pinisi* was a simple enlargement of a common Indonesian design called *pajala;* the European rig was probably added toward the end of the nineteenth century or later (P. I. Manguin, personal communication). Ketch-rigged and high-pooped, the mizzen mast and sails have all but disappeared in recent years, giving way to four- and six-cylinder diesel-powered marine engines housed in makeshift engine rooms beneath small deck houses. These motorized *pinisi* are larger than their predecessors, ranging in capacity from eighty to five hundred tons (230 to 1400 cubic meters); overall lengths vary from forty to eighty meters, with distances from stem to stern post and keel lengths varying proportionally, that is, from twenty-seven to fifty-five meters and from fifteen to over thirty meters, respectively.[3]

The two other principal types of vessel are the *lambo* and the *baggo,* both from South Sulawesi.[4] While the *baggo* retains the gracefully curved keel of the *pajala* hull, the *lambo,* with straight keel meeting tilted stem and stern posts, is similar in design to the nineteenth-century European small trading sloop or cutter. Formerly, the *baggo* was outfitted with a Western gaff rig (see figure 9.2A) while now both carry a gunter rig, locally called *nadé* or *lambo.* A variation of the gaff rig, the gunter features a single mast with a jib and gaff-headed main in which a long spar is drawn up vertically to the mast, extending the main above the masthead (see figure 9.2B).

Hull construction for both *baggo* and *lambo* remains uniquely Indonesian. The *lambo* and *baggo* generally range in capacity from five to forty tons (14 to 110 cubic meters) with keel lengths from seven to twelve meters, length from eight to twenty meters, beams from two to five meters, and heights, keel to deck, from 0.5 to 1.5 meters. Of the two, the *baggo* tends to be smaller; in recent years *lambo* of over seventy tons have appeared.

With the introduction of marine engines, the sterns of both hull designs have been modified to take a motor and screw (cf. the modification of the Pacific Island canoe design to accommodate outboard motors; e.g., Donner this volume). A thick, vertical post through which the shaft passes is set up on a shortened, straight keel. The curved stern post then continues aft from about one-half meter up the vertical member. A center rudder compliments or replaces the two traditional quarter rudders, and it is not uncommon to see these rudders used in combination. Newer

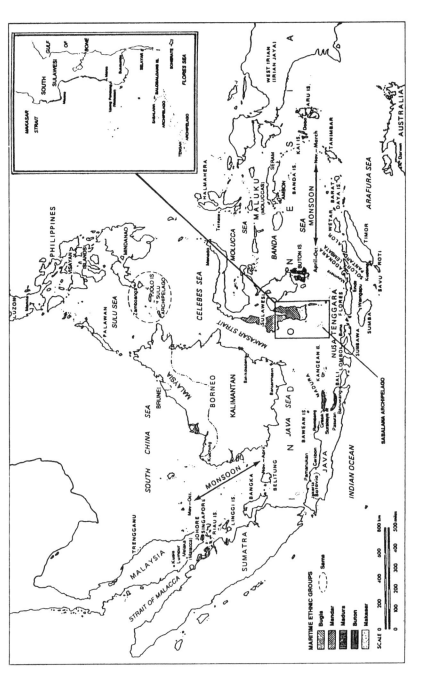

FIGURE 9.1. Island Southeast Asia including homelands of six major maritime ethnic groups, dates and directions of the monsoon winds, and inset of southern South Sulawesi and adjacent islands. (Partly adapted from Horridge 1985)

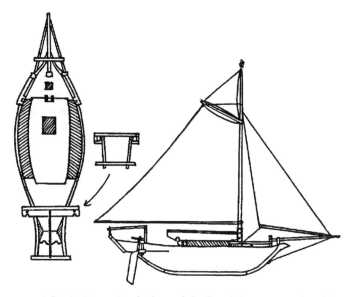

FIGURE 9.2A.   A Bugis *Baggo:* Decked *Pajala* hull with bowsprit and gaff rig.

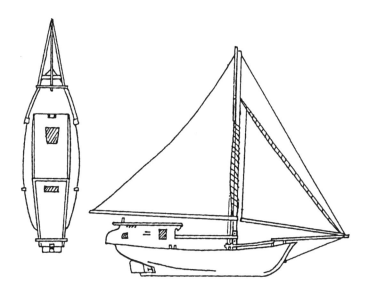

FIGURE 9.2B.   A Bugis *lambo* with *nadé* 'gunter rig' and hull modified for engine.

lambo, however, which are originally constructed to carry an engine, are usually not equipped with quarter rudders. In any case, Bugis ships rely in large part upon the jib for steerage (see also Horridge 1979a, 1979b; Dick 1975, 1987a, 1987b).

In an effort to encourage small private enterprise and to organize its vital interisland shipping services along more efficient and cost-effective lines, the Indonesian government began in the 1960s to subsidize, through credit, the motorization of private commercial sailing ships. At present, virtually all *pinisi* are equipped with auxiliary engines and, by law, with navigation instruments, including magnetic compasses, charts, and radios. Bugis navigators do not appear to have adopted other forms of European instrumentation such as the sextant or radar, but do occasionally refer to charts and maps when traveling to a port for the first time. Meanwhile, owners of *lambo* and *baggo* have begun to install auxiliary engines to remain competitive. Until the installation of marine engines, beginning in the mid-1970s, crew members were known to row the smaller *lambo* and *baggo*, using four long oars, when the wind failed. It seems that the tedium and occasional danger of being adrift, along with economic considerations, are key factors motivating this extraordinary effort and the subsequent rush to motorization. Rapid introduction of new technology raises questions concerning the extent to which local navigators, including the Bugis, are retaining and adapting their traditional knowledge of navigation.

While several people have written about sailing aboard Bugis schooners (Collins 1936, 1937; Judd 1980; Clad 1981), the largest body of scholarship has focused on ship building and design (Burns 1980; Horridge 1978, 1979a, 1979b, 1982, 1985; Kayam and Peccinotti 1985; Manguin 1980; Macknight and Mukhlis 1979; Pelly 1977). Additional studies have examined Bugis maritime law and the geographical extent of Bugis seafaring and trade (Cense 1972; Lopa 1982; Tobing 1961). Despite the considerable literature on traditional navigation practices in Oceania (e.g., Goodenough 1953; Gladwin 1970; Lewis 1980a, 1986; Finney 1979; Feinberg 1988), relatively few such studies have been carried out in Indonesia.[5]

THE BUGIS COMMUNITY OF BALOBALOANG

The most heavily populated islet of the Kepulauan Sabalana Atoll, Balobaloang was first settled five generations ago by Bugis from the area around Maros, north of Ujung Pandang.[6] As of July 1988, Balobaloang had a population of 685 in 135 households. The economy of the island is based upon a combination of cash cropping of coconuts (*Cocus nucifera* L.) and small-scale seaborne trade, while villagers rely upon fish and imported rice for subsistence. Local ships typically trade and carry on consignment cargoes of rice, flour, timber, shallots, salt, dried fish, and coconuts between ports in Sulawesi, Kalimantan, and the Lesser Sundas (Nusa Tenggara).

During the period of steady easterly monsoon winds extending from March through September, and the calmer months of October through December, most of the adult male population is shipped out aboard the village's twenty-eight trading vessels. During the west monsoon, which brings especially strong winds, heavy rains, and high seas, most ships are moored in the lee of the island, while the seamen rest and tend to their domestic duties. A few men stay at home throughout the year to fish, harvest coconuts, and carry out construction and repair work for themselves and their neighbors, often for a small wage. Fishing is done with lines from small dugout sailing canoes equipped with a single outrigger and with nets along the shore. Large fish are salted and dried for sale in Ujung Pandang.

The women of Balobaloang manage and maintain the households, spending a large part of each day looking after small children, cooking, splitting firewood, fashioning coconut leaves into wall and roof panels, extracting coconut oil, and gathering shellfish. Their only cash-producing enterprises are agar cultivation and the netting of milkfish fry *(Chanos chanos)* in the shallows between shore and reef, work shared with the men. Only rarely do women leave the island to visit relatives; a few wives, however, are known to follow their husbands to sea.

Kin ties are reflected in the composition of the Bugis crew: frequently the captain selects his closest kinsmen first. Following a pattern of social organization commonly observed in Southeast Asia, crew members are considered a part of the captain's entourage (e.g., Scott 1972), and profits are shared according to a system that dates from at least the seventeenth century (Tobing 1961).

Among the navigators with whom I sailed most extensively were the younger but experienced Pa' Abdul Razak and the active senior navigator Pa' Syaripudding. Syaripudding, perhaps the most respected active navigator on Balobaloang, first put to sea close to fifty years ago and has sailed to all of the major ports of eastern Indonesia. A number of times he has navigated successfully to places he had never been, gaining a general sense of their locations from maps and word of mouth. Unlike his fellow navigators, who most often confine their activity to consigned cargoes and regular trade routes nearer to Balobaloang, Syaripudding is apt to trade opportunistically, remaining away from the island for months at a time. His knowledge of navigation is clearly extensive. He turned to a motorized ship around 1980. The shorter duration of voyages and the ability to set a straight and steady course modify the problem of navigation. Pa' Syaripudding and others like him appear, however, to be retaining their traditional expertise and adapting it to these changing conditions. The following summary explains Bugis navigational knowledge and practices as I learned them from Pa' Syaripudding, Pa' Razak, and a number of other retired and active navigators and crew members from Balobaloang.

BUGIS NAVIGATION

Bugis navigators employ a system of dead reckoning that depends upon a variety of features of the natural environment plus, increasingly, the magnetic compass. Although these features include land forms, seamarks, currents, tides, wave patterns and shapes, and the habits of birds and fish, navigators rely most heavily upon prevailing wind directions, guide stars, ground swells, and the magnetic compass. It is these major features and their interrelated application that I emphasize in my discussion.

Winds and Directions

The major wind patterns of Island Southeast Asia are governed by the monsoons.[7] From approximately May through October, winds from the east and southeast bring generally fair weather and steady breezes; from November through April, the west monsoon brings first calm air, then rain and squalls to the region (see figure 9.1). For the Bugis, these winds are of such fundamental importance that the two monsoons are named for their respective prevailing wind directions: *bare'* 'west' and *timo'* 'east'.

Since Indonesian sailing ships, like Pacific canoes, are not able to sail upwind with great efficiency, Indonesian seafarers, until the introduction of motorization, did indeed sail "with the wind." In the past, the larger Bugis and Makasar ships often completed only one round-trip per year, covering great distances and exchanging cargoes along the way (Collins 1936, 1937). Today this voyaging pattern is still followed by the seafarers of Buton aboard their nonmotorized *lambo*.

For the Bugis of Balobaloang, trade routes are generally north and south across the Flores Sea. In principle, this allows them to take advantage of both easterly and westerly winds by reaching in either direction, although storms and heavy seas usually confine them to port during the west monsoon. Formerly, voyages were undertaken during the west monsoon only if the captain was hard-pressed financially. Now, with motorization and larger ships, the voyaging season has been increasingly extended such that confinement to port is restricted to the period of most severe weather, lasting about two months. Since ships cannot be worked on until the monsoon breaks, this period remains a time for home repair and rest for the captain and crew.

While monsoon winds dominate at sea, land and sea breezes tend to dominate near the larger islands and especially in harbors. Local weather patterns, however, can and often do disrupt both of these. For example, during my first voyage from Balobaloang to Bima, an initially favorable monsoon wind from the southeast shifted to the south, forcing the captain to beat all the way to a point about one hundred kilometers west of Bima, where he hoped in vain to pick up strong land and sea breezes. This change in wind direction turned a one-day voyage into three days of lost time and boredom for the captain and crew.

Wind directions are named after a system of compass directions called *mata anging* 'points of origin of the winds'. And, although the use of winds to name directions is practiced generally, there appear to be discrepant versions of the boxing of the wind compass itself. Two directional systems, both drawn by Bugis navigators, are given in figure 9.3. The first system (see figure 9.3A) has sixteen points; similar systems with variations in names of noncardinal directions have been described by several navigators on Balobaloang. Furthermore, it is explicitly understood that these points correspond to the sixteen points of the international compass. Although the origins of the Bugis system are not known, most local navigators carry aboard their ships a magnetic compass, which apparently has been familiar to the Bugis since European contact. The second system (see figure 9.3B) has twelve points and was shared with us by Pa' Razak and his father, also an accomplished navigator. Note that four of the noncardinal points of the sixteen-point system are absent here, while the system remains symmetrical. In each case, the positions of the four cardinal directions are identical, and the primary axis runs 'east-west'.

Similar discrepancies surround the "wind compasses" of Polynesia and Micronesia (e.g., see Feinberg 1988:94–95). As on the Polynesian islands of Tikopia and Anuta (Feinberg and Firth as quoted in Feinberg 1988:94), although individuals disagree about the boxing of the compass, general agreement exists about the naming of wind directions by points of a compass. In any case, both wind direction and intensity are of vital concern to the people of Balobaloang, and wind conditions are a constant topic of conversation.

Stars and Asterisms

Bugis navigators, like their counterparts in Oceania, have long relied upon the stars and star patterns to set and maintain course. Although most sailors seem to know a few star patterns and their use, navigators know many more. These star patterns, which I will term "asterisms," are known to rise, stand, and set above certain islands or ports when viewed from others and thereby pinpoint the direction of one's destination, forming a "star compass."[8] For example, *bintoéng balué* 'Alpha

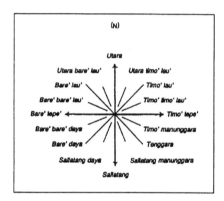

FIGURE 9.3A. *Mata anging* 'wind compass'. The common sixteen-point version.

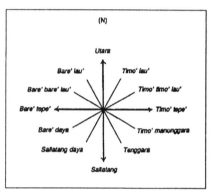

FIGURE 9.3B. *Mata anging* 'wind compass'. The twelve-point variant.

and Beta Centauri' (see A, figures 9.4 and 9.5) is known to appear at dusk in late July and early August in the direction of Bima as viewed from Balobaloang, that is, to the south.

As the night passes and a given asterism is no longer positioned over the point of destination, the navigator's thorough Gestalt-like familiarity with the sky allows him mentally to adjust to the new conditions: he can visualize the points on the horizon at which the stars rise or set relative to wherever they currently appear. When one asterism is not visible, other associated but unnamed stars may be used to remind the navigator of where the original asterism set or is about to rise, or they may be used instead of the missing asterism. This is analogous to the "star path, the

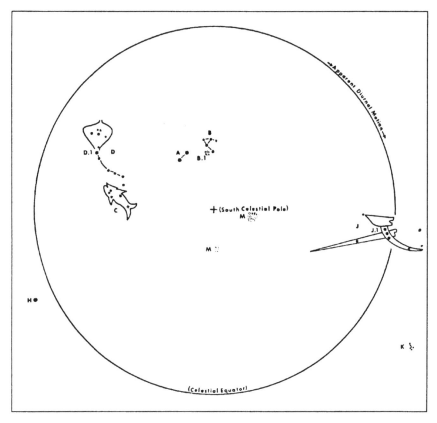

FIGURE 9.4.　Bugis stars and asterisms: the southern sky. (For equatorial view, the horizon passes through the celestial pole, bisecting the circle. Rotate circle clockwise for apparent diurnal motion.)

succession of rising or setting guiding stars down which one steers," described by Lewis (1986:46–47; see also Feinberg 1988) for several Polynesian and Micronesian communities.

Because of the earth's orbital motion about the sun, a gradual annual shift can be observed whereby each star rises and sets earlier each night. As a result, any given asterism becomes lost in the sun's glare and is not visible for approximately one month each year. In addition, the asterism is visible for only a short time each night for weeks on either side of this period of absence. During this extended period, it is not useful for navigation, and other asterisms must be utilized. My study was conducted in July, during the east monsoon. When asked how people navigated during the west monsoon (i.e., the other half of the year), navigators said that they did it by "using different stars." (See table 9.1 and figures 9.4 and 9.7.)

TABLE 9.1.   Bugis stars and asterisms familiar to navigators.

A	*bintoéng balué* *	widow before marriage	Alpha & Beta CENTAURI
B	*bintoéng bola képpang*	incomplete house	Alpha-Delta, Mu CRUSIS
B.1	*bembé'*	goat	Coal Sack Nebula in CRUX
C	*bintoéng balé mangngiweng*	shark	SCORPIUS (south)
D	*bintoéng lambarué*	ray fish, skate	SCORPIUS (north)
D.1	(identified w/o name)	lost Pleiad	Alpha SCORPII (Antares)
E	*bintoéng kappala'é*	ship	Alpha-Eta URSA MAJORIS
F	*bintoéng kappala'é*	ship	Alpha-Eta UMA; Beta, Gamma UMI
G	*bintoéng balu Mandara'*	Mandar widow	Alpha, Beta URSA MAJORIS
H	*bintoéng timo'*	eastern star	Alpha AQUILAE (Altair)
J	*pajjékoé* (Mak.)† or *bintoéng rakkalaé*	plough stars	Alpha-Eta ORIONIS
J.1	*tanra tellué*	sign of three	Delta, Epsilon, Zeta ORI
K	*worong-porongngé bintoéng pitu*	cluster seven stars	M45 in TAURUS (Pleiades)
M	*tanra Bajoé*	sign of the Bajau	Large & Small Magellanic Clouds
[]	*wari-warié*	(no gloss)	Venus: morning
[]	*bintoéng bawi*	pig star	Venus: evening
[]	*bintoéng nagaé*	dragon stars	Milky Way

* Note that the Bugis term for 'star(s)' is *bintoéng*; the suffix *é* may be translated as the definite article 'the' in English.

† Although *pajjékoé* is a Makasar term, it is most commonly used on Balobaloang to indicate this asterism.

Perhaps the most frequently used asterism among the Bugis of Balobaloang is *bintoéng balué*, 'Alpha and Beta Centauri' (see A, figures 9.4 and 9.5).[9] My informants agreed that these two bright stars are used to locate Balobaloang from Ujung Pandang, and Bima from Ujung Pandang or Balobaloang. Pa' Razak observed that, as described above, they appear *sallatang* 'in the south' at dusk during the peak period for sailing, toward the middle of the east monsoon. Pa' Syaripudding further

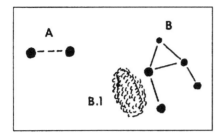

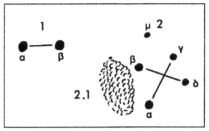

FIGURE 9.5A. Bugis designation: (A) *bintoéng balué* 'widow before marriage stars'; (B) *bintoéng bola keppang* 'incomplete house stars'; (B.1) *bembé* 'goat'.

FIGURE 9.5B. International designation: (1) Alpha and Beta CENTAURI; (2) Alpha-Delta and Mu CRUCIS; (2.1) Coal Sack Nebula in CRUX.

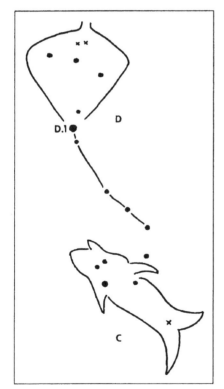

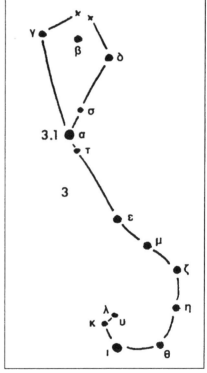

FIGURE 9.6A. Bugis designation: (C) *bintoéng balé mangngiweng* 'shark stars'; (D) *bintoéng lambarué* 'ray fish or skate stars'; (D.1) 'lost Pleiad'.

FIGURE 9.6B. International designation: (3) SCORPIUS; (3.1) Alpha SCORPII (Antares).

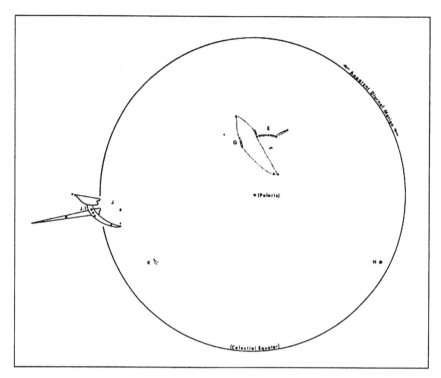

FIGURE 9.7.   Bugis stars and asterisms: the northern sky. (For equatorial view, the horizon passes through the celestial pole, bisecting the circle. Rotate circle counterclockwise for apparent diurnal motion.)

noted that they rise *tenggara* 'southeast', while both navigators agreed that they set *bare' daya* 'southwest'. Their brightness makes them visible even through clouds. The name *balué* is derived from *balu* and means 'the one widowed before marriage'.

Just to the west of Alpha and Beta Centauri is *bintoéng bola képpang* (Crux), visualized as an 'incomplete house of which one post is shorter than the other and, therefore, appears to be limping' (see B, figures 9.4 and 9.5). Crux is used in conjunction with Alpha and Beta Centauri to navigate along southerly routes; like Alpha and Beta Centauri, it is known to set 'southwest'. Interestingly, it was emphasized that Crux is also used to help in predicting the weather. This asterism is located in the Milky Way, which is known to the Bugis as *bintoéng nagaé* 'the dragon' whose head is in the south and whose tail wraps all around the sky. As such, Crux is surrounded by a bright haze of starlight. On the eastern side of the house, however, there is a small dark patch totally devoid of light that is seen as a 'goat', or *bembé'* (see B.1, figures 9.4 and 9.5A). Between the squall clouds of the rainy season, the goat in the sky may be seen standing, as goats are wont to do, outside the house, trying to get in out of the rain. There are nights, however, when the goat is gone from the protection of the house. Hidden by haze, the missing goat portends a period of calm air and little rain.

The Large and Small Magellanic Clouds, small external galaxies neighboring our own, are both known to the Bugis as *tanra Bajoé* 'the sign of the Bajau', referring to the Sama sea gypsies found throughout eastern Indonesia and the southern Philippines. Viewed as a fuzzy patch of light and never rising more than about thirty degrees above the southern horizon as seen from this latitude, *tanra Bajoé* both mark the transitions between the monsoons and serve as aids in setting and maintaining course. The Large Magellanic Cloud is seen to set in early evening in April at the start of the east monsoon, rise in the predawn sky at the monsoon's peak in August, and continue to rise earlier each night as the west monsoon approaches. Pa' Syaripudding further explained that both *tanra Bajoé* rise *sallatang manunggara* 'south-southeast' and set *sallatang daya* 'south-southwest', making them especially useful when sailing from Ujung Pandang to Balobaloang and Bima.

Two additional asterisms were pointed out in the southern sky: *bintoéng balé mangngiweng* 'the shark stars' and *bintoéng lambarué* 'the ray fish or skate stars', which comprise the Western constellation of Scorpius (see C and D, figures 9.4 and 9.6A).[10] Rising and setting to the north of, and between two and three hours later than, Alpha and Beta Centauri, it seemed to me that these prominent and well-known asterisms would likely be utilized as guide stars. Although this was never confirmed, I was told a story about them that reflects the navigators' thorough knowledge of the sky. Positioned literally on the "other side of the sky" from Antares, the brightest star in the 'ray fish' (see D.1 in figure 9.4), one finds *worong-porongngé* 'the cluster of stars', or Pleiades (see K in figure 9.4). Formerly, the 'cluster' had one more star than it does today and is often still called *bintoéng pitu* 'seven stars'. But one day, a long time ago, 'the ray fish' stole one of the seven stars—the brightest one (Antares)—for its tail. Afraid that it will be found out by its victim, 'the ray fish' dares show itself only when 'the cluster' has already set, and, in turn, 'the ray fish' sets before the 'cluster' rises. Thus, the opposition of these asterisms is recalled in Bugis folklore and is likely used as a device to aid in locating these stars.

In the northern sky (see figure 9.7), the asterism that figures most prominently in Bugis navigation is *bintoéng kappala'é* 'the ship stars' in the Western constellation of Ursa Majoris (see E and F, figures 9.7, 9.8A, and 9.9A). The 'ship' is used for traveling north. In particular, it rises *timo' lau* 'northeast' and sets *bare' lau* 'northwest' over Kalimantan from Ujung Pandang and Balobaloang. Associations of this group of stars with the hull of a boat or ship is common throughout Indonesia.

Adjoining the 'ship', and likewise used to navigate northward, is *balu Mandara'* 'widow of the Mandar' (see G, figures 9.7 and 9.8A; two variations were offered— the simple by the navigator, the more elaborate by a young crew member). These two stars, also in Ursa Majoris, remind the Bugis of Alpha and Beta Centauri (thus the name *balu*); Mandar recalls the Bugis' northern seafaring neighbors. While these two stars are seen from northern latitudes to point to Polaris at the north celestial pole, the pole star is not visible from the Java Sea. Their usefulness in locating 'north', however, is well understood.

Of three asterisms described on my first visit as being useful for sailing east and west, only *bintoéng timo'* 'eastern star' (Altair in international usage) was actually pointed out in the night sky (asterism H, figures 9.4 and 9.7). 'Eastern star', according to Pa' Haji Tallé, rises 'east' and sets 'west'. During our voyage in late July, he noted that 'eastern star' "rose after morning prayer" and appeared "two meters above the eastern horizon one-half hour after sunset." Although this application of linear measurement to the altitude of an object at infinity is difficult to interpret, it indicates a definite image of the position of the star in the mind of the navigator.

Two additional asterisms used in sailing 'east' are *pajjékoé,* Makasar for 'the plough' (also known as *bintoéng rakkalaé,* Bugis for 'the plough stars', and *tanra tellué* 'the sign of three') and *wari-warié* or *bintoéng élé'* 'morning star'. Both are said to rise 'east'. In 1988, after I had badgered Pa' Razak for several nights in an attempt to identify these stars, 'morning star' remained unseen and, therefore, unidentified. On my return visit, it was visible and identified as Venus rising in the predawn sky. Later, I also learned that Venus in the evening sky is known as *bintoéng bawi* 'pig star', so named since it is believed that wild pigs will enter and destroy a garden or orchard when this object shines brightly in the west.

Likewise, not visible during my initial visit were 'the plough' and 'the sign of three'. They were, however, provisionally designated, on the basis of a sketch drawn by Pa' Syaripudding, as stars in Orion, including the "belt" (see J and J.1 in figures 9.4, 9.7, and 9.10A).[11] I was told that if I wanted to see them, I should return at a date later in the year. Fortunately, I was able to do just that, and on my second visit, this identification was visually confirmed. Both the 'pig star' and 'the plough', it should be noted, speak to an agrarian lifestyle not practiced by Bugis seafarers but culturally shared with their kin who farm the lands of Sulawesi as well as other islands of the archipelago.

Although stars are useful guides, they are not always visible. Navigators plan their voyages to maximize the possibility of making landfall during daylight. On my voyage from Balobaloang to Bima, the captain scheduled our departure for mid-afternoon, allowing us to back-sight on Balobaloang and other islands of the atoll until dusk, when Alpha and Beta Centauri appeared in the sky. There was a period of about thirty minutes where both the receding island and the stars could be seen, providing a good opportunity to maintain course as attention was shifted from land forms to the stars.

Except during the height of the west monsoon, it is uncommon to experience extended periods of totally overcast skies. Should the primary guiding asterism be concealed, the navigator depends upon his knowledge of other asterisms or unnamed stars to fix his direction. If it is very cloudy, day or night, the navigator turns to wave directions and the magnetic compass to maintain course.

Magnetic Compass

Observations aboard Bugis ships have revealed a pattern of wayfinding in which the magnetic compass plays a key role along with wind, stars, and swells. Once at sea, a simple magnetic compass, or *pedomang,* is commonly found lying on the deck close to the helmsman, giving the appearance that it is quite heavily used. Both the

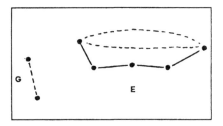 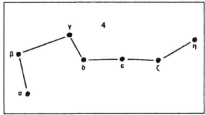

FIGURE 9.8A. Bugis designation: (E) *bintoéng kappala* 'ship stars'; (G) *bintoéng balu Mandara'* 'widow-of-the-Mandar stars'.

FIGURE 9.8B. International designation: (4) Alpha-Eta URSA MAJORIS.

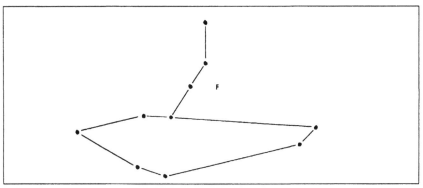

FIGURE 9.9A. Bugis designation: (F) *bintoéng kappala* 'ship stars'.

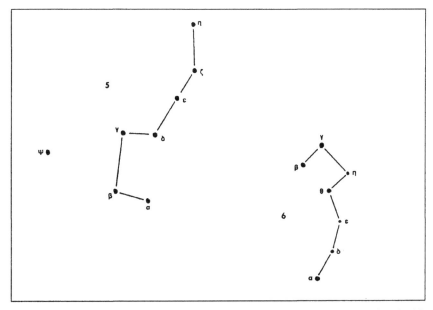

FIGURE 9.9B. International designation: (5) Alpha-Eta URSA MAJORIS; (6) Beta and Gamma URSA MINORIS.

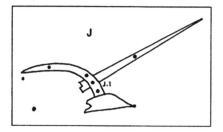
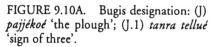

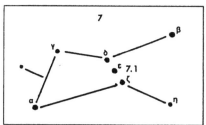

FIGURE 9.10A. Bugis designation: (J) *pajjékoé* 'the plough'; (J.1) *tanra tellué* 'sign of three'.

FIGURE 9.10B. International designation: (7) Alpha-Eta ORIONIS; (7.1) Delta, Epsilon, and Zeta ORIONIS.

testimonies of the navigators and my own experience indicate that the level of dependence upon the compass varies with navigators and circumstances.

Apparently long familiar with magnetic compasses, only the younger generation of Bugis sailors have come to depend upon them. Because of their high cost and rarity in the past, a mariner's compass, even a broken one, was prominently displayed on the ship and was the source of great pride (Collins 1937). Local retired navigators speak of formerly making their own compasses but finding them too inaccurate to be relied upon. Since 1962, however, sailing ships of over fifty cubic meters in capacity have been required by Indonesian law to carry a compass. Within several years of the enactment of this law, prosperity on Balobaloang had reached the point where ships of over fifty cubic meters were being built, and captains could afford a relatively inexpensive dry compass. Currently, every ship on Balobaloang is equipped with such an instrument.

Although the more experienced navigators say that they could do without it and rely on wind, waves, and stars, the magnetic compass plays a central role in contemporary Bugis navigation. On frequently sailed routes, the helmsman knows from experience or from the navigator's instructions the proper compass bearing that will guide the boat toward its objective. At night under mostly clear skies, the helmsman points the ship's bow toward a succession of guide stars whose own azimuths change as the night passes. To compensate for this change, he checks the compass about once per hour, sometimes after several minutes of calling to a sleepy crew member for a flashlight or match by which to see it. On cloudy nights, when few or no stars are to be seen, the helmsman's job is much harder. Complicated by the inherently unsteady helm of the *lambo*, the helmsman is forced to check the compass every minute or so with a flashlight whose batteries quickly run down through constant use. By day the compass is generally observed more often, regardless of the weather, although the sun, when low in the sky, is used as a reference. Both day and night, the directions of waves and swells also are noted and used to maintain a heading, as discussed in the next section.

Even though the compass is marked with the English symbols N-E-S-W and so forth, the naming of directions when using the magnetic compass agrees with those of the wind compass, and the correspondence between the two is generally taken for granted. Occasionally, numerals, representing degrees on the face of the compass, are referred to and used in place of one of the points of the wind compass. In use, the compass rests on the deck with the desired heading aligned with the ship's keel. It is the helmsman's job simply to keep the compass needle lined up with the N-S axis.

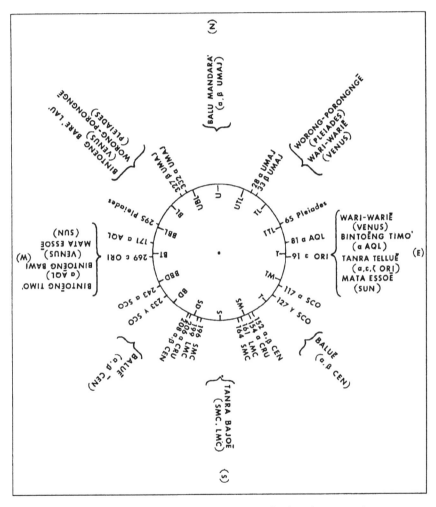

FIGURE 9.11.   Bugis star compass. Directions are displayed in a rotating pattern after illustrations made by Bugis navigators. In the inner circle, Bugis 'wind compass' directions are presented in an abbreviated form; see figure 9.3A for full terms. The middle circle consists of international designations for Bugis navigational stars with azimuths of their rise and set points. The outer circle shows directions associated by Bugis with their navigational stars; it includes international designations.

When setting and maintaining course or determining wind direction, navigators use the magnetic compass in the same ways that they use the star and wind compasses. That is, the navigator memorizes the stars or compass points, or both, that will guide him between any two locations, bearing in mind the effects of drift from wind and current. For example, it is known that, to sail from Balobaloang to Bima during the east monsoon, one must head due south, while during the west monsoon one heads south-southwest to southwest, depending on the strength of the wind and current. Likewise, to reach Ujung Pandang from the island during the east monsoon, one travels somewhat east of north, while during the west monsoon a heading to the north-northwest is preferred. This difference, as navigators are quick to point out, takes into account drift from wind and currents, while true directions are also known. Practiced navigators have many of these bearings committed to memory and will refer to the experience of others as well as to charts and maps when they travel to new or infrequent destinations.

On my initial voyage aboard a Bugis ship, we traveled along the route best known to the seafarers of Balobaloang: Ujung Pandang to Bima via the island, a distance of about 212 nautical miles. Over the course of four days and five nights at sea without an auxiliary engine—and on later voyages after an engine had been installed—only occasionally did I see the helmsman or captain refer to the compass, and rarely at night or when in sight of land. When asked about this, both the captain and the helmsmen agreed that the compass could be used through the night, but to do so, one would have to light the flashlight, "so why not just use the stars?" Even if the compass were thrown overboard, we were assured, the navigator could find his way.

This testimony is quite credible in that temporarily getting lost with an experienced navigator is not uncommon. Since major ports are on high islands, once landmarks are memorized, the only problem is getting within sighting distance of a familiar mountain or two. Even in bad weather, those experts can eventually and safely find their way using features of the sea and sky; so when a ship finds itself a few hours off course, it may be cause for frustration but not alarm.

Not every navigator, however, can do without a compass. Some older men never learned to use other means of wayfinding, while others are just not experienced enough. The latter was the case on a routine southbound voyage from Ujung Pandang to Balobaloang. Departing in the early evening, the young captain and his helmsman were unaware that the ship's compass was broken. They thereby failed to realize that the wind had changed and that they were heading too far to the west. As a result, they became lost for a number of hours. Had the captain known the guide stars, it was said, he would have known that his compass was broken and been able to navigate without it.

The magnetic compass has become an integral, if not necessary, part of the Bugis navigator's tool kit. Whether the boasts of many Bugis sailors are justified— and I suspect that the best of them could, indeed, manage quite well without a compass—is not the point here; what is more interesting is the manner in which it is used and by whom. That senior navigators are able to rely exclusively upon the stars while younger ones depend upon the magnetic compass signifies, I believe, a transition in progress that could have interesting repercussions for the navigational art among this seafaring people.

Waves and Swells

Waves and swells provide Bugis navigators with important clues about currents and winds. Since waves at sea move with prevailing winds, they can be used to ascertain wind direction, or vice versa, if one or the other is known in terms of a general system of direction, such as the wind compass described earlier. They are also relied upon to maintain course and to warn of reefs and shallows. Not unlike their Oceanic cousins (e.g., see Lewis 1980a, 1986), the Bugis speak of feeling the motion of the ship with respect to the swells and are thus able to know without looking if the ship is keeping to the desired course. Once a course has been established, any change in the motion of the ship requires the attention of the navigator. Navigators, I was told repeatedly, use this method when they are sleeping in the cabin or below deck. My own observation is that some Bugis captains sleep a lot, both day and night, but rouse quickly when a sudden change in direction causes the ship to undulate in a different manner.

Changes in heading relative to waves, however, are not the only source of fluctuation in the motion of the ship. Navigators are also alert to the rocking motion caused by *kala-kala*—any waves, large or small, that come from many directions at once, whether from a prevailing current, from waves clashing with an opposing wind, or from the coming together of two opposing currents, usually tidal. Often the result of changing winds, *kala-kala* may also indicate that the ship has wandered into a shallow area, fraught with danger. Some navigators claim that they can sense the difference between these types of *kala-kala*, again by the feel of the ship's motion.

While the magnetic compass and celestial phenomena may be the primary means used by the Bugis to set and maintain course, waves play an increasingly important role on cloudy days and, especially, nights, when the sun and stars are not visible. And at all times when waves are present, they provide a constant rhythm by which the navigator and helmsman maintain course.

CONCLUSION

Bugis seafaring, in many ways, contrasts with that of the Pacific Islanders described in the remainder of this volume. The Bugis sail large ships resembling European schooners, which are increasingly equipped with auxiliary inboard diesel engines. They make their livelihood as traders who reside aboard their ships for major portions of the year. And navigational techniques routinely involve the use of a magnetic compass. Nonetheless, these people represent one end of a continuum of Austronesian maritime activity.

Similarities are evident in ship-building procedures, relying upon a carpenter's ability to estimate proper relationships without reference to written diagrams or measurements, and in a hull design that limits one's ability when sailing to beat into a head wind. The clearest point of continuity, however, is in navigational techniques. Bugis navigators, like their Pacific Island counterparts, depend upon star paths, supplemented by wind patterns, wave configurations, seamarks, currents, tides, the sun, and animal behavior. These supplemental aids will be the subject of ongoing research.

Like that of their Austronesian cousins in the insular Pacific, Bugis maritime technology and practice has been modified in such a way as to incorporate techniques and objects from other cultural traditions. In this manner, the compass has been fully integrated into Bugis navigation. Older techniques remain prominent during a period of rapid growth in the use of marine engines and international navigational technology, but change is accelerating. Additional investigation not only should help preserve a passing tradition but also should elucidate a living, evolving body of indigenous knowledge, affording a case study in the relationship between cognition and practice as these expert navigators renegotiate their relationship with the economic, social, and natural environment of which they are a part.

NOTES

Acknowledgments   The research for this essay was made possible by financial support from the National Science Foundation and the Center for International Education Fulbright-Hayes Program. Local support and assistance was provided by the Lembaga Ilmu Pengetahuan Indonesia and the Office of the Harbor Master at Ujung Pandang. To my friend and colleague Mary Judd, who introduced me to the Bugis, and to the navigators and their families of Balobaloang, especially Pa' Syaripudding, Pa' Abdul Razak, and Pa' Haji Tallé, I would like to extend my sincerest thanks. Finally, I am grateful to Niko Besnier, Harold C. Conklin, Richard Feinberg, Charles O. Frake, Pierre-Ives Manguin, and Harry A. Powell, who offered helpful comments on earlier drafts.

1. This chant is translated from a Bugis inscription displayed at the Benteng Cultural Center at Fort Rotterdam, Ujung Pandang.

2. More on interisland shipping in eastern Indonesia may be found in Dick (1975, 1987a, 1987b).

3. For purposes of comparison with Western ships, it is noted that the keel of the *pinisi* has long extensions morticed to it at each end such that the first plank above the keel is longer than the keel itself (Horridge 1979b:13). Locally, keel length is most often used to describe the size of a ship.

4. *Lambo* were first described by Collins (1936, 1937) and Nooteboom (1930, 1936, 1947). Construction, at that time, was carried out in small villages along the Mandar Coast of South Sulawesi and the south coast of Flores at Ende, and later, in Konjo villages of Bulukumba, South Sulawesi. Today, construction sites are scattered and remote.

5. Lopa's dissertation (1982) on traditional maritime law in South Sulawesi contains a concise summary of Mandar navigation and is the best available to date. Lewis' results appear in two brief unpublished reports to the Lembaga Ilmu Pengetahuan Indonesia (1980b) and in a short popular article (1980c:122–27).

6. Ethnographic data for this essay were gathered on Balobaloang and aboard its ships during an exploratory study in 1988 and seventeen months of dissertation research in 1991–1992. I first met Pa' Razak and Pa' Syaripudding at Paotéré Harbor, Ujung Pandang

(formerly Makasar) in 1988. At that time I joined Mary Judd to conduct a preliminary study of Bugis navigation in conjunction with her study of the economics of Bugis commercial shipping and trade. Through Judd's contacts among local shipping agents and the office of the Harbor Master, we were able to locate and travel from Ujung Pandang to Bima via Balobaloang aboard Razak's forty-ton *lambo*, the *Alam Bahari*, which was newly launched and still lacked an auxiliary engine.

7. In Indonesia both the easterlies and westerlies are known as "monsoon winds," in contrast with the western Pacific where the east and southeast "trade winds" are distinguished from the westerly "monsoons."

8. In international astronomical usage, a distinction is made between the terms "asterism" and "constellation." Constellations are bounded regions of the sky, like political boundaries on a world map, that derive their names from imaginary, often mythological figures, which, when drawn upon the sky, more or less encompass most of the stars in that region. Often it is extremely difficult to see the figure in a constellation (e.g., the "crab" in Cancer). Asterism refers to a simple connect-the-dots pattern of stars that may form a subset of a single constellation (e.g., "the Big Dipper" in Ursa Major, the Great Bear), or may incorporate stars from several constellations (e.g., "the Summer Triangle" in Cygnus, Aquila, and Lyra). Since Buginese stars form simple patterns and do not directly correspond to international usage, the term *asterism* is preferred.

9. *Bintoéng*, the Bugis term for 'star' or 'stars', occasionally may precede the name of the specific star or asterism in spoken language. For example, *balué* generally stands alone while *bintoéng élé* ('morning star' [Venus]) is commonly heard.

10. Scorpius also contains Nukumanu's 'shark' (Feinberg this volume).

11. Identification of *tanra tellué* with the three stars of Orion is not surprising since cognates of *tellu* (e.g., *tolu*) are used to describe Orion's Belt in other Austronesian languages.

REFERENCES

Ammarell, E.
1995   Bugis Navigation. Ph.D. Dissertation, Yale University.
Burns, M.
1980   All hail ye Bugis schooners. *Orientations*. June:43–49.
Cense, A. A.
1972   *Pelayaran dan Pengaruh Kebudayaan Makassar-Bugis dipantai Utara Australia*. Jakarta: Bharata.
Clad, James
1981   Before the wind: Southeast Asian sailing traders. *Asia* 4:20–23, 43.
Collins, G. E. P.
1936   *East Monsoon*. London: Jonathan Cape.
1937   *Makassar Sailing*. London: Jonathan Cape.
Dick, H. W.
1975   Prahu shipping in Eastern Indonesia, Part 1. *Bulletin of Indonesian Economic Studies* 11:69–107.
1987a   Prahu shipping in Eastern Indonesia in the interwar period. *Bulletin of Indonesian Economic Studies* 23:104–21.
1987b   *The Indonesian Interisland Shipping Industry: An Analysis of Competition and Regulation*. Singapore: Institute of Southeast Asian Studies.
Feinberg, Richard
1988   *Polynesian Seafaring and Navigation: Ocean Travel in Anutan Culture and Society*.

Kent, Ohio: Kent State University Press.

Finney, Ben R.
1979   *Hōkūle'a: The Way to Tahiti*. New York: Dodd, Mead and Company.

Gladwin, Thomas
1970   *East Is a Big Bird: Navigation and Logic on Puluwat Atoll*. Cambridge: Harvard University Press.

Goodenough, Ward H.
1953   *Native Astronomy in the Central Carolines*. Philadelphia: University of Pennsylvania Press.

Horridge, G. Adrian
1978   *The Design of Planked Boats in the Moluccas*. Monograph No. 38. Greenwich: National Maritime Museum.
1979a   *The Lambo or Prahu Bot: A Western Ship in an Eastern Setting*. Monograph No. 39. Greenwich: National Maritime Museum.
1979b   *The Konjo Boatbuilders and the Bugis Prahus of South Sulawesi*. Monograph No. 40. Greenwich: National Maritime Museum.
1982   *The Lash-Lug Boat of the Eastern Archipelagoes*. Monograph No. 54. Greenwich: National Maritime Museum.
1985   *The Prahu: Traditional Sailing Boat of Indonesia*. Singapore: Oxford University Press.

Hughes, David
1986   The prahu and unrecorded inter-island trade. *Bulletin of Indonesian Economic Studies* 22:103–13.

Judd, Mary
1980   I will sail on with the wind. *GEO*. Hamburg: Gruner and Jahr.

Kayam, Umar, and Harri Peccinotti
1985   *The Soul of Indonesia: A Cultural Journey*. Baton Rouge: Louisiana State University Press.

Lewis, David
1980a   *The Voyaging Stars*. Sydney: Collins.
1980b   Navigational techniques of the prahu captains of Indonesia. Reports to LIPI. Unpublished.
1980c   Navigators of the narrow seas. *Hemisphere* 24:122–27.
1986   *We the Navigators*. (1972) Honolulu: University of Hawai'i Press.

Lineton, J. A.
1975   An Indonesian Society and Its Universe: A Study of the Bugis of South Sulawesi and Their Role within a Wider Social and Economic System. Ph.D. Dissertation, University of London.

Lopa, Baharuddin
1982   Hukum Laut, Pelayaran Dan Perniagaan: Penggalian Dari Bumi Indonesia Sendiri. Ph.D. Dissertation, Universitas Diponegoro, Semarang.

Macknight, Campbell
1976   *The Voyage to Marege': Macassan Trepangers in Northern Australia*. Melbourne: Melbourne University Press.

Macknight, Campbell, and Mukhlis
1979   The Bugis manuscript about praus. *Archipel* 18:225–82.

Manguin, Pierre-Ives
1980   The Southeast Asian ship: an historical approach. *Journal of Southeast Asian Studies*

11:266–76.

Nooteboom, C.

1930   Vaartuigen van Ende. Tijdschrift voor Indische. *Taal-, Land-, en Volkenkunde* 76:97–126.

1936   Vaartuigen van Mandar. Tijdschrift voor Indische. *Taal-, Land-, en Volkenkunde* 80:22–23.

1947   The study of primitive sea-going craft as an ethnological problem. *International Archive of Ethnographie* 45:216–24.

Pelly, Usman

1977   Symbolic aspects of the Bugis ship and shipbuilding. *Journal of the Steward Anthropological Society* 8:87–106.

Scott, James C.

1972   Patron-client politics and political change in Southeast Asia. *American Political Science Reviews* 66:91–113.

Tobing, P. L.

1961   *Hukum Pelayaran Amanna Gappa (Amanna Gappa Navigation Law)*. Ujung Pandang: Yayasan Kebudayaan Sulawesi. Selatan dan Tenggara.

EPILOGUE

Seafaring in the Pacific, Past and Present

Ward H. Goodenough

and

Richard Feinberg

• Although the essays in this volume are diverse in focus, they draw upon a common heritage. The diversity of Oceanic seafaring techniques and practices gives testimony to how phyletic cultural traditions change over time. These essays were not written to illustrate such change; that they do so enhances their collective value. In this epilogue, we shall discuss the common heritage out of which the various traditions have grown and how they testify to the phyletic evolution of cultural traditions.

Human settlement of the Pacific Islands began some thirty to forty thousand years ago with a movement of people from Indonesia to the big island of New Guinea (Irwin 1992). From New Guinea they went south into Australia and Tasmania, and eastward into the Bismark Archipelago and the Solomon Islands. It is not known how this settlement was accomplished; we know only that it was ancient, apparently took a long time, and involved some travel by sea but not over great distances. There is no evidence that these early settlers had a highly developed seafaring tradition.

About four thousand years ago, a new people entered the Pacific. They established coastal settlements in northern New Guinea, the Bismark Archipelago, and the Solomon Islands, then continued on to become the first settlers of all of the Pacific Islands beyond. They were a maritime people, and what they did was truly remarkable.

Their coming into the Pacific was a product of a vast diaspora, apparently of seagoing traders whose ultimate home was what is now Fukien Province in China. From Madagascar in the west, through Southeast Asia and the insular Pacific, all the way to Easter Island off the coast of Chile, people speak demonstrably related languages—members of the so-called Austronesian language family (Blust 1980a). Until European discovery of the Americas at the end of the fifteenth century, there was no comparable spread of people with common cultural and linguistic ancestry by sea over such a vast area. This Austronesian diaspora began about six thousand years ago, and by one thousand years ago, it had largely run its course, making it a process almost entirely confined to prehistory.

Archaeology yields clues regarding early Austronesian culture and the beginnings of the diaspora; and historical linguists have reconstructed some of the vocabulary of the ancestral languages relating to voyaging and sailing vessels as well as other aspects of ancient technology and social organization (Blust 1976, 1980b). Fishing was an important activity to the early Austronesians, as attested by words for 'bait', 'fish hook', 'basketry fish trap', 'dragnet', 'fish drive', and 'derris root fish poison'. In addition, there were words for 'canoe' or 'boat', 'raft', 'canoe paddle', 'use a paddle', 'rudder' or 'steer', 'punting pole', 'outrigger', 'sail', 'cross-seat' or 'thwart', 'bailer', and 'rollers for beaching or launching' (Blust 1976).

The home area of the ancient Austronesians was clearly a coastal one, where subsistence activities involved fishing as well as gardening and hunting, and where water craft were oriented both toward coastal or near-shore movement and open-sea travel. Linguists and archaeologists have identified Taiwan as the source of the Austronesian diaspora (Chang 1989). Six thousand years ago, Taiwan was closely linked culturally with Fukien across the Taiwan Straits. The Austronesian tongues apparently are distantly related to a number of the non-Chinese languages of what is now South China (Benedict 1975), a finding corroborated by the distribution of cord-marked pottery in Taiwan and coastal regions of South China (Huang 1989; Chang 1969, 1986; Sung 1989). The region just north of this area was undergoing a marked cultural florescence (Chang 1986:193–206, 208–12).

Climatic change, probably combined with population growth, resulted in deforestation in this area. By the beginning of the Christian era, people of South China were importing such tropical forest products as rattan, camphor, bird feathers, rhinoceros horn, and incense (Wang 1958). Progressive scarcity of these resources, we may infer, led the people to turn increasingly to places further south. The Fukien coast would have been one such place.

Warmer conditions persisted on Taiwan for another thousand years, until about 2000 B.C. (Chang 1986:78). It would have been natural for Taiwan to become a source of such products for trade back to the mainland. As Taiwan lost its tropical forests, however, the search for forest products spread still further south into the Philippines; and Taiwan soon became culturally isolated. We can see the early impetus for the diaspora of Austronesian-speaking peoples out of Fukien and Taiwan southward into the Philippines and Indonesia as arising from these early beginnings of the "China Trade," a trade that was conducted exclusively by Austronesians until the eleventh century A.D. (Hall 1985:42). In addition to forest resources, such marine products as bêche-de-mer, trochus, and cowrie shells undoubtedly also played a role in this trade, as they still do.

In the course of this diaspora, the search continued for places from which the products of trade could be obtained. Once traders established themselves at such places, they necessarily entered into relations with people already there. The local people knew where to find forest products, while the traders' sphere of knowledge was the sea. These relations often led to intermarriage. A trader's son who married a local woman acquired access through his wife to the local products of the land and to rights in land for his children. In return, his wife's family had access through him to prestige goods from abroad. The men of his wife's family could use the wealth from abroad for bride-price payments to marry the immigrant man's own female relatives. Thus would have emerged a pattern replicated over much of the Austronesian-speaking world, where women, through their husbands, serve as sources of prestige wealth, while men, through their wives, provide food and other land products for their kin.[1]

Many descendants of the traders became landsmen. As populations grew, they expanded into the interior of the islands and lost all sea-related knowledge. Such knowledge was maintained, however, by those like the *orang laut* 'sea people' of Indonesia or the sophisticated Bugis (Ammarell this volume), who continued to depend on it as traders and fishers.

These orientations toward sea and land have undoubtedly been present for a long time in the South China Sea and its immediately adjacent regions. Repeatedly, a small group must have established a base, intermarried with local folk, had descendants who became differentiated into relatively landless, sea-oriented people and land-owning, landbound cultivators and product gatherers. The Manus and Usiai of the Admiralty Islands (Mead 1931) are well-known examples of this pattern of land versus marine specialization.

In the large islands of Indonesia, the abundance of land led to the emergence of new population centers, and the seafarers associated with these centers increasingly came to play a major role as middlemen in the developing trade between India and China, a trade that was already well established by the beginning of the Christian era (Whitmore 1977). This trade provided the impetus for development of the Indonesian seafaring tradition. The Austronesians who moved to Oceania, however, became increasingly remote from major trade routes, and east of the Bismark Archipelago in Central Melanesia, they became totally separated from them.[2] What remained in most of the Pacific were smaller local networks where the prestige goods that circulated were imports from relatively nearby islands (see Lepowsky; Montague; Powell, all this volume). A result of this decrease in the scope of trade was a progressive loss of aspects of the old cultural heritage and new local elaborations out of what remained, as in Hawai'i, using whatever materials were locally available.

This century has seen enormous changes in maritime traditions as a result of colonial restriction of interisland voyaging in traditional craft and, since World War II, the introduction of such products of Western technology as outboard motors. The degree and kind of change is highly varied, as attested by the studies in this volume. Together these essays depict people adapting to their changing circumstances in a variety of ways. Yet, when we examine these changes more closely, we find that they illustrate some common factors affecting adaptation to changed circumstances throughout the region, both in prehistory and modern times. Perhaps such adaptations also speak to common human tendencies, regardless of divergent cultural traditions.

AUSTRONESIAN MARITIME KNOWLEDGE

Ancient Austronesian sailing craft were probably of two basic types, both still in existence (Haddon and Hornell 1936, 1937). One was a catamaran, consisting of a pair of hulls or floats, connected by a platform; the other had a single hull and an outrigger float. The latter was useful for short trips undertaken by a few people. The former, the double-hulled vessel, was used in long-distance traveling, its platform capable of carrying more people and cargo.

The vessels of the Polynesian aristocracies are impressive examples of the double-hulled type (Haddon and Hornell 1936), and the huge, multiple-hulled *lakatoi* of the Papuan Gulf area (Seligman 1910:96–120) are famous elaborations of it. Other examples include the *orou* of the Mailu area of southeastern Papua New Guinea (Haddon and Hornell 1937:231–40; Montague this volume). Goodenough witnessed smaller, platformed vessels of this type employed in coastal trading and as mobile homes by the frequenters of the native market at Koke, east of Port Moresby, in 1951.

On the more remote islands of Polynesia, there was little outside influence on boat construction, design, and navigational practices until European contact. By contrast, the maritime industries of many western Malayo-Polynesian societies evolved in a highly competitive and cosmopolitan milieu. Still, local Southeast Asian sailing ships, although apparently influenced by Arab and Western design and technology, continue to display features that reveal their evolution from an ancestral Austronesian dugout technology (Hornell 1970; Horridge 1978). Thus, even the largest Bugis sailing ships are built up from a keel reminiscent of the dugout, and, while local ships have almost universally adopted plastic sails and cordage and installed marine engines, most new ships are still built without metal fasteners. Moreover, the hulls of local ships display shallow keels, allowing them both to avoid the hazardous reefs that abound in the region and to be beached for repair without damage to the keel. As with Pacific Island sailing canoes, however, this added maneuverability in shallow water limits a ship's ability to sail upwind.

As boat construction has evolved in response to local pressures, so have Austronesian navigational techniques. Travel between islands located hundreds of kilometers apart, once they were settled, was not uncommon; and even finding places that lie not far over the horizon requires aids to setting and maintaining course. Back-sighting on landmark alignments; knowing the directions of prevailing winds, currents, and swells; making use of the stars both for direction and general spatial orientation at night; using seamarks such as reefs and shoals; and noting clouds that hang over land, lagoon-water reflections in the sky, and the presence of sea birds that roost on land at night are all presumably a part of an ancient legacy that has been adapted in its specifics to local conditions and needs.

In Micronesia, the Carolinians have elaborated the use of stars (Goodenough and Thomas 1987), and the Marshallese have taken advantage of the complicated patterns of currents and swells found in their atoll chains (Davenport 1960; Carucci this volume). Unfortunately, outside of Micronesia and some of the Polynesian outliers (Feinberg 1988, this volume), few traditional navigational systems in the Pacific are now remembered in detail. The possibility that the ancient Austronesians used a compasslike directional system whose points were named (somewhat arbitrarily) for the rising and setting of convenient stars is implied by Frake's reinterpretation (1994) of the Carolinian sidereal compass as an abstract, directional system of equal intervals of arc. The Carolinian sidereal compass is, therefore, presumably a local elaboration on an older tradition.

As already indicated, many Austronesians lost their maritime skills and knowledge. They kept them and honed them as needed, and they let them lapse where there seemed little need to maintain them. The studies in this volume illustrate conditions under which seafaring traditions are kept alive and those under which they die out. What is common to the people who maintain seafaring traditions is that they have a practical need for them. The traditions have been preserved to serve a particular specialty in a regional economy, as among the Bugis, or have been preserved as part of a strategy for survival, as among the landless Manus or the atoll dwellers of Micronesia and the Tuamotus in Polynesia. Seafaring was also preserved as an instrument of war, as in connection with head-hunting raids among peoples of the western Solomons (Hviding this volume) and New Zealand's Maori. In both of these cases, the outrigger canoe was replaced by large, planked, single-hulled vessels that did not use sail but relied on crews of paddlers for greater speed and directional control. Paddle canoes outclassed sailing vessels for military purposes in the Pacific, as galleys did in the ancient and medieval Mediterranean.

People on isolated islands who do not have neighbors close enough to visit seem to have lost their maritime abilities, except for what was needed for fishing close to shore or for coastal transport. Such was the case with Sikaiana and Rotuma (Donner, Howard this volume), and it was the case with the people of Nauru and Kosrae in Micronesia (Goodenough 1986) and the Polynesian Moriori in the Chatham Islands (Irwin 1992:115). Many of these islands continued to receive immigrants from other places, but they did not voyage out.

People on islands, and in localities within island groups, that were rich in resources had little reason to travel to their neighbors, while their less well-endowed neighbors had good reason to travel to them. Thus, the high islanders of Pohnpei, Chuuk, Yap, and Palau in the Carolines relied on people from the atolls around them for sailing canoes and navigational knowledge (Goodenough 1986). For atoll dwellers, by contrast, the sea and voyaging played a central role in how they structured their world, both symbolically and practically (Carucci; Donner; Feinberg, all this volume). The high chiefs of the large islands of Fiji similarly relied on the Lau Islanders for their navies. And in the Santa Cruz Islands, seafaring was maintained by the Reef Islanders, not by the richer inhabitants of Santa Cruz (Ndeni) Island itself (Davenport 1964, 1968, 1969).

It is tempting to look at centers of power and wealth as maintaining fleets that voyaged out to islands in their spheres of influence. Actually, it was the outer islanders who sailed in to visit them and who conveyed their influence back home, as with the so-called tribute system involving Yap and the atolls of the Central

Carolines (Lessa 1950; Alkire 1965). Whatever fleets the centers maintained for military or prestige purposes were constructed and manned by outer islanders. This same tendency is illustrated by Kiriwinans in the Trobriand Islands (Powell this volume), where the wealthy and powerful people of Omarakana, who are not particularly good seamen, use canoes almost solely for *kula* trading purposes. They make a relatively poor show in sailing. Those who take a more prominent role in *kula* voyaging are the people who use canoes all year in practical economic pursuits, being less richly endowed with agricultural land (Montague, Powell this volume).

REGIONAL DIFFERENTIATION

Once the Pacific was settled, a series of regions (aside from truly isolated islands) emerged, some greater and some smaller, within which water transport tended to be confined. The Massim of southeastern New Guinea was one such region (Lepowsky; Montague; Powell, all this volume). The Vitiaz Straits area between New Guinea and New Britain was the hub of another (Harding 1967). Samoa and Fiji constituted the east-west axis and the Tokelau Islands and Tonga the north-south axis of another such region. The Marshall Islands were yet another, as were the atolls of Kiribati; and the Central Caroline Islands formed the hub of another region, or overlapping set of regions, that extended from Yap in the west to Pohnpei in the east.

Over time, each of these regions modified its boat designs and navigational methods in accordance with local needs. Such atoll clusters as the Marshall Islands, Kiribati, and the Tuamotus had special needs that appear to have stimulated experimentation with single-outrigger sailing canoes that could be handled easily by a small crew of two or three people and that also could be taken onto the open ocean. The atoll crews had to cover considerable distances to exploit the marine resources of the reefs and surrounding ocean and the land resources of distant islets across large lagoons (as in the Marshalls). At the same time, these lagoons afforded relatively safe areas within which to experiment with hull and sail design.

Micronesia is justly recognized as the region in which the most sophisticated design of single-outrigger sailing canoes was developed (Haddon and Hornell 1936). The design involved a lateen sail whose upper yard stepped into a socket in whichever end of the hull was serving as the bow. The mast, attached at the upper yard, held up the sail and inclined forward to make a triangle with the yard and the canoe's hull. Because the canoe performed best with the outrigger kept on its windward side, changing to the opposite tack required unstepping the yard from the bow and swinging the luffing sail around to the other end of the hull, which now became the bow. This procedure resulted in one side of the hull (the outrigger side) always being the windward side and the other always being the lee side, except when sailing directly before the wind. It also resulted in the two ends of the hull serving equally as bow and stern.

Taking advantage of this situation, the Micronesians developed a hull that was symmetrical on its lateral axis and asymmetrical on its longitudinal axis, the opposite of the usual hull design of most sailing vessels (Gladwin 1970). The resulting hydrofoil design along the keel worked something like an airplane wing, giving the hull lift to windward, with the amount of lift increasing as the canoe heeled over. This made it possible to sail fairly close on the wind without losing way, and, hence, it greatly reduced the need to tack. The weight of the outrigger assembly served to keep the canoe from capsizing from the force of the wind, the best performance being when the outrigger float was lifted just enough so that it skimmed the water's surface. The canoes on which Goodenough sailed in Kiribati had shrouds only on the outrigger (windward) side, and they could be readily adjusted to incline the mast toward the outrigger or away from it as needed.

We hypothesize that this design evolved in the large lagoons of the Marshall Islands, perhaps about one thousand years ago. It revolutionized the possibilities for water transportation and soon spread to Kiribati, where it was adapted to be effective in the light winds of the doldrums. The design then was carried by adventurers from both the Marshalls and Kiribati westward to the Caroline Islands. We believe it made possible the permanent settlement and exploitation of the small coral islands and atolls between Chuuk and Yap, where trips over more than one hundred kilometers of open sea to fishing grounds became routine (Thomas 1987). In Chuuk, the ancient double-hulled vessels of ocean transport came to be remembered only in the form of stylized models that served as shrines to spirits of dead ancestors (Krämer 1932:239–41, 334–36). Clearly, it is improper to take the canoe designs and navigational lore of Micronesians, where they still survive, if shakily, and assume that they represent the ancient body of maritime lore of the early Austronesian settlers of the Pacific. In their present form, they are relatively recent developments.

UNITY IN DIFFERENCE

Despite regional differentiation, common themes are underscored by contributions to this volume. Prominent among these is the role of geographical and ecological pressures in the maintenance and loss of old equipment and techniques. Sikaiana, an atoll lacking close, hospitable neighbors, has almost entirely abandoned its old seafaring activities, although interest in ocean voyaging is maintained in stories, songs, and travel via ship and airplane. Rotuma, equally isolated, larger, and with more abundant resources, may have given up its voyaging tradition even earlier.

Of all communities depicted in this volume, Nukumanu is perhaps best situated to preserve its older seafaring technology and practice. It is sufficiently isolated that European shipping cannot meet all transportation needs, money is scarce, outboard motors and fiberglass boats are expensive to acquire and maintain, and fuel shipments are sporadic. At the same time, Ontong Java provides a relatively large, resource-laden, friendly destination that can be safely reached with older maritime technology and skills.

The islands of the Trobriand and Louisiade Archipelagoes are also characterized by isolation from Western resources and contacts, yet they have effective access to other islands of their region. And, like Nukumanu, they have retained a considerable proportion of their old maritime traditions. Enewetak is in some ways similarly situated. United States dollars, however, have made modern boats and motors relatively easy to obtain, and canoes have been abandoned for normal activities. Marovo in the western Solomons is much less isolated, both geographically and economically, than most other communities discussed in this volume. Its people maintain close symbolic and emotional attachment to the sea and seafaring, but boats and canoes of a new style, often equipped with outboard motors, have replaced older craft.

Geographical and ecological considerations affect these communities in other ways as well. Continued Kiriwinan participation in overseas *kula* trade, despite considerable geographical and technological liabilities, underscores the activity's importance. And the availability of a good natural harbor has made Kaduwaga village a voyaging center for the entire Massim area.

The communities appearing in this volume share a symbolic system that reflects their ancient common heritage. Male is consistently identified with sea, female with land. Thus, women cultivate and tend to stay at home while men engage in travel, deep-sea fishing, trade, and overseas employment. This pattern is illustrated in every one of these studies, with the partial exception of Vanatinai, where women sometimes organize trading expeditions and pilot canoes. Even on Rotuma, where women and their husbands often fish together, such fishing is done inside the reef. As elsewhere, lagoon and reef are meeting places between land and sea, where men and women may pursue common activities.

Throughout the Pacific region, seafaring provides a metaphor for daily life and construction of local identity. This is made explicit in the essays on Rotuma, Sikaiana, Enewetak, Nukumanu, and Marovo; and it is implied for the Louisiade and Trobriand Archipelagoes as well as the Bugis. Similarly, men build their renown by traveling to other lands and coming home to tell of what they have experienced. Such travel is a major theme in the essays on Enewetak, Sikaiana, and Rotuma, and its importance is strongly implied for Nukumanu. Likewise, for the Massim, voyaging is vital to procuring renown through the *kula* trade, an activity that also carries with it tales of intrigue and adventure.

The sea is a source of danger as well as adventure; indeed, danger is what makes its mastery a source of prestige. This ambivalence is highlighted particularly in the essays on Sikaiana and Rotuma, and it exists to some degree in all seafaring communities. In most instances, however, the positive associations far outweigh the negative.

RECENT CHANGE AND THE FUTURE

As the contributions to this volume testify, much has changed since Europeans, Japanese, and Americans entered the Pacific—first as explorers, whalers, traders, and missionaries; later as plantation-labor recruiters; and finally, until very recently, as colonial rulers. Access to modern technology led first to the adoption of European sailcloth and, in some places (e.g., Kiribati) the importation of lumber for hull construction. Traditional vessel designs continued, but they were implemented with new materials, paid for by exporting copra and by working on plantations or in phosphate mines. Prior to the introduction of steel tools and other products of Western technology, anything larger than a small paddle canoe represented a sizable investment in labor and required access to the necessary raw materials, especially suitable trees from which to make the hull. Chiefs and heads of large kin groups were in the best position to mobilize the construction of sailing vessels and war canoes, and the availability of sea transport was relatively limited. With steel tools, imported lumber and sailcloth, and access to wage labor or other sources of cash needed to purchase them, it became possible for many more people to acquire sailing canoes. On Onotoa in Kiribati in 1951, Goodenough counted two sailing vessels per three adult men in the village of Aiaki, a startling increase over what was possible in earlier times. This, in turn, significantly affected fishing patterns and, as a result, how people organized their family relations (Goodenough 1963:337–43). Similar effects are reported for Polynesian Kapingamarangi (Lieber 1993).

An increasing use of outboard motors has led to the construction of new types of boat or to modifications of traditional craft to accommodate them. Heavy boats designed exclusively for outboard engines have introduced a new hazard—drifting helplessly when the motor fails (see Carucci, Feinberg this volume). Time spent in school has deterred many young men from learning the traditional skills associated with the construction and handling of sailing canoes; and even when school is not a competing factor, young men are inclined to want to be modern and to show only perfunctory interest in what they perceive as old-fashioned.

The extent to which local economies can provide access to the products of modern technology varies greatly. The long-run potential of Papua New Guinea, the Solomon Islands, and Vanuatu is quite different from that of Micronesia, the Tuamotus, or such relatively isolated places as Enewetak, Sikaiana, Nukumanu, and Rotuma. Since the latter places have little to export but labor, they must continue to depend on traditional subsistence activities and the traditional technology for conducting them, or they must go away to work and send remittances or emigrate permanently.

In any event, those who keep on plying the waters of their home areas, whether in outrigger canoes or motor-driven vessels, must know how to navigate their local seas. They must know the shoals, reefs, currents, and appropriate course settings, whether by star compass or magnetic compass. These are things that Indonesian and Pacific sailors will continue to learn out of practical necessity. However much they may be changing, seamanship and some parts of traditional maritime lore will remain important for at least some islanders for as long as we can foresee.

Future seafaring, however, will be increasingly affected by the adaptation of Western marine technology to local conditions and local financial resources. As is already being done in some areas, Pacific Island boat builders will continue to evolve designs for small, motor-powered boats adapted to their needs for carrying cargo and passengers in response to growing regional demands. Participation in commercial fishing by Pacific Islanders, both as laborers and as entrepreneurs, is also likely to increase. More people in the Pacific may follow the example of Rotumans and enter the service of shipping companies as seamen on modern freighters and tankers that travel the world over. Whatever time may bring, the island people are now committed participants, though in varying degrees, in the global economy. How that participation develops will largely shape the course of their seafaring future.

NOTES

1. This pattern of exchange of prestige goods and other products between brothers (and their wives) and sisters (and their husbands) has been well described in such places as the Trobriand Islands (Malinowski 1929; Weiner 1976), Palau (Smith 1983), and Sumatra (Bruner 1963). The association of sea with male and land with female is illustrated throughout this volume.

2. For a review of the evidence regarding the spread of Polynesians in the central and eastern Pacific, see Rouse (1986).

REFERENCES

Alkire, William H.
1965   *Lamotrek Atoll and Inter-Island Socioeconomic Ties.* Illinois Studies in Anthropology No. 5. Urbana and London: University of Illinois Press.

Benedict, Paul K.
1975   *Austro-Thai: Language and Culture with a Glossary of Roots.* New Haven: HRAF Press.

Blust, Robert
1976   Austronesian culture history: some linguistic inferences and their relations to the archaeological record. *World Archaeology* 8:19–43.
1980a   Austronesian etymologies. *Oceanic Linguistics* 19:1–189.
1980b   Early Austronesian social organization: the evidence of language. *Current Anthropology* 21:205–47.

Bruner, Edward M.
1963   Medan: the role of kinship in an Indonesian city. In *Pacific Port Towns and Cities,* edited by A. Spoehr, pp. 1–12. Honolulu: Bernice P. Bishop Museum Press.

Chang, Kwang-chih
1969   *Fengpitou, Tapengkeng, and the Prehistory of Taiwan.* Yale University Publications in Anthropology No. 73. New Haven: Department of Anthropology, Yale University.
1986   *The Archaeology of Ancient China.* 4th edition. New Haven and London: Yale University Press.
1989   Taiwan archaeology in Pacific perspective. In *Anthropological Studies in the Taiwan Area: Accomplishments and Prospects,* edited by Chang, Kwang-chih, Kwang-chou Li, Arthur P. Wolf, and Alexander Chien-chung Yin, pp. 87–97. Taipei: Department of Anthropology, Taiwan National University.

Davenport, William H.
1960   Marshall Islands navigational charts. *Imago Mundi* 25:28A–34A.
1964   Social structure of the Santa Cruz Islands. In *Explorations in Cultural Anthropology,* edited by W. H. Goodenough, pp. 57–93. New York: McGraw-Hill.
1968   Social organization in the Northern Santa Cruz Islands: the Duff Islands (Taumako). *Baessler-Archiv* (Neuefolge) 16:207–75.

1969   Social organization in the Northern Santa Cruz Islands: the Main Reef Islands. *Baessler-Archiv* (Neuefolge) 17:151–243.

Feinberg, Richard
1988   *Polynesian Seafaring and Navigation: Ocean Travel in Anutan Culture and Society.* Kent, Ohio: Kent State University Press.

Frake, Charles O.
1994   Dials: A study in the physical representation of cognitive systems. In *The Ancient Minds: Elements of Cognitive Archaeology,* edited by C. Renfrew and E. Zubrow, pp. 119–32. Cambridge: Cambridge University Press.

Gladwin, Thomas
1970   *East Is a Big Bird: Navigation and Logic in Puluwat Atoll.* Cambridge: Harvard University Press.

Goodenough, Ward H.
1963   *Cooperation in Change.* New York: Russell Sage Foundation.
1986   Sky world and this world: the place of Kachaw in Micronesian cosmology. *American Anthropologist* 88:551–68.

Goodenough, Ward H., and Stephen D. Thomas
1987   Traditional navigation in the Western Pacific. *Expedition* 19(3):2–14.

Haddon, A. C., and James Hornell
1936   *Canoes of Oceania,* Vol. 1: The Canoes of Polynesia, Fiji, and Micronesia. Special Publications No. 28. Honolulu: Bernice P. Bishop Museum.
1937   *Canoes of Oceania,* Vol. 2: The Canoes of Melanesia, Queensland, and New Guinea. Special Publications No. 28. Honolulu: Bernice P. Bishop Museum.

Hall, Kenneth R.
1985   *Maritime Trade and State Development in Early Southeast Asia.* Honolulu: University of Hawai'i Press.

Harding, Thomas G.
1967   *Voyagers of the Vitiaz Strait: A Study of a New Guinea Trade System.* Seattle: University of Washington Press.

Hornell, James
1970   *Water Transport: Origins and Early Evolution.* (1946) Devon, U.K.: David and Charles.

Horridge, G. Adrian
1978   *The Design of Planked Boats in the Moluccas.* Monograph No. 38. Greenwich: National Maritime Museum.

Huang, Shih-chang
1989   A discussion of relationships between the prehistoric cultures of Southeast China and Taiwan. In *Anthropological Studies in the Taiwan Area: Accomplishments and Prospects,* edited by Chang, Kwang-chih, Kwang-chou Li, Arthur P. Wolf, and Alexander Chien-chung Yin, pp. 59–86. Taipei: Department of Anthropology, Taiwan National University.

Irwin, Geoffrey
1992   *The Prehistoric Exploration and Colonization of the Pacific.* Cambridge: Cambridge University Press.

Krämer, Augustin
1932   Truk. In *Ergebnisse der Sudsee-Expedition 1908–1910,* II.B, Vol. 5, edited by G. Thilenius. Hamburg: Friedrichsen, De Gruyter and Company.

Lessa, William A.
1950   Ulithi and the outer native world. *American Anthropologist* 52:27–52.

Lieber, Michael D.
1993   *More Than a Living: Fishing and the Social Order on a Polynesian Atoll.* Boulder, Colo.: Westview.

Malinowski, Bronislaw
1929   *The Sexual Life of Savages in Northwestern Melanesia.* New York: Liveright; London: G. Routledge and Sons.

Mead, Margaret
1931   *Growing Up in New Guinea: A Comparative Study of Primitive Education.* London: G. Routledge and Sons.

Rouse, Irving
1986   *Migrations in Prehistory: Inferring Population Movement from Cultural Remains.* New Haven: Yale University Press.

Seligman, C. G.
1910   *Melanesians of British New Guinea.* Cambridge: Cambridge University Press.

Smith, DeVerne Reed
1983   *Palauan Social Structure.* New Brunswick, N.J.: Rutgers University Press.

Sung, Wen-hsun
1989   Unity and diversity in prehistoric Taiwan: a cultural perspective. In *Anthropological Studies in the Taiwan Area: Accomplishments and Prospects,* edited by Chang, Kwang-chih, Kwang-chou Li, Arthur P. Wolf, and Alexander Chien-chung Yin, pp. 90–110. Taipei: Department of Anthropology, Taiwan National University.

Thomas, Stephen D.
1987   *The Last Navigator.* New York: Henry Holt and Co.

Wang, Gungwu
1958   The Nanhoi trade: a study of the early history of Chinese trade in the South China Sea. *Journal of the Malayan Branch of the Royal Asiatic Society* 31.2(No.182):1–135.

Weiner, Annette B.
1976   *Women of Value, Men of Renown.* Austin: University of Texas Press.

Whitmore, John K.
1977   The opening of Southeast Asia: trading pattern through the centuries. In *Economic Exchange and Social Interaction in Southeast Asia: Perspectives from Prehistory, History, and Ethnography,* edited by Karl L. Hutterer. Michigan Papers on South and Southeast Asia No. 13. Ann Arbor: Center for South and Southeast Asian Studies, University of Michigan.

Index

www.ingramcontent.com/pod-product-compliance
Ingram Content Group UK Ltd.
Pitfield, Milton Keynes, MK11 3LW, UK
UKHW040803120225
454975UK00002B/48